OPERATION BULLPEN

Kevin Nelson

SOUTHAMPTON BOOKS

Copyright © 2006 by Kevin Nelson

All rights reserved. No part of this book may be reproduced or transmitted in any form or by any means, scanned or distributed in any printed, mechanical or electronic form, including photocopying or recording, or by any information storage or retrieval system without permission in writing from the publisher. Please do not participate in or encourage piracy of copyrighted materials in violation of the author's rights. Purchase only authorized editions.

An application has been submitted to the Library of Congress to register this book.

ISBN 0-9786340-0-4

Cover: This FBI evidence photo of Mickey Mantle bears a Greg Marino forgery. It is under Mantle's chin.

FBI evidence photos on interior pages: Mike Mains, photographer

Please visit the official website at www.operationbullpen.com. For orders, inquiries and correspondence, contact Southampton Books at 707-747-4705, or email southamptonbooks@sbcglobal.net.

Cover and Interior Design: Lorraine Rath
Printing and Binding: United Graphics, Mattoon, IL

Printed in the United States of America

10 9 8 7 6 5 4 3 2 1

OPERATION BULLPEN

The Inside Story of the Biggest Forgery Scam in American History

By Kevin Nelson

SOUTHAMPTON
BOOKS

For Jennifer,
who has shown me that true love is never a fake

CONTENTS

Introduction • vii

Part One
Half Moons • 1

Part Two
Operation Bullpen • 59

Part Three
Rings and More Rings • 237

Epilogue • 271

Sources and Acknowledgments • 285

INTRODUCTION

The order came in through Rino Ruberti, the blue-eyed, blond-haired handsome man who had been coming on strong in the racket, especially since taking over Stan the Man's account. In just one month Rino—pronounced "Reno," like the city—had written $200,000 in new business from Stan and more was on the way.

This order was a little strange, though, so strange that Rino wasn't sure if Greg would fill it.

Greg was Greg Marino, "the master forger" (as the media invariably referred to him later), who had filled some very strange orders over the past five years but nothing quite like this one. It was for five baseballs—official Rawlings World Series baseballs, to be exact—all to be signed on the sweet spot with the autograph of Mother Teresa.

"It shocked me when they asked for it," said Marino, who was not easily shocked. "I never thought anyone would be interested in a Mother Teresa forgery. On a baseball, no less. I'm thinking, 'Who the hell can they be selling these to?' But at that point it didn't matter. It was all the same to me."

Little did Marino know that when he filled the order—apparently signing three Mother Teresa photos as well as the balls—he was creating some of the most sensational, and unique, counterfeit products in the 2,300-year history of forgery. Marino also could not know that as he was doing this, an FBI undercover investigation—code-named Operation Bullpen—was planning to come down on his head.

On October 13, 1999, four hundred federal agents staged coordinated morning raids across five states on sixty homes and businesses—one of the largest one-day takedowns in FBI history, breaking up the biggest, most profitable forgery ring in the annals of American crime. They raided Greg's house, Rino's, Stan the Man's and a whole bunch of others, seizing $10 million in forged goods and a half-million in cash on that day alone. It was one for the record books.

Seven months after the takedown, the FBI, IRS and United States Attorney's Office held a joint press conference in San Diego to crow about the results of their investigation. This was when the Mother Teresa ball hit the news. The existence of a ball—*a baseball!*—with the fake signature of a future saint on it was too juicy a tidbit for reporters to pass up. CNN "Headline News" led with it. The Associated Press featured it at the top of its wire service story. Barbara Walters used it in her lead-in for "20/20," and it popped up again on a companion piece by "Primetime Thursday." More evidence that the ball had touched something in the national consciousness, Jay Leno did a riff on it on "The Tonight Show," and the characters in "Dilbert" joked about buying and selling a football signed by Jesus.

The Mother Teresa forgeries excited so much comment not only because they seemed so absurd, but also because they provided an insight into the men and women involved in the ring—their "brazen" and "outrageous" nature, as *Reader's Digest* put it. The ring in fact produced lots of brazen and outrageous work. They were the McDonald's of forgers, cranking out hundreds of thousands of forgeries and peddling them on eBay and the Internet, the cable TV home shopping channels, mail order, auctions, card shows and retail shops in every state in the Union. In all, say government investigators, the Bullpen ring ripped off American consumers for more than $100 million.

Signed memorabilia—photos, posters, cards, balls, jerseys, helmets and the like—is a $1 billion annual industry in the U.S. Collecting autographs is no longer child's play. It has become the province of adults who invest in autographs the way others invest in stocks or antiques or art. It's a big business, and the ring exploited it in a big-time way, living the high-flying criminal lifestyle of drugs and booze, partying with hookers, buying new vehicles and boats and homes, and taking cash-happy gambling trips to Vegas and the Caribbean.

But interestingly, the gang members were not people one would normally associate with a gang at all. Rather they were, in legal jargon, Category Ones—people who, for the most part, had never received anything more serious than a traffic ticket. These high-flying, incredibly successful crooks were decent blue collar and middle class folks who loved their children, drove them to school in SUVs, held backyard barbecues, enjoyed sports and the movies, paid taxes, and otherwise lived fairly ordinary lives.

What made them run wild on the other side of the law was the lure of easy cash—mountains of life-altering, gloriously untraceable cash. Many in the ring were just scuffling along, trying to make a living and not doing a very good job of it. This forgery thing was their one chance in life for a big score, and they grabbed it.

They were not all men; women were in on it too. The scam was so good that wives and mothers joined in, including one mother and grandmother in her sixties who became a Bullpen kingpin. The operation described by the IRS as "a nationwide criminal racketeering enterprise" was, at heart, a family business.

But when takedown day arrived, they did not all go down together. One ringleader secretly changed sides and cooperated with the government, going undercover to provide evidence that sent his friends and former associates to prison. The FBI saw this informant's actions as the right thing to do; those in the ring saw it as betrayal, pure and simple.

"They were," said one of the agents who busted them, "a bunch of loose-knit guys who were just scraping by. But they became, by far, the largest and most prolific forgery ring ever uncovered by the FBI."

This is the story of how they came together, the intense loyalties they formed with one another and how those loyalties cracked apart under the pressure of a criminal enterprise that was both the greatest and the worst thing they ever did.

This book contains information derived from federal documents and affidavits; interviews conducted by the author with FBI, IRS and Justice Department officials and others involved in the investigation; interviews with members of the Bullpen ring; videotapes, audio transcripts and photographic evidence; firsthand observations of people and places; and supporting research. The dialog quoted in these pages is drawn from government documents, video- and audiotapes, and the recollections of those who actually participated in the conversations as they were taking place. The accounts on these pages are factual. Every attempt has been made to be accurate; nothing has been made up.

PART ONE

HALF MOONS

1

One lazy afternoon in 1994 Wayne Bray was sitting around W.W. Sports Cards anxious for something to do. This was not unusual for him. He often found himself searching for stimulation outside the realm of baseball cards and sports and celebrity memorabilia, which was the nature of his business. The front door of his shop was open. He liked to keep it open to let the air in, but also to not feel so closed off from the larger world that existed beyond the tiny constricted universe that was W.W. Sports Cards. He was a man with barely contained energy; the open door provided an outlet for it. Bray hated the same old thing, day after day, and that open door gave him the sense that something new could happen in his life, something different.

He could not know that something very different was about to happen to him. Through that open door walked a man in his mid-thirties with soft hazel eyes and dark wavy hair with a thick black beard. "He looked like a bearded, scruffy pirate," said Bray, and a big one at that. People who saw Greg Marino invariably pegged his height as two or three inches above six feet, but he was actually an inch under it. The reason for this impression may have been the heft of his substantial shoulders—he was "kick-the-shit-out-of-you-big," in Bray's words—but apart from his size, little about him was intimidating. His T-shirt was old and grungy and hanging out of his sweats, which were themselves only in slightly better shape than his beat-up sneakers.

Carrying a large plain black portfolio bag as faded and worn as his clothes, he approached the front display counter where Wayne was sitting and began what passed for his sales pitch. He was selling lithographs, he said, painted by his father who was a successful artist.

If your dad is so successful, thought Wayne, how come you look like a bum?

Greg put the bag on the counter and unzipped it, pulling out a succession of brightly colored, handsomely rendered lithographs of famous sports stars: Michael Jordan, Larry Bird, Troy Aikman, Nolan Ryan, Mickey Mantle.

As put off as he was by Greg's looks, Wayne liked the art, especially a Muhammad Ali lithograph that showed two facial portraits and three different action poses in the picture. "Okay, so what do you want for them?"

"You do trades?" Greg asked in a hopeful tone.

Marino's voice was deep with a lazy quality to it, like the warm hazy day outside and most every afternoon Wayne had spent in this tiny shop on this nowhere street in this nothing little flatland North County town called Vista, vista-less Vista, which was about as far away as you could get from New York—the other quality you could hear in Greg's deep, lazy voice. Three thousand miles away and New York was still in him. It was in every syllable he uttered.

"Yeah I do trades," said Wayne, whose voice and manner could never be described as lazy. Everything about him suggested energy, ambition, desire, however frustrated these feelings may have been. "What do you like?"

Greg started looking around, leaving the bag on the counter as he wandered around the shop to find something that interested him. On the outside W.W. Sports Cards, a specialty shop, appeared to be nothing special, easily overlooked if you were passing by on the street. But if you happened to stop and poke your head in, you saw instantly its unique shiny appeal. Unlike most memorabilia shops, which have the gloomy, slightly claustrophobic feel of someone's attic, crammed with ancient, forgotten, unwanted things, Bray's was a mixture of cool new and cool old. In an unstylish business it had style. There were the usual display cases full of baseball cards, both old and new, singles and in packs, but there were other things too—a framed photograph of Marilyn Monroe clad in white fur, Hot Wheels, posters of "Easy Rider" and "Goodfellas," Spawn action figurines, a Beatles album cover, a Darth Vader mask and a white Storm Trooper's mask with its simulated breathing filters and communications link units—all arranged with an eye for how they looked, the aesthetics of it. If you were into that sort of thing, it was a nice place to hang out.

Similarly, the owner of W. W. Sports Cards bore some resemblance to his shop: rough on the outside but compelling within. Also in his thirties, but a few years younger than Greg, Wayne described himself as "the type of guy who would only stick out in a crowd if one was paying attention." Depends on the crowd, of course, but Wayne did wear some conventional hats—small businessman, husband, father—while projecting the image of an outsider, somebody who did not belong and who did not wish to. Skinny as a stick, he would not have weighed one hundred fifty pounds with a ten-pound rock in his pocket. Consistent with his lack of heft, his face was lean and angular with a modified Fu Manchu, two thin lines of hair extending from the corners of his lips down to his sharp chin. He looked like an outlaw biker on a diet. Reinforcing this bad-boy impression was the body ink starting from his wrists on both arms and swirling in patterns up to where it disappeared under the sleeves of a Hawaiian shirt. Underneath the shirt were more tattoos covering wide swaths of his back and shoulders. Bray himself designed some of these tattoos as a means of telling the significant stories of his life, and there have been some stories to tell.

Teen rebellion lasting into his late twenties, fast cars and choppers, drinking and partying and chasing girls, bad jobs ("Any crappy job there is, I've had it"), drug misadventures, rehab, more drug misadventures, more rehab, marriage, divorce, and spinning out of that break-up a three-year run on methamphetamines that he won't talk about. "It was a horrible run," he said. "I don't want to get into it. All the car crashes and all that."

But after all that he ran into some luck. He got off crack. He met a woman, they fell in love, he gave marriage a second try, and this time it worked. They had a baby and made a home and he settled into the life of a middle class burgher trying gamely to fit his square-peg personality into the round hole of respectability.*

You got a sense of the sadness he carried under the surface of his painted skin from his eyes. There was a deadened or blank quality to them, almost like a convict's. Even in the middle of the day his eyelids drooped and he appeared only half-awake. Contributing to this feeling of sleepiness was how often he rubbed his eyes and fully closed them, as if letting them take a one-second nap. But this may have been nothing more than a response to the banging inside his head. Suffering for years from intense headaches, every day he swallowed a handful of pills to back the pain off. He never went anywhere without his pills, carrying the bottles in his briefcase when he went on a work errand. His medicine cabinet at home was filled with more bottles.

Oddly perhaps, considering he was in the hobby business, the owner of W.W. Sports Cards was not a hobby person. He did not collect cards as a kid and did not even like sports that much, except for tennis, which he loved. But he knew his business, and he of course knew the value of the card Greg was pointing to on a shelf in a display cabinet.

It was a Don Mattingly. Worth maybe ten, fifteen bucks tops.

"How 'bout that one?" Greg asked with a kind of boyish eagerness, excited about seeing the card. The Hollywood posters and novelties meant

---

*Many in the Bullpen ring had wives and children. If they didn't commit crimes or play a role in the conspiracy, their names will not be used.

nothing to him next to the Mattingly. "You trade for that?"

Wayne brought the piece of cardboard out from under the glass and handed it to Greg, who treated it with care and respect, looking it over front and back, pleased as punch. "I'll give you twenty lithographs for it," he said.

Wayne was a man not usually caught off guard, but this proposition surprised him. Like any good businessman he was always looking for an advantage in any deal he entered into, probing for weaknesses, looking to ferret out any underlying motives in the other party. For him the surface appearances of things were to be relentlessly examined because in his experience they could not be trusted.

"Twenty?" he said with a questioning look.

At least in terms of business, the bearded, scruffy thrift store pirate could not have been more unlike Bray. Greg was no hard-nosed negotiator, clearly; nothing about him appeared hard-nosed at all. His instincts and inclinations were more intuitive, less analytical. He seemed a floater in some respects, floating along doing the best he could with what he had and then moving onto the next thing when the thing he had been doing didn't pan out. What he was doing at the moment was cooking at the Welk Resort over in Escondido, which he liked—well, some of the time. Being a chef in a hot, busy restaurant kitchen was a creative grind; the creative he enjoyed, the grind he hated. The tourists and old folks would come in for dinner or Sunday buffet and marvel at the wonders he made out of plain vegetables and jello, deftly slicing off a cross-section of a giant banana squash with a paring knife, hollowing out the large main piece and filling the bottom of it with small blue jello squares so that it looked like water—the ocean. From the leftover slab of squash he'd chop up pieces of it and put them to use as islands in the ocean. On these island outposts stood palm trees with bell pepper fronds and peeled carrot trunks, and on the jiggling but perpetually becalmed sea were celery boats with red pepper sails that never went anywhere, kind of like his life.

To boost his restaurant income, which was in sore need of boosting, he peddled his dad's artwork in his spare time, lugging his faded black bag around to card and memorabilia shops in the area. His father was a big sports fan, and when Greg was a kid growing up in Long Island, Angelo would take him and his little brother John on the train up to the Bronx to see the Yankees play. Greg loved that, loved everything about that: going with his dad and brother, bumping along on the subway, walking into that old stadium with all its ghosts and seeing that big green grass field and then rooting his team on to two back-to-back world titles in the late seventies. After that he was a complete goner, totally hooked on the Yankees despite the long, dry, championship-less trough they fell into in the late eighties and early nineties. But you couldn't blame that on Mattingly; he was, as Greg said, "just about all we had in those days," a guy who gave it everything he had every day, a hard worker but gifted too, and Greg's favorite player by far.

Marino was not simple, not at all; he had plenty of smarts. It was just that he tended to accept things at face value whereas his future partner in crime was constitutionally unable to do that. What you saw with Greg was what you got. He had no hidden agenda, no underlying motive except a sentimental desire to own the baseball card of one of his boyhood heroes who was close to hanging up his spikes.

"Sure," he said. "Twenty."

Bray took the offer. He figured he could sell the twenty lithos for forty to fifty bucks apiece, netting maybe a grand from a card that had cost him virtually nothing. It was the most lopsided trade he had ever done, and yet the guy on the short end of it seemed tickled pink by it. At that point, Wayne recalled in his inimitable fashion, "I decided that anyone who would let me bend him over that bad, I wanted to keep him in my life."

After the deal was done the two men talked some more, getting to know each other a little bit on a non-business basis. Then Greg headed off and Wayne, left once more to prowl the shop alone, stepped outside to smoke a cigarette and check out the scene on the street under bland, cloudless skies. Nothing much, as usual, was stirring. Then the phone sounded inside. He took one last drag of his cigarette, flicked it still burning into the gutter, and went back in to stop the noise.

2

The best way to sell the fake is to pair it with the real. In the niche business of autographed sports memorabilia Stan Fitzgerald had mastered this lovely corruption, regularly scamming some of the biggest names in sports, men whose fame was of such a nature that when they affixed their signature to a photo or jersey or ball, these ordinary articles of merchandise became instant collectibles that fans and hobbyists paid astonishingly large sums to acquire. These athletes, both active and retired, ventured out from New York City via limousine to the suburbs of New Jersey where Stan lived and worked his hustle. For a fee, naturally, they sat down at a table in his Washburn Place office in Caldwell and signed everything set in front of them for an agreed-upon period of time. Then, with the limo idling outside ready to take them back to the big city, they posed, as a goodwill gesture, for a souvenir picture with Stan or Donna Fitzgerald, his smiling, good-natured wife and accomplice. This seemingly innocent photo op was part of the scam.

At various times over the years Donna posed with Gary Carter, Roger Clemens, David Cone, Bret Favre, Randy Johnson, Mark Messier, Pete Rose, Ted Williams and many other stars. Her husband tended to be more camera-shy but on at least one occasion he and Donna posed with Wade Boggs, Boggs standing between them with his arms affectionately around their shoulders. This photo appeared, as did the ones with Donna and the other athletes, in full-page Stan's Sports Memorabilia advertisements in *Sports Collectors Digest* and other journals of the collecting trade. Other stars hired by Stan for these private signing sessions—Yogi Berra, Bob Feller, Jake LaMotta, Mariano Rivera—also appeared in these ads with a pen visible in hand, signing a ball or photo of their likeness.

What these athletes did not realize was that they were being duped. By associating his company with them, Stan the Man, as many called him—not to be confused with Stan the Man Inc. of Missouri, which was affiliated with Hall of Famer Stan Musial—gained respect and credibility not only for the legitimate products he sold, but also for the illegitimate ones. Donna, half owner of Stan's Sports Memorabilia, knew the score. So did Stan's late middle-aged, slightly graying, dignified mother Josephine, who became her son's accountant and helped him dodge the IRS by disguising his illegal earnings for tax purposes.

Every signed item sold by Stan's Sports Memorabilia came with a certificate of authenticity, also known as a COA or cert. By any name it was an essential part of the con. These pieces of paper, often issued by Stan himself, cannot be described as worthless, however, because they provided cover for his counterfeit products and helped to fill his bank account with millions of non-counterfeit U.S. dollars.

When Stan met Wayne Bray for the first time, at a card show at the Meadowlands in New Jersey, Stan was in his late twenties, a young man on the make in a $1 billion annual industry many people still associate with kids. Wayne had come east to sell things, do some industry schmoozing, party a little. His W.W. Sports Cards table happened to sit close to the big, bustling, customer-rich sales space of Stan's Sports Memorabilia. Whereas W.W. Sports Cards was strictly a one-man band, Stan's Sports Memorabilia had several well-groomed young employees hustling around in matching polo shirts talking up the virtues of autographed photos, autographed posters, autographed baseballs, autographed bats, autographed caps, autographed footballs, autographed helmets, autographed mini-helmets. Even more impressive than their sales moxie and the gaudy display of merchandise were the bills exchanging hands, the checks being written, the credit card orders being processed.

At the center of this beehive of commercial activity was Fitzgerald, a soft-bodied, clean-shaven man with short dark hair and horn rim glasses nestled into a white fleshy face. He had a nerdy look about him, someone who might wear white socks and tennis shoes to a solemn occasion. "Ever see 'The Family Man' on TV?" said Bray. "He kinda looked like the dad in that show. Glasses, sort of puffy, a fatherly type. But a real aggressive businessman."

A mutual friend, Gene the Postman, introduced the two. But after a brief exchange of pleasantries each drifted off to his own hustle with nothing important being said. Since this was a big East Coast show, attracting exhibitors from around the country, there were hundreds of booths in the hall, seemingly every one of them featuring a sign that said BUYING! even though what every vendor really wanted to do was SELL! On sale were every piece of sports ephemera known to man: balls, bats, helmets, jerseys, bobbleheads, figurines, photos, posters, books, magazines, CDs, old-fashioned LPs and novelties. But the prime objects of attraction were the tables and tables of baseball cards. Supplanted by football as the nation's most popular sport, baseball remains king among collectors, in part because of the ongoing appeal of baseball cards. Worth hundreds or even thousands of dollars, the priciest cards were displayed under glass—look but don't touch. Every card was arranged face up with the image of the player visible to the curious eyes peering down through the glass. When a potential buyer wanted to see one up close, the salesperson brought it out from under the glass and set it lovingly on a viewing table with a black high-density desk lamp. The sharp light exposed the card's flaws—slightly blurred photo, dull colors, rounded edges—any one of which could be evidence of poor quality, thus reducing its price. Other less valuable cards were housed in open cardboard boxes that shoppers could flip through as they pleased. Even these cards, though, were encased in hard plastic sleeves that protected them from being torn or stained or having their edges dulled by rough hands.

Nearly all the hands holding the cards, nearly all the eyes inspecting them, nearly all the voices talking loudly on the floor, belonged to men. A card show, like a strip club, was a mostly male environment, a guy thing. Like at a ballgame, the lines to the men's room were the longest, while the women's john appeared deserted. You saw a few women shoppers and some female salespeople, but the boss of every booth, who came in to close the major deals, was invariably a man—and frequently a rather beefy one at that, his pinkish forehead and armpits moist with sweat under the pressure to move merchandise in this noisy, crowded, aggressively competitive atmosphere.

Naturally, with so many men milling about, NFL cheerleaders, Playboy Playmates and swim suit models hosted some of the best-attended booths. Clad in full battle regalia—teased hair, tight blouse, tight short skirt, spike heels—they hawked their posters, calendars, 8x10s and screen savers to guys who could also pay five bucks a pop to get their picture snapped with them.

In another part of the hall was a special section reserved for celebrity signings. Baseball cards were the red meat of shows but celebrities brought the sizzle. They were the headliners, arriving in black stretch limos and entering through a side entrance off limits to the public. Escorted to the autograph section, the star took his seat in a folding chair behind a table, the focus of attention for hundreds of people who had stood in one line to buy a ticket for the right to have him sign their treasured keepsake, and another line so he could actually do it. A handler assigned to each star monitored his interaction with fans—making sure he had plenty of different-colored pens at hand, supervising the picture-taking, often wielding the camera himself, and in general keeping things moving briskly along. An usher with a megaphone walked the lines reminding people to have their items out and ready for signing. In-demand superstars command $50,000 or more per appearance, and show promoters make money by selling tickets and moving lots of customers through.

Bray noted with interest the crowds in the autograph section and the clamor at Stan's booth and the booths of other autograph sellers in the hall. If, as he claims, he was still only selling baseball cards at this point, this may have been when it dawned on him that he was in the wrong business and Stan was in the right one. In any event, when Stan came up to him at the end of the show and got suddenly talkative, Wayne decided to listen.

Why Stan approached him is not clear. Maybe the tattooed Californian's looks piqued his interest. Or maybe Gene the Postman had filled him in on Wayne's backstory. Stan's backstory had some kinks in it too. He was an ex-deputy sheriff who had quit law enforcement to pursue his booming sports memorabilia business full-time. Having done police work in the past, he may have had a nose for people who were up to no good, or who wanted to be. Whatever the reason, he presented Wayne with an autograph order.

"He gave me this list of about twenty names—Michael, Magic, Bird, Dan Marino, Joe Montana, John Elway, those types of guys, all superstars," said Bray. "It was a big order. Footballs, jerseys, 8x10s, maybe a hundred different items in all. He told me how much he'd pay for this order and if I could fill it, give him a call. We'll do some business."

Left unsaid was how Stan expected Wayne to lay his hands on all these valuable but impossible-to-get superstar sigs. Stan never spelled it out, never said the f-word; he spoke in code, leaving his listener to puzzle it out for himself. It was no puzzle to Wayne. The two shook hands, sealing their unspoken criminal pact, and peeled away from each other as quickly as they had come together.

On the plane flight back home Wayne gave more thought to Stan's murky but clear proposition. These thoughts were not of the "Should I do it?" variety, rather they were more on the order of "How do I do it?" Wayne knew himself well enough to know that he was sick to death of sitting on his ass all day watching dust balls form in the petrified air of his shop. Count him in.

When he got back to town he called Mike Lopez, a forger whose talents became known to him "through the grapevine." The short and chunky Lopez was pure East LA: baggy T-shirt, baggy pants, black combed-back hair. What the grapevine said about him was that he was fast, dependable, and careful to the point of paranoia. Like the rich and famous people whose autographs he forged, he zealously guarded his privacy, renting or leasing cars in which to conduct his business and regularly changing his cell phone number. His specialty was team-signed NFL helmets, the bogus sigs all placed at varying angles with different pens so as to make it appear they were signed by a squad of players, rather than one secretive scribbler sitting at home at his kitchen table. As a forger Mysterious Mike was as prolific as he was ordinary. But in the early days of the racket, quality was not as highly esteemed as it later came to be, mainly because the idea of sports memorabilia fraud was relatively unknown. The buying public still believed in the truth of what they saw—that if a star's autograph was on a given object, the star was the one who had put it there.

Bray told Lopez about the order—the quantities needed, the variety of items involved, the names of the superstars.

"I'll take care of it in a day," said Mike blandly.

"Take care of it"—that was Lopez talking in code. A quick study, Bray listened and understood, eager to fill Stan's order so Stan would fill up his wallet with cash.

Wayne got the blanks—unsigned merchandise—and sent them up to Lopez in LA. A day or so later the phone in W. W. Sports Cards rang. Hustling in from the outside, Wayne grabbed it. It was Lopez. The order, as promised, was done. Ecstatic, Wayne said he'd pick it up personally. He drove up to LA, got the stuff, drove back to the shop, packaged it up and sent it off to New Jersey, thinking this was the start of good times for him.

In the uneasy weeks that followed, Bray realized he had made a bonehead rookie mistake. In talking to Lopez he had bragged about his new customer and mentioned him by name. Mike said nothing at the time but made a mental note of it. Sometime after this he called Stan the Man in New Jersey and started dealing with him directly, squeezing Wayne out. Bray had gotten shut out of the game even before he had started playing.

He felt burned and stupid for being so careless, a traitor to his own normally sharp instincts. But he never forgot that lesson as long as he was in the racket. Nobody would ever screw him over like that again.

3

The pioneering counterfeit career of Mike Lopez came to a temporary stop after he pulled off the biggest and sweetest scam of his life. While doing his deals with Stan the Man and others, he made a connection with a national cable TV home shopping network. One of its programs sold signed sports memorabilia, and Mike had loads of signed memorabilia to offer them—specifically 2,500 of his team-signed NFL helmets. Not only did he burn the network for a cool $750,000 on the deal, he had the added satisfaction of watching his bogus stuff being peddled on TV and snapped up by suckers across America who thought they were buying the real thing.

Crafting this big of a scam, in such a high profile way, brought the normally reclusive Lopez a bit more attention than he wished. He said later that things got so hot for him that he had "to lay low because everybody was on my trail." Before dissolving into the scenery, though, Mysterious Mike played a small, accidental role in jump-starting the career of the man who would far surpass him in the racket, a man the FBI would later describe as one of the most gifted forgers in the annals of American crime.

It happened at the monthly warehouse card show in the City of Industry, one of the popular stops on the southern California collecting circuit. Making a rare personal appearance to show off his wares, Lopez happened to bump into Greg Marino, who was there doing the lithograph shuffle. Both being regulars on the scene, the two knew each other and talked some business, Greg mentioning how much he liked the photos of Barry Sanders and Emmitt Smith that Mike was selling. They worked out a lopsided trade in favor of Lopez, and Greg walked off happily with a handful of star-signed pictures for his personal collection.

By this time Greg had lost his chef's job at the Welk; either he had quit or was fired, he won't say which. Whatever the story, his sole means of making money was selling his dad's art. His wife Kathy had a steady job at a bank so that covered the rent and groceries but after that there wasn't a whole bunch left over. It was frustrating. Here he was, one of the world's worst salesmen, trying to make a living (or if not a living, at least *something*) in sales. Adding to his frustration was how hard it was to move Angelo's art.

His father was a trained artist. Back east he'd gone to school at Farmingdale College, Westport Fine Arts, and the School of Industrial Art in New York City. He had worked as a graphic designer at a Manhattan ad agency before leaving to start his own business, a hair salon on Long Island. But even when he was running the salon, Angelo painted. He'd set up his easel in the back of the shop, and paint before the customers came in the morning and after they left at night. Among his favorite subjects were Indians of the Old West—a dignified Sioux woman in traditional dress, braves on horseback crossing a river, a Navajo tribe in winter—but his bread and butter as an artist was sports. After announcing his retirement from soccer Pele played his last game at the Meadowlands in the late seventies. Angelo painted the great Brazilian star as his fans wished to remember him—exulting with clenched fists, sliding on a field, leaping to kick a ball—and souvenir stands sold more than 10,000 of his lithographs that day.

Greg, who had some drawing talent himself, taking a semester of art classes in college before dropping out, admired his father's art, and it irked him that people didn't appreciate it the way he did. Time after time, when trying to convince foot-dragging shop owners to take Angelo's pieces on commission, they'd say to him:

"Too bad they're not signed."

"Do you have any ones that are signed?"

"I'd take them if they were signed. But sorry, no."

Even with their modest price tags, Angelo's artistic visions were regarded as incomplete. "People always asked for autographs on the pieces I was selling," said Greg with barely disguised scorn. He thought it was unfair but he had no choice but to pack up his bag and troop off to some other shop in the faint hope of finding someone interested in buying art for art's sake, signed only by the artist.

It was after he returned home from the City of Industry that Greg realized there might be another way.

Taking a closer look at the Lopez photos, "I started noticing things about these pieces," and the things he noticed weren't good. Some of the sigs were mixed up, as if Emmitt had gotten confused what his picture looked like and signed Barry's photos instead. And some of the autographs "didn't look too good," putting it delicately.

Greg understood the grift immediately but rather than feeling screwed for trading for such obvious fakes, he felt inspired. If Mysterious Mike could do it and get away with it, why not him? He could make some dough—God knows they needed it—and he could give a boost to his dad's art career while he was at it.

So, as he says, he started "messing around," just playing, nothing serious at first, seeing if he could duplicate, with his own hand, the autograph of Mickey Mantle. "It was probably the most popular autograph in the hobby at the time," he explained. "And the signatures I'd seen of Mantle were either real or really bad fakes. I'd never seen anybody do a real good Mantle. I figured if I could do him, I'd be doing something."

Mantle-signed memorabilia was as valuable as it was popular. A signed Mantle photograph [these are mid-nineties prices] sold for about $100; a signed ball, $200; a bat, $800; and the auction prices for rare pieces soared into orbit.* Being one of the all-time greats on the Marino family's favorite team, the Oklahoma-born slugger also held sentimental appeal. Mantle's final season was 1968, so Greg, only a small boy then, never saw him in action at the Stadium. But his father did, and Angelo probably painted Mantle more than any other player.

Greg gathered some paper and pens and sat down at a table in his apartment. In his sales calls for his dad he had collected samples of the genuine Mantle sig from magazines and photos, so he set these exemplars on the table to study. He was alone. Kathy was at work. Bright sunlight poured through a window, and he clicked on a lamp to get an even sharper view, looking at the famous signature hard, harder than he had looked at anything before, trying to burn its image into his mind. Finally he felt ready to give it a try.

Not quite. Something wasn't right. He knew what it was. He stood up, got a bag of weed, found some papers, and rolled a joint. He lit it and took a couple of long tokes breathing in real deep.

Now he was ready.

As he studied the signature, paying close attention to its lines and spacing, it occurred to him, again, how much he enjoyed looking at it. Besides the money and sentiment, this was what also drew him to Mantle. Unlike so many other athletes and celebrities who scribble their signature in a rush to be done with it, Mick had clean, highly legible handwriting. Greg noted this with satisfaction in the samples spread out before him: how consistent his hand was and how much pride he clearly took in his signature despite having done it tens of thousands of times in his lifetime. The young Mantle

---

*In a 1999 Sotheby's auction, former HBO chairman Michael Fuchs paid $123,500 for Mantle's 1956 World series ring. In that same auction comedian Billy Crystal outbid another person for a glove worn by Mantle in a 1960 game. Crystal's winning bid: $239,000. Prices for the rarest Mantle baseball cards have topped $120,000. Although these purchases took place after the period described here, they give an accurate picture of Mantle's commercial clout among collectors, which continues today.

signed his name plainly, like a diligent student trying to earn a good grade in penmanship. But as his fame and stature grew he achieved through the style and delicacy of his pen strokes something completely unexpected for a man of immense power who hit some of the longest home runs ever. He created a truly beautiful signature.

What made his signature so striking, and handsome, were the two *M*s of his name. Each had a graceful curving shape like a stylized half moon. Those two half moons, Greg saw, would make the difference between a good and bad Mantle. Each half moon had a certain size and shape to it, almost in the form of a triangle. So Greg began by drawing a simple triangle on the page; then, a crude half moon inside it. Everything was wrong at first—the triangle, the half moon, the angle of the strokes—everything but his desire to get better, to get it right. Putting the half moon inside the triangle helped because of instead signing free hand, he was using a geometric shape within which he could experiment.

As much as he enjoyed drawing cartoons and cartoon figures, if the signature looked drawn, he knew it was a dud. "I had to do it without a kink. You look at how you sign your name and there's a flow to it. There's no stoppage. It's fluid. Everything I did had to have a flow to it, same as Mantle. It had to be fast like he was signing it himself. The angles had to be right. It had to be perfect, and it had to be fast."

He drew pages and pages of half moons inside triangles, running out of paper and getting more and then rolling and smoking another joint. Gradually he felt confident enough to drop the triangle and write the first half moon while flowing directly into the rest of Mickey's name. Mantle lifted his pen, creating a definite space, before beginning that second half moon and finishing his last name with a flourish: a curlicue *e*. Greg tried to do the same, realizing that success would come only when he stopped trying and just did it—unthinkingly, unconsciously, effortlessly.

He practiced a while, took a break, and practiced some more until Kathy came home. In her mid-thirties, an upbeat, brown-haired native southern Californian, she met Greg at a party, which is fitting because that was what they did a lot when they started going out together: smoke, drink, run around. "We were partying kids," she said. But she liked and eventually fell in love with the big, bearded New Yorker because he was so different from the bland and blond beach boys she had grown up with. He made her laugh with the things he said and the way he said them. First they lived together. Then they got married in Vegas but not before Greg, like a scene out of "Diner," asked Kathy to recite the lineup of the Yankees. She aced the exam, naturally starting with Don Mattingly at first base. They had been married about a year when she came home to have Greg excitedly greet her with his pages of Mantle squiggles.

For her it was just giggle stuff. "Just play," she said. "Fluky stuff." In the spirit of fun she even took up a pen and gave those Mantle half moons a go herself, playing a while before stopping for dinner and then some TV after. Tired from the day and knowing she had to face the bank again in the morning, she kissed her husband good night and slipped into bed as he returned to his writing table and pens and paper.

For Greg, this was more serious fun. Alone once more, day having turned to night, his wife asleep in the next room, a galaxy of half moons started springing from his pen, the same signature written so many times over and over that as his eyes grew bleary and tired, the two words seemed to form one unbroken stream of letters in his mind: MickeyMantleMickey MantleMickeyMantleMickeyMantleMickeyMantleMickeyMantle—at which point, it occurred to him that maybe it was time for him to go to bed too. But he was back at it the next day, practicing for hours and hours and days and days and nights and nights until it no longer felt like practice anymore. The pen seemed almost to flow of its own accord without his direction, forming the angles it needed to form and moving rapidly and flawlessly in one unbroken motion across the page. Through sheer endless repetition those half moons were becoming second nature to him.

His goal was not to do one perfect Mantle, it was to do perfect Mantles all the time, to sign Mantle's signature with the same careless ease he signed his own name. Feeling like he'd achieved that, or something close to it, he showed some of his forgeries to a few people in the business, including Mike Lopez. "They said to me, 'If you can do Mantle, you can do anybody.' But even after I started doing him I still didn't think anybody would pay me for it." He was wrong about that. As it turned out lots of people were willing to pay him lots of money for it, and the first one to do so was a curt, sharp-spoken Orange County memorabilia dealer named Shelly Jaffe.

Most everybody in the racket between LA and San Diego knew Shelly Jaffe, or knew of him, because he had been dealing fakes as long as anyone. On one level you had to respect that: a man ahead of his time. In his sixties, balding, with a white mustache, his large glasses hanging at his chest on a string holder, he was an elder of the tribe, crafting his dubious deals while padding around in gym shorts and sports shoes in his home office on

Yaqi Court in Tustin. A native of Cleveland and a sports fan all his life, Jaffe scalped football tickets while an undergrad at Ohio State, eventually dropping out because "there was more money out in the street than there was in school." His occupation, his passion, was always sales. He sold women's clothing before becoming a broker for a steel company, and a job transfer brought him and his wife to California. When asked what makes a good salesman, he said, with characteristic dismissiveness, "Please. There's no answer. There's no definitive answer to that. A good salesman is what he is. You can't teach it. It's instinctive. You gotta know how to sell in your own way. That's why college can't teach it."

He started collecting baseball cards when his son was born—as keepsakes, not as investments or to resell. But as more money came into the hobby, his interest grew and he developed a pleasurable side business called Shelly's Cards. Then came the 1994 baseball strike that wrecked everybody's fun. When major leaguers walked off the job in August, causing the playoffs and World Series to be cancelled, the card market crashed. Who wanted to buy cards with pictures on them of overpaid, selfish brats who were ruining the national pastime? From a high of $1.2 billion in 1991, new card sales fell almost by half the season after the strike. The resale or secondary market where Shelly's Cards operated got pounded, as did sports memorabilia in general. Speculators were burned badly, and in at least one case the consequences were tragic.*

To stay in business Shelly shifted out of cards and into autographs, where the money suddenly was. From autographs it was a nimble sidestep into forgeries. "I couldn't make an honest living," he said. "I'd pay ninety bucks for an item. I'd go to a show and the guy at the table next to me would be selling four of the same items, clearly fakes, for twenty-five bucks apiece. Forgeries were becoming so prevalent you either quit the business or you joined them. I joined them."

Once he joined, it was impossible not to appreciate the corrupt beauty of the scam. Complaints about the authenticity of a sig occurred, but not often, and even when they did they hardly rose to a level that attracted the interest of law enforcement. Somebody rips you off for $10,000 or $50,000, you're going to be pissed and take it up with the authorities. Somebody sells you a signed Andre Agassi tennis ball for seventy-five bucks (assuming you even realize it's bogus)—well, you're not going to feel the sting quite as sharply.

Duane Garrett, a San Francisco raido talk show host and major Democratic Party fundraiser, was an avid collector who engineered a number of possibly illegal schemes to sell vintage memorabilia. These ventures collapsed in part due to the drop in fan interest after the strike. On the verge of bankruptcy, apparently fearful his questionable dealings were about to be exposed, Garrett killed himself by jumping off the Golden Gate Bridge in the summer of 1995.

And that was what was so brilliant about the thing: its sheer dumb ordinariness. It wasn't like robbing a bank for one big score; it was like picking the pockets of every person in the bank, including the bank vice president who proudly displayed his collection of Hall of Fame memorabilia that, poor fool, he thought was actually signed by the Hall of Famers. But it wasn't even like picking pockets because the vice president and most every other customer happily forked over their money and at such bargain prices, often came back for repeat business.

Now, some of the cannier customers may have strongly suspected they were buying a forgery, based on its below-market sales price and easy availability. But, having sunk a small fortune into the emperor's new clothes, they were not about to do or say anything that would jeopardize the resale value of their investment. The signed memorabilia they owned had value because people believed the signatures were real; once that belief disintegrated, so did the value of their collection. So they stayed mum about it. Another group of customers were in simple denial about the true nature of what they had purchased. Others may be fooled, but not them. The effect was the same in any case: They kept their mouths shut. The victims themselves, then, became silent partners in the crime, co-conspirators. Oh, what a lovely swindle it was!

Mike Lopez did some work for Shelly but Shelly considered him a crappy forger whose products were everywhere, destroying any competitive advantage he might have had in selling them. He asked Mike if he could recommend anyone else in the trade. In a gesture atypical of the screw-or-be-screwed world of counterfeit memorabilia, Mike generously gave him Greg's name. So Shelly invited Greg and Kathy up to his place to see what this new kid could do.

From Escondido, where the Marinos lived, it is about an hour and a half north up Interstate 5 to Tustin. Greg was nervous and smoked a joint on the way up. From the freeway they turned into a residential section whose streets were so clean they looked as if they had been hosed down that morning. Many of the streets had Indian names; Shelly's house was on Yaqi Court. The homes were all four- and five-bedroom tan and brown stucco houses with late model SUVs parked in front. One house had an American flag flying outside and there was a basketball hoop on the street. When the Marinos rang the front bell Shelly poked his head out the window of his upstairs office and yelled down for them to let themselves in and come on up. They followed the stairs up into the privacy of his office where Shelly, who was not big on formalities, gestured for Kathy to have a seat on the couch and quickly set to work with her husband.

Greg sat down at a desk. A computer was against one wall, a phone next to it. Shelly pulled down the window blinds for reasons of privacy and to cut down on the glare on the desk. The walls of the office featured framed photos of Joe DiMaggio, but it was Mick, not Joe, who was the man of the moment. Shelly set some Sharpies in front of Greg and a short stack of 8x10 black and white Mantle photographs in need of Mantle sigs.

Practice was over; this was show time. The photos were all the same: a young, handsome Mantle in his Yankee cap and pinstripes, facing the camera with a serious clear-eyed gaze. Greg spun out the two half moons with bold strokes diagonally across the lower right corner of the picture, staying clear of Mantle's face but in a spot where the autograph could be clearly seen and where a buyer would most want it to be placed. When he finished he handed the picture to Shelly and went on to the next in the stack. On some of the photos, per Shelly's instructions, he added a 7 to the sig, Mantle's number on the Yankees, a flourish that boosted the price of the piece.

Taking his big glasses off his chest and placing them on the bridge of his nose to better assess what he was seeing, Shelly examined each signature rolling off Greg's pen with the intensity of a scientist studying the results of an important laboratory experiment. Half the photos he regarded as worthless, awful, crap, tossing them into a reject pile. But the other half—ah, they were "great."

"Greg was always high," said Shelly fondly in retrospect. "But he was a helluva forger."

In gratitude Shelly dropped a thousand bucks, cash, on Greg and Kathy. They couldn't believe their eyes, exchanging wide, secret grins when he was counting out the bills. Then when they got outside their smiles turned to bright, happy gusts of laughter.

"Wow." They said over and over on the drive back home. "Wow."

A thousand bucks—and for what? A few hours of work, if you wanted to call it work, which it wasn't, not really, not like slaving away at the Welk or any other job Greg had ever done. It was too easy to be called work, and the money was much, much better. And Shelly had only bought some of the photos. What if he'd bought all of them? What would he have paid then? And as they were leaving, the cynical old pro—Greg called Shelly "a scandalous guy, very paranoid. He worried way too much"—was eager as a kid to do more business with him.

It was crazy, thought Greg, just crazy enough to interest his pal Wayne Bray.

Since their first meeting at W.W. Sports Cards the two had become close friends—Greg coming into the shop to hang out, Wayne buying more of

Angelo's stuff, Wayne and Greg and Angelo going in on some art deals together, with Wayne fronting the money for the printing costs in exchange for a percentage of the sales. Kathy had gotten to know him too. The bank where she worked was in the same neighborhood as his shop, and she'd come over during her lunch hour to buy Yankee cards and knickknacks for her husband.

During this time Greg hadn't said anything to Wayne about his private Mickey Mantle obsession, not showing him any of his samples or telling him about his rendezvous with Shelly. But if he ever did come clean with his new friend, he felt certain that Wayne would be into it just the way he appeared to be into other activities of a questionable nature. "Wayne was always into this and into that," said Greg knowingly. "He was that kind of guy."

His instincts proved correct. With a flair for the dramatic, Greg decided to reveal his new-found talents at W.W. Sports Cards. A Mantle souvenir plate hung on the wall of the shop. Greg asked Wayne to bring it down for him, which he did, setting it on the front display counter. Greg said, "Watch this," and with a gold pen he had brought for the occasion, signed a perfect Mantle sig on the plate.

Suddenly another dull, purpose-less day in Vista radiated with meaning.

Wayne's droopy, heavy-lidded eyes popped wide open and "his face turned red," said Greg. Wayne agreed: "I looked at it, and I went bing-bing. It was perfect, a perfect Mantle."

He challenged Greg to do it again, giving him a piece of paper to see if lightning could strike twice. It did—two, three, four, five times in a row. Greg's half moons were even better than Mantle's!

Bray has described his personality as "spontaneous—spontaneous combustion." This was the moment of combustion, the moment that lit the fuse. In this instant, the instant he laid eyes on Greg's perfect Mantle, he grasped the raw potential of what they could do together. He could see the next thing, and he could see how the next thing, if they could make it work, would lead to another, bigger thing, and how the next thing after that could be bigger still, bigger than all the other previous things combined, and it could all keep snowballing like that and the money could be gargantuan. Life-changing, brain-spinning, Super Lotto jackpot-type money.

No more small-time trading card deals. No more pinching pennies to get ahead, when you never get ahead anyway. No more worrying about paying the rent or the bills or anything else. Nothing would be out of reach for them. The only thing they'd have to worry about was how to spend all the money they'd be making.

In his endless days and months and years at W.W. Sports Cards Wayne had learned patience, a trait that did not come naturally to him. Patience he now had in bunches; what he lacked was money, and this lack, and how to remedy it, was what dominated his waking thoughts.

Well, here was the answer. Think no more. Wait no more. Their main chance had arrived.

Greg wasn't so sure, though. It was one thing to do a few jobs for Shelly and some other people. It was kind of a kick, like Kathy said. But if they started doing this seriously it sort of put them into a different category, right?

Wayne, hearing Greg's hesitation, talked about it with him. Yeah, this was criminal, no doubt. They would be breaking the law. This wasn't something they could chat about with other people, particularly if those other people wore blue uniforms with badges. They had to be very, very careful because they'd be committing fraud and ripping people off and lying about it. The stakes were high. They risked screwing up their marriages, hurting their families, and if they were caught they could go to prison for a long time.

Aw to hell with it, said Greg with a shrug. Let's go for it.

It turned out Greg not only looked and dressed like a pirate, he had the soul of one too. In this sense he and Wayne were kindred spirits, brothers, and he signed on fully for the vision Wayne mapped out for them. It would be tempting to see the pair as two half moons—the one's vision and drive and organizational skills fitting perfectly with the other's artistic talents to form this grand criminal enterprise they were about to embark on. Tempting, but not correct. For there was a third piece, a third person whose participation truly made the enterprise whole. That was Stan the Man.

With Mike Lopez dropping from the scene, Stan and Wayne had re-established business ties and were back on deal-making terms. Quickly Wayne got on the horn and without mentioning Greg by name, to avoid the possibility of a double-cross, "I hinted to Stan that I had a better forger than Lopez and that I could get anything he wanted." Interested, Stan said sure, he'd take a look at the guy's "talent"—talent being another code word for forgery—and placed an order for some bulkies and flats.

The bulkies were baseballs to be signed with Mantle's sig, and the flats were photos of him. The balls came from one of Stan's equipment distributors, and the photos from a photo supply house. He shipped them to W.W. Sports Cards. When they arrived Wayne waited till he could wait no more, closed the shop, then hurried over to Greg's place. When he rolled up Greg had just gotten out of the shower and was in his underwear, so Wayne carried the boxes in by himself and set them in the living room, burning to get going.

Greg's internal clock had a different timing mechanism, though. Before going to work he needed a joint. "I'd do it before, during, after. It helped me relax. Wayne didn't smoke pot so much. He smoked cigarettes and popped pills." Next Greg slipped in a Bob Marley CD and turned up the volume. "We'd always play music when I was signing. Reggae mostly—Bob Marley, Shaggy. A little Sinatra too." A stick of weed, some sounds, and Greg was ready to rock, though he still hadn't gotten out of his boxers.

"Greg had a big ol' gut," Wayne recalled, "and he wore white boxer shorts. He'd sweat because he was so big, and after a shower he'd put baby powder all over himself. So we had to brush the powder off some of the stuff he was signing."

Smoke filling the air, music blasting, baby powder flying, Greg started in with the photos. He worked in the kitchen, on the flat surface of the table, signing one after another and moving quickly through them. When they were done Wayne put them back in their box, and the pair turned to the balls.

Balls represented more of a problem. The writing surface was made of horsehide or cowhide, and was rounded and small and awkward. Greg signed some in the classic way of players autographing for fans at a ballpark, holding the ball in his left hand and the pen in his right. But after a while he sat down on the living room couch and used a couch cushion to prop his right arm up. He sunk his arm into the cushion so that it was slightly above or level with the ball. The cushion supported his forearm and wrist, and he felt more comfortable and made fewer mistakes as he went through the balls.

Wholesalers sell baseballs in cases, ten dozen to a case, each dozen enclosed in smaller boxes within the case. Wayne slit the seams of a case with a knife, pulled out one of the boxes, and opened it. Every ball was wrapped in plastic and sat perched in an egg carton-like container. Carefully unwrapping the plastic he took each ball out and placed it so the sweet spot was facing up, so that Greg didn't have to fumble around looking for it. The sweet spot is the blank space opposite the commissioner's signature on a baseball where the stitching comes closest together. It's the money spot where autograph seekers universally want it to be signed.

After the ink dried on a signature Wayne restored the ball to its plastic cocoon and put it back in its egg crate. After a dozen balls he returned the crate to the box and the box to the case, always making sure Greg had fresh balls to do, the sweet spot perfectly positioned, no delays, keep it moving. When they finished they loaded everything back into the vehicle and Wayne drove it over to UPS to ship to New Jersey.

Stan responded promptly. He liked what he saw, so much so that another shipment of blanks was soon arriving at W.W. Sports Cards. Included in this shipment was an envelope bulging with cash. Wayne took his cut and drove the goods and the rest of the money over to Greg's, and they went after it again. It was total lunacy. They were criminals, and their weapon was a friggin' Sharpie, man. Fire up another reefer: They were in business.

4

As soon as they filled Stan's first order—no, before that: as soon as he saw perfection etched in gold on the Mantle plate—Wayne knew if they were really going to get this thing going, they needed to do more names than just Mantle.

"If you can do Mantle," he told Greg, echoing what others had said, "you can do DiMaggio."

There are three baseball autographs every serious collector has to have: Mantle, DiMaggio and Ted Williams, known in the trade as the Big Three. Greg had emotional ties to his Mantle, but his motive for learning DiMaggio was pure commerce. He agreed with Wayne that if he learned him and got him right, they'd make more money.

The first letter of a person's signature is almost always strongly written even if the letters that follow are a mess. Similarly, when a prospective buyer looks at an autograph, his eyes naturally travel to the two capital letters. So when Greg returned to his work table to tackle his new assignment, he started by filling up sheets of paper with just *J*s and *D*s.

"Some people said you could never do DiMaggio," he recalled. "His signature was too perfect, always consistent. The big thing on Joe's name was learning the *J*. That was the most important. He was very consistent in the way he signed his *J*. Both the *J* and the *D* had to be consistent, and the *D* had to be at a certain angle. It was easy to mess up the *D*."

Greg messed up a lot in the beginning, a fact his taskmaster of a coach was not shy about pointing out. Wayne thought Greg's DiMaggio looked like his Mantle, only without the half moons, and that simply wasn't acceptable. It had to be the way DiMaggio himself signed it—nothing else would do. "Wayne was very persistent about things, very detail oriented," said Greg with some exasperation. "Things had to be a certain way. It pissed me off because sometimes he could be a real stickler. Other times when he had a big order from Stan that needed to be filled right away, his attitude was, 'Get it done.'"

Even though most of the people who saw these autographs wouldn't know the difference between DiMaggio's *J* and Jersey Joe Walcott's, Wayne knew how Joe D. did it, and he felt strongly this was the way it should be done. Furthermore, he knew another stickler for quality, Stan Fitzgerald, was eyeballing each and every piece they sent him, so they had to be good, better than good. Wayne also believed, as did Stan the Man, that their insistence on quality gave them an edge over the hacks in the racket who were turning out slop just to make a fast buck.

Greg's personal style was more easy-going than Wayne's, but he worked just as hard. Like his hero Donnie Baseball, he put demands on himself and strove to fulfill them. Seeing the profit that could be had in being the best, or close to it, he too cared about getting the details right. Then there was that sense he had—call it an aesthetic impulse, though he would have never used this term and might even be embarrassed by it—that his creations should look a certain way, and that was as close to genuine as possible. So when Wayne asked him to do a sig again, he did it. And he did it again and again and again and again, however many times it took before he felt he had it and didn't need to practice it anymore. There was no bullying or coercion; he made a choice, and Wayne had made the same choice. They were a team.

"Greg had a gift," said Wayne. "But he practiced too. A lot."

After DiMaggio, they moved on to the last of the Big Three. "With Ted," said Greg, "the *d* and the *W* would run together. Then Ted would come down on the first loop of the *W* but not quite finish it and then go into the *i*. It was like with Joe and Mickey. I did all these letters over and over again until I felt I got it."

His Muhammad Ali caused him more trouble. "The whole sig was hard," he said, recalling his efforts to learn Ali. "Each year his signature seemed to get worse and a little different than the year before. You know, because of his Parkinson's. It changed so many times over the years. There was not a certain Ali you could stick with."

Challenging as it may have been, he applied his Ali to photos (8x10, 16x20), posters, boxing gloves (single or pair), boxing trunks, baseballs, even golf balls. That was the thing, they were finding, about this new business they were in: There were so many different product possibilities. Michael Jordan alone could have filled a warehouse with all the merchandise associated with him: individual photos, team photos, individual and team posters, magazine covers, cards, books, toy figurines, statues, Bulls jerseys, basketballs,

Dream Team basketballs, caps, baseballs, golf balls, collectible plates, banners, pennants, cachets, Air Jordans, cereal boxes, and the mountains of other merchandise issued by companies he had endorsed.

The *M* of Michael's name was written in the shape of a 23, his number for the Bulls. "He was very consistent in the way he did it," said Greg, who tried to be just as consistent when forging him. "It was exactly the same every time, probably because he signed so much himself."

An autograph was a form of personal expression, and yet each one conformed to a pattern such as the triangle underlying the Mantle half moons. Once Greg discovered this pattern he felt he could lock into a sig and nail it. The *o* in Dan Marino, for instance, looped around his last name with an expressive curve, accompanied often by his number on the Dolphins, 13. But Dan's 3 was sharper and less rounded than the way Shaquille O'Neal did the 3 in his number, 34. Whereas Bret Favre's 4 looked nothing like the numeral; it more resembled the letter *f*.

Other famous signatures frequently came in pairs: Joe Montana and Jerry Rice, Larry Bird and Magic Johnson. Since the public associated these players together, there was great demand for material signed by them both. Another popular duo was DiMaggio and Marilyn Monroe. Despite the fact that Joe publicly stated that he would not sign photos of him and Marilyn, nor any Marilyn-related memorabilia, people still longed for autographed pictures of them together—a wish Greg and Wayne and Stan the Man were happy to grant.

Celebrity fugazzis were part of the mix too, and Greg worked on his Marilyn and his Elvis and his Julia Roberts and his Tom Hanks and his Madonna and his Michael Jackson as surely as he did the sports guys. But the celeb side of the racket never drew as much play as the jocks. One reason for this was that with celebs, you could basically only sell flats such as 8x10s and posters. In sports, though, you could sell flats and bulkies—all those balls and bats and jerseys that the public considered to be of higher value, and thus was willing to pay more for than mere paper products.

Still, Greg couldn't do any sig unless he first saw a genuine example of it. This was one of the early challenges they faced: digging up exemplars. Some days Greg and Wayne would meander into a memorabilia shop and while Wayne chatted up the sales clerk, occupying his attention, Greg would stand over by a far wall studying a star's photo with his or her signature on it, practicing how to forge it on the sly. Seeing how important exemplars were to the growth of the business, Wayne rapidly took this duty over, relentlessly combing through magazines, books, autograph handbooks and sports cards in search of them. When he found one he made a copy and inserted the page into a black three-ring binder. The "black book," as they jokingly called it, was no joke, for every sig in it potentially represented money.

The more exemplars they had, the more sigs Greg could do—the big names as well as the lesser ones, though they concentrated on the superstars for the obvious reason that their signed memorabilia commanded the highest prices. Their autographs were also better known among collectors, so if something seemed screwy about them, they might be more easily spotted. To get objective appraisals of Greg's work, Wayne sent his best sigs to the leading sports autograph experts in the country who, for a fee, inspected them for authenticity. They did not know, of course, that what they were inspecting was fake. In the unanimous opinion of these experts, the material appeared genuine.

Inevitably, as the months passed by, other guys found out what was going on and wanted in. One of these was Big Ricky Weimer, a chubby, low-key veteran of the card business who always seemed to have a lit cigarette hanging from his mouth. His specialty was old bats and sports gear of marginal value. People brought him baseball bats from the '60s and '70s that they had scavenged at garage sales and swap meets, and Big Ricky always overpaid for them. If a bat was worth a hundred bucks he paid two hundred—and the guy who sold it to him walked away feeling sorry for poor Ricky because he'd fleeced him so bad.

What this guy did not realize was that Big Ricky turned this bat over to his buddy Greg Marino, who applied the sig of Mantle or DiMaggio or Roger Maris—or all three. This piece-of-crap store model bat then sold for a couple thousand bucks.

Another guy who got involved early was Dick Laughlin, a nice, respectable frame shop owner in San Juan Capistrano who developed a nice, respectable counterfeit business on the side. Like Big Ricky, he trafficked mainly in the vintage market, driving down from Capistrano to drop off a Glad trash bag full of old junk on Greg's doorstep in Escondido. Then, after Greg did his thing, Dick picked up the goods and put them on sale at his shop.

Some of the guys, like Big Ricky, were middle men and distributors; others like Laughlin mostly sold retail. Smokey's in Las Vegas combined retail with a brisk mail order business that sold to people around the country. Located on the Strip between the Monte Carlo and Bellagio, the "world famous" card shop—so said its sign out front, ringed by flashing neon lights—was run by David and Phil Scheinman, neither of whom appear smoky in any way. Late middle-aged, with a neatly trimmed mustache, David Scheinman, known as "Doc," resembled a high school teacher marking the days until retirement. He was lean and somewhat severe looking, in contrast to his thirty-something son Phil, who was a little on the pudgy side, sporting around the vast Smokey's showroom floor in jeans and a ball cap. Greg had gotten to know them on his trips to Vegas, and they quickly became a solid account for him.

Amidst the wide array of merchandise at Smokey's were lithographs and baseballs painted by Angelo Marino, who also threw in with his talented son. Slender and quiet and inwardly drawn, Angelo—those close to him call him Andy—was a personable, dark-haired family man in his sixties who seemed at times a tad preoccupied, as if he had other, more important things on his mind—those other things being art, art and art. Just like Greg, he felt frustrated by the public's apathy toward his work, and earlier in his career he had pulled a fast one on Dan Marino (no relation), then a star quarterback for Miami and now a broadcaster. The two Marinos entered into a legitimate business transaction of the type artists and celebrity athletes often arrange, with Angelo painting a portrait of Dan that was sold as a limited edition lithograph with a set number of pieces in the print run signed by Dan. Only, as Angelo later confided, the autograph run "was not as limited as Dan thought." Angelo forged Dan's signature on many of the lithos and sold them to the public as the real thing.

There is evidence to suggest that in addition to Wayne, Angelo helped Greg with his forgery techniques in the beginning. Certainly the elder Marino could see the profit in it too. One of his unsigned Ali or Bret Favre or Jack Nicklaus lithographs sold for twenty-five to fifty dollars apiece, if they sold at all. Add the star's signature and the same picture went for twice that, and jumped off the shelf. Finally Front Page Art—the name of Angelo's business—was giving the public what it demanded: art and signatures.

With his father involved, Greg's mother Gloria came to know about her son's activities as well. "I guess it seemed harmless [to her]," Greg said matter-of-factly, when asked what his mother's response was when he informed her about his new career. "It was a supply and demand type of thing. People wanted these things and we were supplying it to them."

Gloria and Angelo lived in Escondido not far from Greg and Kathy, and it wasn't long before Greg started meeting some of those supply and demand obligations at his parents' house. Naturally John Marino, who lived with his parents, wasn't going to be kept out of it for long. A true six-footer and then some, John was bigger and huskier than his older brother with black hair and a mustache. A talented athlete when he was a teenager, he had once entertained dreams of becoming a pro golfer. But what had once gotten into Wayne Bray, crystal meth, got into him too, and away flew most of his ambitions save for the ones having to do with getting his next fix. He married a woman who was into the junk as well. They split up but not before they had three kids together. In between stints in rehab John peddled his dad's art too, but he was an even worse businessman than Greg and far less reliable. This forgery thing—he helped with setups, ran errands, picked up and delivered merchandise—at least gave him a job and a steady source of income.

Then in August 1995, for John and the rest of them, this steady flow of cash turned into a raging torrent.

Earlier that summer the sixty-three-year-old Mickey Mantle, an ex-alcoholic who was suffering from liver cancer, had received a liver transplant. Doctors found, however, that the cancer had spread to other parts of his body. Knowing he was about to die, looking old and frail and emaciated, the man who had been a hero to a generation of boys and men held a televised press conference at the medical center in Texas where he was a patient. He delivered some of his remarks directly to the nation's children. Don't be like me when you grow up, he said. He was nobody's role model. A few weeks later he was dead.

The grace in which he held himself at the end, the humility he showed, only deepened the public's affection for Mantle, causing a frenzy of orders for memorabilia associated with him. Seemingly every sports fan in America who had been touched by him during his life wanted to stay connected to him now that he was gone. But Wayne and Stan were prepared, stocking up on Mantle merchandise during his sad, public demise. So when the end came they were ready to act, Wayne rolling up to Greg's place in a vehicle full of photos, posters, balls, bats, jerseys and whatever else he could fit in.

"Wayne showed up at my door with piles of Mantle merchandise," Greg recalled with a kind of astonishment. "He said to me, 'You're gonna buy a new Explorer next week,' and he was right. I did. We did that much in business. Just tons and tons of orders. We went crazy."

Wayne did the setups and Greg, wearing gray sweats and white socks and no shirt—his other favorite work outfit besides boxers—spun out half moons till he was dizzy, smoke and reggae filling the room at all times and the two of them laughing and moving to the music and having the criminal time of their lives. In the evening when Kathy got home they took a break and she fixed them dinner. Then after dinner they went right back to it.

In September, after the rush had slowed down some, Greg and Wayne flew off to see Cal Ripken break Lou Gehrig's consecutive game streak at Camden Yards. It was strictly a spur of the moment thing. They got the most expensive rooms at the classiest Inner Harbor hotel they could find on such short notice. Nobody at the hotel or anywhere else asked where their money came from; cash was cash, and when you have it people are just happy to take it from you. Tickets for the game were impossible to come by, but they threw money at the problem and the problem went away. They got choice seats and witnessed history.

The next month Dick Laughlin hooked Greg up with a ticket to see the Yankees play the Mariners in the fifth and deciding game of the American League Division Series. So, again, totally spur of the moment, Greg hopped on a plane to Seattle. The Yankees lost, which bummed him out, but he lived it up like a rich man and had a grand time. That's what happens when you've got a wallet stuffed with bills and the knowledge that when it empties out, it's going to fill right back up again. In November Stan the Man ordered a thousand more Mantle photos, and the forgery brothers and their growing band of confederates were off and running again.

Another big event in sports put money in their pockets that fall: the return of the world's best basketball player to full-time play. Mourning over his father's death and feeling as if he had been to the top of the basketball mountain and seen all there was to see, Michael Jordan had left the game in 1993 after leading the Chicago Bulls to three consecutive NBA titles. His dream was to play professional baseball but after a year and a half of struggle in the minors he finally gave up the little round horsehide ball for the bigger leather one that had made him rich and famous, coming back to the Bulls in time for the playoffs in the spring of 1995. Jordan's performance was uncharacteristically poor, which seemed only to make him more determined when he returned for his first full season after retirement, joining his old running mate Scottie Pippen and the newly-acquired bad boy rebound king, Dennis Rodman, to form the best, most exciting, most glamorous basketball team on the planet.

Jordan's comeback put a charge in commerce as well as basketball. *USA Today* reported that the stock of the companies that used him as their promotional spokesman rose $2 billion on the speculation that he would again suit up for the Bulls. When he did indeed suit up, for his first game General Mills gave away 10,000 posters and 5,000 T-shirts with the slogan, "Jordan's Back. And He's Eating His Wheaties." Larry Brown, then coaching the Pacers, said it was "like Elvis and the Beatles are back." A TV commentator joked that Bulls fans were in "a state of Jorgasm." Equally fervid were the folks in the collecting industry, especially the Upper Deck Company that owned the exclusive commercial rights to Jordan's autograph.

Located in Carlsbad, California, about a half hour north of San Diego and within minutes of where the Bray-Marino ring was based, Upper Deck is a leading trading card and memorabilia manufacturer with annual sales of $200 million. In 1994 it entered into a multimillion dollar pact with Jordan, one of the first of its kind in the autograph industry, which essentially stipulated that except for love notes to his wife and children and occasional freebies for fans at games or personal appearances, he could only sign his name on Upper Deck merchandise. He was prohibited from signing at private sessions or card shows or anywhere else without the company's permission. Even those times when he was allowed to sign products made by another company, such as when Nike displayed autographed Air Jordans at its stores around the country, the signings occurred only under Upper Deck's strict supervision. Another time General Mills decided to give Wheaties boxes signed by Michael to its top executives as holiday gifts. If Upper Deck had chosen to play Scrooge, it could have forbidden him from signing them. As it happened the execs all got their gift boxes. Upper Deck even supervised the signing of a life-sized cardboard standee of MJ in his Bulls uniform grinning and holding a basketball that was used at a trade show by another firm.

Through its relationship with Jordan, Upper Deck had a competitive advantage unmatched by any other card or memorabilia company. Its products featured the genuine Jordan signature, not a facsimile, and Jordan-signed cards were inserted randomly into its packs as an incentive for people to buy, which they did in large numbers. The success of this arrangement led Upper Deck to tie up other brand name superstars—Dan Marino, Joe Montana, Bret Favre, Troy Aikman, Ken Griffey, Jr., Mickey Mantle, Ted Williams, to name only a few—to similar autograph deals.

Whether it was basketball, baseball or golf season, Jordan signed every month for Upper Deck. These signings took place at the Omni Hotel on North Michigan Avenue in Chicago where he had a penthouse office suite. Each signing followed the same procedure, with Upper Deck sending a shipment of unsigned merchandise to the Omni. There to meet the truck was Anthony West, who handled security for the sessions. West made sure none of the boxes had been opened in transit and everything was as it should be. From the delivery bay he accompanied the goods upstairs to a suite on a lower floor of the hotel where he and another company official unpacked the boxes and set the material out. When everything was ready, the call went up to the penthouse. In due course Jordan and an assistant appeared, and Jordan set about the process of turning nothing into something. Like a wizard waving a magic wand, he transformed a dime card into a one hundred dollar card, a ten dollar poster into a two hundred dollar poster, a twenty dollar basketball into an eight hundred dollar basketball. His touch gave every piece of merchandise in the room a new, more lucrative identity. Then Michael and his assistant said goodbye until the next time, and departed.

It was the job of Anthony West and the other Upper Deck representative to pack everything back up and apply security seals to the boxes. West then rode the elevator down with the boxes to a waiting delivery truck, and helped load them in. As the truck drove away he called the home office to let them know when its precious cargo was scheduled to arrive back in California. His duties done, he caught a cab to O'Hare and flew back to Carlsbad where he resumed his regular duties as an investigator for the company.

West, a soft-featured man who speaks so quietly it is sometimes hard to hear what he is saying when seated across the table from him, originally joined Upper Deck as a security guard. He conducted foot patrols of its offices and manufacturing plant, and surprise searches of employees at the end of the work day to make sure they weren't leaving with anything they weren't supposed to. In his first weeks on the job he foiled one would-be thief by finding a number of uncut sheets of Ken Griffey Jr.'s rookie card hidden between pieces of flattened cardboard in a palette outside the plant. Baseball cards come off the printing press in sheets, to be cut individually for distribution in packs. An uncut sheet of the rookie card of a superstar like Junior was, in West's phrase, "like a Mona Lisa" and worth thousands of dollars, a fact no doubt understood by the employee who returned to the plant that night when no one was around, reached under the cardboard in the palette, and came up with air.

Machine operators cut around the bottom of a WD-40 can used to lubricate the presses, inserted cards up into it, and replaced the bottom piece so the can looked normal. Trash cans and dumpsters were also popular places to hide cards, not to mention the insides of jackets. West watched one employee in a puffy silver and black Raiders jacket leave the plant, go out to his car, come back in, then go back outside again. Raider Guy did this several times before West asked him to unzip his jacket, which had been slit open on the inside on both sides to hold Ted Williams cards. When West escorted him out to the parking lot, in the back seat of his car, in full view of anyone who happened to pass by, were hundreds of Williams cards with a street value probably worth double what Raider Guy made in a year.

Raider Guy may not have been the world's smartest thief but he knew what he was after, as did other employee-thieves working with dealers on the outside. "They knew exactly what they wanted," said West. "These stolen cards were often preordered. Guys would try to get hired at Upper Deck in order to be an inside man and steal cards. Then they'd sell the cards to a dealer who sold them for big bucks."

It was only natural, then, as West's role with the company grew, that his investigations went beyond Upper Deck's posh, glass tower headquarters on Sea Otter Place in the hills of Carlsbad and out into the hurly-burly commercial marketplace. He wanted to track the movement of these stolen cards and find out who these dealers were. "For some reason," he said, "I took an interest in getting these guys." A former hotel security man, West had previously worked under an ex-LAPD detective at the Century Plaza in Los Angeles where political figures and celebrities in need of tight security frequently visit, and he had learned a lot about the business from him—what to look for in assessing a subject and how to observe someone without being observed yourself. As he started to snoop around the guy ghettoes of card shows and card shops he applied these techniques, not knowing he was about to pick up the trail of far bigger game.

With thinning hair, a mustache and a chunky but solid build, in many ways West resembled many of the subjects he was investigating, except, as he knew, in one visible way. He was a black man moving around a scene heavily populated by white and Asian men.

"I was easy to identify," he said. "I'd go to a show and see maybe one or two other blacks in the entire hall."

West knew he was being watched, but not because of the color of his skin. Dealers feared, correctly, that he was gathering information on them to bust them. At the popular City of Industry show he suspected that spies were posted at the front door who, when they saw him enter, relayed a message back to corrupt dealers who then stashed their contraband cards.

On these "look-outs," as he called his visits to these places, dealers began to look out for him, causing him to change tactics. Rather than go into a shop where the owner recognized his face, he sometimes sent in an assistant to check the place out for him to see if all the goods being sold were on the level.

While doing these lookouts, and flying back and forth across the country for the sessions at the Omni, West started to see things he wasn't sure he was seeing. Having witnessed Jordan sign his name a zillion times, he knew his signature better than any man alive save for Michael himself. This was why he found it so troubling, and baffling, to see the autograph with the M as a 23 showing up for sale at airport souvenir shops and other places he passed through on his travels. Some of the sigs were clearly fake, but others appeared so close to real as to be real. Even to his trained eye it was hard to tell.

Michael was only signing for Upper Deck, but this 8x10 of him thunder dunking was not an approved Upper Deck product. So how did his autograph get on it then? Could Michael be signing things on the sly in violation of his contract to make more money? This troubling thought occurred to West and Upper Deck management as they pondered the mystery of why all these Jordanesque items were appearing here, there and everywhere.

At one of the Omni sessions a company representative finally asked Michael about it. "Not being accusatory," said West, "just wanting to know." Michael basically said, Oh for crying out loud, he didn't sign that crap, he hated signing all this stuff, and besides, he had more money than Donald Trump so why would he sign more than he had to? And no, he wasn't doing wholesale free signings for fans before games or on the golf course, so that eliminated that possibility.

Okay, so if MJ wasn't signing behind their backs, what about some of these other superstars under exclusive contract with Upper Deck? Genuine-looking material with their signatures on it was becoming as widespread as the Jordan stuff. West said that Upper Deck discretely checked up on a few of these stars to make sure their signing habits did not conflict with their contractual commitments to the company. But the volume of signed material appearing in the marketplace argued against individual duplicity of this sort. One person couldn't do all this, or even a few people. Something else was going on, something bigger and more insidious, and the focus of West's investigations shifted from stolen card product to forgeries.

On his look-outs, now charged with a new purpose and new targets, West, the first investigator in the U.S. to spot the widespread existence of forgeries, often teamed with an assistant at Upper Deck, Kathy Wichmann. Bright, fast-thinking and pretty with long dark hair, she would chat up the dealer or sales clerk, allowing her boss to poke around the premises with more freedom, both of them paying close attention to the shipping labels on any UPS boxes that were sitting around. If Kathy and Anthony spotted a Michael Jordan forgery, they would make up a story, explaining to the dealer that they worked at a company that was holding a party and how neat it'd be if they could hand out autographed pictures of Michael to the employees.

"Can we order a dozen of them?" they would ask, innocently, the unstated message of their question being: "Will you sell us counterfeits?"

Authentic signed MJ items are not like jelly beans at the jelly bean factory; you can't order bags of them. But if the dealer said, "Sure, I can do that. Gimme a week or so," it suggested to them that although the guy was not himself a forger, he was doing business with one. And their roving eyes would go to the boxes with shipping labels that would say the name and address of the person the dealer was getting his products from. Then these names and addresses—the fraudulent dealer's and his forgery source—would go on a list of subjects that West had begun to compile, a list that kept growing as he and Wichmann did more investigations.

Upper Deck had sought monopoly control over Jordan's signature and largely achieved it among legitimate companies. But by making his signature even harder to obtain than it already was, it had inadvertently helped foster a black market for fakes. West was struck by how quickly they had appeared in the marketplace, and in such astonishing numbers. It was like everyone of a certain bent of mind had the same idea at the same time, and converted this idea into action.

His list of subjects consisted of individuals and businesses around the United States and Japan. In the forgery business it helps to have a reputation as someone who has access to celebrities. Whether it's true or not doesn't matter; it's the reputation that counts. Most celebrities in this country live in New York and Los Angeles, which may explain why West found so many active forgery nests in the New York–New Jersey area and in his home turf of southern California. Stan Fitzgerald was but one of the New Jersey operators who made it onto his list. In the Los Angeles area, Mike Lopez was on it. So was Shelly Jaffe. West had done look-outs at W.W. Sports Cards and knew Wayne Bray personally. Bray was on the list too.

Early on, West had seen Angelo Marino's sports lithographs on sale at various places—unsigned except by the artist. Then he started seeing Angelo's art also signed by the star athlete who was featured in the painting. How could an obscure Escondido artist get access to the likes of Muhammad Ali and Magic Johnson and Joe Montana and have them sign his lithos? West suspected he knew the answer to that, and the Marinos joined the list.

ה

Every budding organization has its growing pains, and the Bray-Marino network was no different. At the center of everything was Greg; nothing happened without him. After Greg the other center of everything was Wayne, and that was where people encountered problems.

The dealings with Stan ran smooth; no problems there because Wayne controlled things, which was the way he liked it. Stan only dealt with Wayne, never Greg. Wayne almost never mentioned Greg by name to Stan, an arrangement all three of them preferred because too much information, too freely discussed, was dangerous. Stan paid Wayne (either by cash or through Wayne's American Express account), and Wayne paid Greg. Stan never paid Greg directly, never did anything with him directly. Wayne was the conduit through which goods, information and money flowed.

Things got messier as more people came in. Different business arrangements had to be made. Wayne didn't trust John Marino and didn't like him being involved but there wasn't much he could do about it, him being Greg's brother and all. Greg was close to his family, and that was that. The same was true of Big Ricky, Dick Laughlin and the Scheinmans. Greg had known them for years and so the Marinos sold to them directly, independent of Wayne.

Not so with Shelly Jaffe, who started out buying directly from Greg but lost this privilege as Wayne's position in the ring grew more powerful. If Shelly wanted Greg Marino products, which he did, he had to deal with Wayne and go through him. This was not a match made in crooks' heaven, for it was a toss-up who despised each other the most. "From the very beginning," Jaffe said about Bray, "he was an asshole." Always coming on strong, always trying to intimidate people, though not Shelly who was too smart and too ornery to be bullied by someone thirty years his junior whom he viewed as a skinny-ass punk. Shelly disliked Bray's "demeanor, his looks, his business practices. But he was the conduit to Greg so you had to deal with him."

Bray's opinion of Jaffe was equally sharp—"an irritating old man who never shuts up"—and he kept a sharp watch to make sure Shelly didn't try to go around him and gain access to Greg some other way. Bray's attitude toward Shelly was no different than his approach to anyone else; this was the way he operated, determined not to be tricked the way Mike Lopez had tricked him when he was just starting out in the racket. "I made it my business to know everything about everybody so they wouldn't steal Stan," said Wayne firmly. "The same with Greg. I wouldn't let anybody get close to him. His brother I couldn't stop. But others I could."

Bray did not mind being seen as an intimidator; it was a successful business tactic. He issued blunt warnings to anyone whom he suspected of trying to encroach on his relationships with Greg and Stan, telling them, in effect: You can go here but you cannot go there, get it? Most people got it, including Shelly. Shelly's animosity towards him may have been caused in part by the fact that he now had to pay a mark-up to Bray for Marino merchandise, and so he was padding the pocket of a guy he couldn't stand.

Nevertheless, united by an emotion stronger than hate—love of money—the two antagonists did business together, and each of their businesses grew. Shelly brokered autographs much like he brokered steel, functioning as a middle man and supplying signed memorabilia to big retail and mail order outfits, auctions—including auctions for charities and nonprofits—and on the home shopping channels. Shelly found that as long as his clients made money, and they were making plenty, they did not investigate too closely the authenticity of the items he was selling them. Thus, many legitimate businesses and organizations became complicit in the scam. They may not have known these signatures were counterfeit, or they may have suspected as much and chosen to look the other way. The effect was the same in any case.

"To me that was one of the reasons why forgeries took off," said Jaffe. "Anybody who was anybody could see that they [the forgers] were getting away with it."

But people were beginning to notice, particularly those in law enforcement. One afternoon the phone rang in Anthony West's Upper Deck office in Carlsbad, and he picked it up thinking it was a routine business call. But it was anything but routine.

"Hello," said the voice on the other end of the line. "This is Bob Walker of the FBI."

Walker was calling from Chicago, where he was a special agent in the field office there. He said he was beginning an investigation into counterfeit sports memorabilia and wanted to speak to West about it. Unwilling to talk unless he was sure about who he was talking to, West asked the agent to fax him his business card to verify his ID. Walker said fine. West recited his fax number, and they hung up. Seconds later the fax machine was humming.

West pulled the sheet from the fax and inspected it. In upper case letters at the top of the card it read: FEDERAL BUREAU OF INVESTIGATION. To the left was a miniature replica of the FBI seal. Bob Walker's name occupied the center of the card, just above his job title of Special Agent. At the bottom in smaller print were his contact numbers and the street address of the Chicago FBI. West punched in the numbers immediately.

On his look-outs around the country West had given his business card to various people, and some of these people had told Walker about him. Walker said he knew almost nothing about sports memorabilia and needed to talk to someone who was familiar with the business. West not only knew the business, he could shed some light on its seamy underside too. He explained that he was about to come to Chicago for a signing session with Michael Jordan and they could talk in person if Walker wished. They set a time and date to get together, and agreed to continue their conversation then.

At this meeting the agent asked West lots of questions and West answered them, explaining about his list of subjects and how he had come to compile it. Walker, in West's words, was a "a tough, go-get-the-crooks kind of guy," which pleased the Upper Deck investigator because the crooks Walker was now about to go get were in the autograph trade. Clearly if the FBI swept up some of the dirt in the industry, it would make his job easier. West turned over his entire list of names, including Bray, the Marinos, Stan the Man and some Chicago guys. Since Walker's investigation, code-named Operation Foul Ball, was centered on his home turf, he was most interested in the Chicago guys.

Operation Foul Ball was said to have started when a baseball fan bought a glove supposedly signed by Chicago White Sox first baseman Frank Thomas. Discovering it to be a forgery, this person complained about it to the local FBI. While this complaint may have triggered Walker's investigation, the FBI's focus soon became the criminal cottage industry that had sprung up around the exclusively-held signature of Michael Jordan. In April, May and June of 1996, when the Bulls were making their sweep through the playoffs, a twenty-nine year old South Side memorabilia dealer named Anthony Alyinovich was making a small fortune trafficking in bogus Jordan and Bulls merchandise. With an office and warehouse in suburban Des Plaines,

Alyinovich was a businessman, an earnest striver, not a forger. Those duties belonged to Kevin Walsh and Jon "Hit It" Schwarz, two other twenty-somethings who were willing to do "a bit of the soft," as 19th century English crooks called fraud. They affixed Jordan's and Pippen's and Rodman's autographs to the merchandise, which Alyinovich then distributed to dealers and retailers around Chicago.

Walker, who went undercover in the investigation, secretly tracked all this activity, acquiring a good deal of this phony Jordan material which the FBI showed to West when he came to town. From what he saw, nearly all of it was fake. One time West, Walker and Assistant United States Attorney David Rosenbloom, the prosecutor in the case, squeezed into the back seat of a cab to go see Michael at his penthouse suite at the Omni, carrying with them some of the evidence collected by Walker and his colleagues. Jordan reacted with disgust when he saw the stuff and like West, declared the bulk of it to be pure fakery.

During Foul Ball, Jordan became fascinated with the investigation, keeping up on its progress by quizzing West for updates when they met at their monthly signing sessions. He became conversant enough to be able to refer to Alyinovich and his cronies by name.

The FBI raided Alyinovich's warehouse about the same time the Bulls were popping the corks on their NBA championship, and in July the FBI and United States Attorney's Office announced his indictment at a heavily attended press conference at the Dirksen Federal Building. [The indictments of Walsh, Schwarz and others in the ring followed early the next year.] Neither Jordan nor any other pro athlete attended the press conference, although they were very much on the minds of those present. Spread out on tables in the front of the room were work samples from the Alyinovich crew: basketballs, No. 23 jerseys, Air Jordans, Wheaties boxes, plus Pippen and Rodman stuff and some non-Bulls material such as a Jeremy Roenick Chicago Blackhawks jersey and a Grant Hill Detroit Pistons jersey, all with fake signatures. Authorities estimated Alyinovich's haul to be in the neighborhood of $2.4 million.

The soft-spoken West, who attended the press conference, probably got off the best line to reporters, saying that "if Michael had really signed most of what people think he signed, his arm would have fallen off by now." The most telling words, however, came from United States Attorney James Burns. Tall and lanky, a former pro basketball player, Burns warned, "This is a nationwide case. It is not just located out of Chicago." He was referring to the fact that although authorities had taken down Alyinovich, they had hardly stopped autograph crime in the U.S. All those involved in the case, including Bob Walker, knew this to be true.

From West and other sources, Walker had developed the names of subjects around the country. But his efforts concentrated on Chicago and what was happening in the racket there. And although the investigation was continuing and more arrests were expected, these arrests would center on the Chicago area. Operation Foul Ball was a limited local fix to a problem that was far bigger than a handful of guys in one ring in one city.

The Alyinovich indictment attracted TV and radio attention and front page coverage in the *Chicago Tribune* ("That sports hero's autograph may be sign of larceny," read the headline) as well as other papers in the city and elsewhere. Later coverage of the scandal dominated the front page of the *New York Daily News* with an enlarged photo of a baseball with a crudely rendered Mickey Mantle autograph, one of the non-Chicago forgeries done by Hit It Schwarz and Walsh. The headline shouted "FOUL BALL" with the copy at the bottom of the page saying that "a new wave of forgeries has hit the memorabilia business."

Especially in Jordan-crazy Chicago, the case generated so much attention it may have surprised the FBI to some degree. Clearly, the combination of superstar athletes and consumer fraud made for good copy—and excellent image-building PR for those responsible for bringing the crooks to justice.

Even as the Chicago FBI was secretly conducting Operation Foul Ball, the Upper Deck Company was privately lobbying federal authorities to take action. It dispatched its corporate counsel to San Diego to speak to Phil Halpern, an AUSA—the acronym everyone in law enforcement uses when referring to an Assistant United States Attorney—in the United States Attorney's Office there. Halpern and John Newell had been classmates in their undergraduate days at Hamilton College in New York, but the purpose of Newell's visit was not to reminisce about old times. He wanted to discuss memorabilia fraud and how it was hurting Upper Deck.

"We had dinner at my house and we talked about the counterfeit problem," recalled Halpern. "He explained that as soon as Upper Deck tried to crack down on it somewhere, it would spring up somewhere else. So he wanted to know if the federal government could do anything about it."

Despite its image as a sleepy, postcard-pretty, touristy beach town, San Diego is America's seventh largest city. Part of the southern judicial district

---

* *Alyinovich's group dealt with retailers and distributors in Massachusetts and California, including a Huntington Beach sports shop that sold Greg Marino products. This was evidently the only link between Alyinovich, who pled guilty and cooperated with the government, and Bray-Marino.*

of California, it includes the port of entry at San Ysidro, the busiest land border crossing in the world. Annually more than 50 million people and 20 million vehicles pass between Mexico and the U.S. using San Ysidro and another border crossing point. Some of these people and vehicles are smuggling dope, but the dope they are smuggling is not always heroin or cocaine or pot. Some of it is the kind that illegally enhances athletic performance, and in the late 1980s Halpern, a bright, driven, dark-haired ex-marathon runner, became the top federal steroid smuggling prosecutor in the U.S., bringing cases against a number of high-profile smugglers. In so doing he earned a reputation as the man who handled the big sports cases at DOJ, an attorney who might be interested in taking on a sports case of a different kind, that of counterfeit memorabilia.

This was why Newell had approached him. But before he would commit Halpern needed to know more. "How big of a problem are we talking about here?" he asked.

The question was central because, in Halpern's view, for the federal government to get involved, it had to be a big case. "A one million dollar Ponzi scheme is not enough to interest the government," he said. "It's got to be large dollars. We have more crime than we can handle here. People ask me if I've ever convicted an innocent person and I tell them, 'Look. We don't need to convict innocent guys. We've got plenty of guilty ones.'"

It was also crucial that the case, like steroids, go beyond San Diego's boundaries to make a national impact. While listening to Newell, Halpern wasn't persuaded that counterfeits crossed the threshold into a matter of federal concern. It seemed strictly a sideshow, somebody else's case. So he was surprised when the attorney gave his dollar estimate of the size of the problem.

"Hundreds of millions of dollars," said Newell.

Well, thought Halpern, that certainly crosses the threshold. Making no commitments, he said he'd look into the matter further. When dinner was over Newell gave him the business card of Upper Deck's investigator, Anthony West.

Halpern and an associate at the IRS met with West, who turned over his list of subjects just as he had done with Bob Walker. (Though West said nothing about the ongoing Operation Foul Ball investigation.) Doing some preliminary gumshoe work of their own, Halpern and the IRS agent found little to excite them, as many of the names on West's list were located outside Halpern's prosecutorial reach. Halpern called over to the Aero Drive office of the San Diego FBI to see if there was any interest in the case, but there were no takers. So the matter slid by the wayside amidst the press of other business until the blitz of publicity that followed the Alyinovich indictment.

Operation Foul Ball was a law enforcement and media success. Not immune to the intoxicating effects of good publicity, the San Diego FBI noticed this, and by the time Halpern called again in reference to the Upper Deck complaints, the formerly cool mood inside Aero Drive had warmed. Feeling like he wanted to be part of the action and could bring something valuable to it, Halpern joined the case as AUSA while the FBI assigned two of its agents to head up the investigation, Tim Fitzsimmons and Jeff McKinney.

Fitzsimmons was the case agent with overall management responsibilities for the investigation. McKinney was co-case agent, supervising the surveillance ops and other duties in the field. If, as has been said, an investigation takes on the personality of the man or woman in charge of it, then this case had a dual identity, for both men put their imprint on it. First, Fitzsimmons:

With clear blue eyes and brown hair that is lightly graying at the temples, he stands slightly under six feet tall with solid shoulders that fill out his suit coat. Wearing a suit and tie is required for male FBI agents when on duty, although Fitzsimmons will shed his jacket when seated at his desk or in the privacy of his car when driving to and from an assignment. At his belt underneath his jacket, in a worn leather holster, is his nine millimeter Sig Sauer, which he has drawn many times in the line of duty but never fired. Earnest and self-contained, serious about his job and his life, a devout Catholic who does not drink or smoke or swear, Fitzsimmons was, said a colleague, "like your priest. As straight as straight gets and I say that in the most admiring way possible."

Then in his thirties, he resembled "an old-fashioned G-man," a man who followed the rules and expected others to do the same though he was seldom surprised when they did not. Unlike, perhaps, those G-men of yore, Fitzsimmons was a college graduate with an MBA. Highly organized, with a mind and memory for details, Fitzsimmons analyzes every problem set before him like the McDonnell Douglas avionics engineer he was before joining the Bureau, always watching what he says about an investigation, never revealing more than he has to.

Anthony West remembers being intimidated as hell by Fitzsimmons the first time they met. "What is he thinking about?" West kept asking himself, as the agent said almost nothing during their conversation. "Why doesn't he say something?" West figured it was an investigative technique of Fitzsimmons'—let the other guy do most of the talking so he'll know more about you than you know about him. "Tim is the type that doesn't say more than he has to. It drives you crazy when you talk to him on the phone because there are these long pauses when you think it's his turn to say something and yet he doesn't."

Fittingly, given his sober, steady professionalism, in his first years with the FBI Fitzsimmons acted as a SWAT team sharpshooter on the drug and organized crime squad in the Honolulu field office, helping to bring down, among others, a Korean gang that was manufacturing ice, the smokable form of methamphetamine. While it is considered a good bust in law enforcement circles to seize a few ounces of ice, Fitzsimmons's squad uncovered pounds of it in a raid on a Korean restaurant. A separate seizure in the case garnered $1 million in cash.

He later moved into white collar crime and transferred to San Diego, and he had just finished working on a local political corruption investigation when Operation Bullpen crossed his desk and piqued his interest. (Phil Halpern had worked on the same case and they knew each other.) Most white collar cases are dry, complex affairs that require extensive knowledge of the banking, mortgage and securities industries. They typically target corporate cheats—bland but arrogant individuals who work in corner offices in downtown skyscrapers and whose behavior is stereotypically normal (wife, children, dog, cat, home in the 'burbs) except for the millions they are stealing from their employer or company shareholders through illegal accounting and business practices. This case, Fitzsimmons saw immediately, did not fit that mold.

For one, it was about sports, which was different in itself and pretty cool. As the son of an Air Force pilot, living in various places around the country according to where his father was stationed at the time, Fitzsimmons followed the Dallas Cowboys as a boy, watching their games every Sunday on TV and plastering posters of Roger Staubach on his bedroom wall. When he was in the sixth grade and living in Florida with his dad away in Vietnam, a friend of the family's offered to take him and his brothers to Miami to see the Cowboys play the Colts in the Super Bowl. The plan was for them to meet Dallas defensive tackle Larry Cole before the game, but there was a mix-up and the boys didn't get in to see him. When Cole found out about this unintentional snub, he sent them an autographed football which, decades later, the hard-boiled G-man still owns and regards with sentimental affection.

The Cole football gave Fitzsimmons the sense that more was being ripped off in this scam than just money. Parents and grandparents and aunts and uncles bought autographed memorabilia for children who idolized these star athletes whether they deserved it or not. He didn't like the idea of a kid putting up an athlete's poster on his bedroom wall that was signed not by the athlete, but by some crook. His attitude was that adults who had given in to cynicism should not muck around with the innocent dreams of children. It offended him on some level; got under his skin.

This was also true of his partner, Jeff McKinney, who was appalled by the corruption he saw in the industry. "I like the idea of preserving memories but the money-making side of it was disgusting," he said. "Athletes and legitimate businesses, and parents and kids who were spending a fortune on these bogus Jordan jerseys were all being ripped off by these guys."

With sandy blond hair, glasses and a goatee, McKinney was a big man (six-foot-three, 210-plus pounds) with a big laugh that when it emerged, seemed to emanate from a chamber deep inside him. Possessed of a sharp, sarcastic sense of humor, it was McKinney who coined the code name of Operation Bullpen, fitting because bullpen was a baseball term and much of the bogus stuff being made by the forgers was baseball-related. It was also a play on words—the pen referring to the forger's primary tool and all the bullshit it produced.

McKinney's manner has some of the characteristics popularly associated with Californians (he's a native): laid-back, easy-going, casual. But occasionally one can hear an edge to the things he says and how he says them that suggests he is not a person who is going to be pushed around or lightly dismissed. His first assignment for the FBI was in Provo, south of Salt Lake City, and his duties there more resembled a policeman than typical FBI, as he handled murder, rape, and assault with a deadly weapon cases. One of his investigations targeted a gang that sold guns and stolen goods. To do business with the gang, the FBI opened an undercover storefront operation in which a hidden door was built inside the store. When gang members came to see the FBI agents posing as gun buyers, because the threat of violence was always there, McKinney and others hid behind the door, weapons in hand, ready to act if the threat ever became reality. The investigation brought down more than fifty members of the gang.

Eventually McKinney left the guns and drugs squad and went into the tamer world of white collar crime, coming back to southern California and settling in as an agent at the Carlsbad RA. In FBI-speak, RA stands for "resident agency," a satellite office in an outlying area away from the field office. Aero Drive, where Fitzsimmons worked, was the main base of operations for the San Diego FBI, while the Carlsbad RA covered North County. This was partly why McKinney drew the Operation Bullpen assignment. The FBI wanted to have a man close to the action, and the action in this case figured to be in North County.

Both McKinney and Fitzsimmons talked to Bob Walker, who told them things about Operation Foul Ball that the public knew and things it did not.

Anthony West had turned over his ever-useful list of subjects, which he kept adding to even after the Alyinovich bust. This suggested to the agents—rightly, as it turned out—that while Foul Ball may have had a dampening effect on the racket initially, the memorabilia boys had resumed their activities and business was brisk as ever. Their suspicions were confirmed in late 1996 when a FBI raid in Los Angeles uncovered counterfeit material linked to Bray and Marino.

Fitzsimmons had run background checks on the two and while they had no criminal history to speak of, that had not discouraged them from going over to "the dark side," as the agent put it with a slight smile. They were a couple of nobodies at the center of a corrupt national racketeering enterprise and that, in the FBI's view, made them a couple of somebodies. And what was so extraordinary about them, among many extraordinary things, was that they were doing it in the backyard of Upper Deck, the company they were hurting so badly with their forgeries. It was like a modern twist on an old-time movie Western with the FBI, in the role of sheriff, chasing after the bandidos in a dusty corner of the country down Mexico way.

And so, for now, the investigative team was set: Fitzsimmons case agent; McKinney co-case agent; Halpern prosecutor; and Anthony West providing outside assistance. In January Fitzsimmons submitted a request to his supervisor to formally begin the investigation. The request bounced back marked O&A: Open and Assigned. The chase was on.

PART TWO

OPERATION BULLPEN

6

That was the thing about it, the one real and true and completely unbelievable thing: the money. The money was the beginning, the end, and everything in-between. Their crazy-ass dreams were coming true. Suddenly it had all opened up for them.

Imagine this: You're an unemployed cook and you walk into a Mission Bay boat center on an insanely blue and sunny morning and you put down forty grand—cash—for a brand-new thirty-five-foot Maxum Sun Cruiser 2400, and on that same day, that very same day, you take ownership and launch it in the water, water as ridiculously blue and perfect as the sky. And before you know it you and your brother are gliding south down into Mexican waters in your new boat that you name—hey, it never hurts to have a sense of humor about these things—the *Bada Bing*.

The *Bada Bing* became the home away from home for Greg and John—the party boat. They loved fishing as much as they loved partying, and they'd take it out into the ocean up to Catalina or down to Cabo and they'd bring back yellowtail tuna, bass, barracuda, shark. John's biggest catch was a fifty-pound yellowtail; Greg's was a nearly two-hundred pound striped blue marlin that he hauled in off Baja. They brought fish home and cooked it up with Kathy and their parents and had so much left over they gave some to the neighbors. After a while they got so tired of it they started throwing everything back, printing up T-shirts for themselves that said, "Save the Yellowtail."

From Escondido it was a forty-five minute hop down to Quivera Basin at Mission Bay where they docked the boat. They'd go down early on a Friday, after their forgery work week was over, and spend the long weekend fishing and partying, heavy on both. They'd spend the day on the water and at night get rooms in a swank hotel with a view of the bay. Some of the other guys in the scam would join them, and they'd have parties with drugs and liquor and women who were not their wives. These women were not skanks either but real high-class hotties, the best money could buy. Their every secret desire could be explored; fantasyland was only as far away as their bulging wallets. Now they were really living the ballplayer's life.

"We all had secret lives," said Greg candidly. "Nobody was innocent in this thing."

The wives knew but they didn't know, y'know? Some of them deliberately looked the other way because they were enjoying the benefits of the scam, whether they directly participated in it or not, and they did not wish to risk doing anything that might endanger those benefits. Boys will be boys, but money is money and they liked nice things too, same as their husbands.

Wayne and his wife had a baby. Baby needs new clothes. Mom needs a new, bigger vehicle to chauffeur baby around in. The house needs fixing up to make room for baby, or maybe the house just isn't big enough anymore. So you trade in the old house for a new one just like you traded in that old car for a new set of wheels. Gas! Groceries! Mortgage! Diapers! Day care! Car payments! Credit cards! Clothing bills! It just keeps coming and coming when you have a family, only now Daddy had found a way to sink those worries to the bottom of the sea.

"Fifteen thousand bucks was nothing," said Wayne without exaggeration. "Fifteen thousand bucks was a day at the mall."

He'd walk into a mall and drop eight grand in an afternoon buying watches or diamond jewelry, which he loved. He bought diamonds while entertaining thoughts of possibly opening a jewelry store. That was the way his mind worked, always spinning, always thinking of the next thing, and that was what money did for a person too: You could entertain whatever thoughts you pleased, knowing you now had the ability to indulge in them if you chose.

For a couple of guys who had been doing okay, or less than okay, Wayne and Greg had taken a sudden, exhilarating leap up in class—at least the sort of class money can buy. Wayne would stroll into an electronics store saying "Give me this, give me that," and the sales staff would fall over themselves to do it for him. There'd go another eight or ten or twelve grand. Just like that. All cash. No questions asked. Whatever his heart desired—new big screen TV, new home sound systems, new car sound systems, custom this, custom that—his heart could have it. Tired of the furniture, honey? Here's all new stuff. Want new clothes? More new clothes? Want to buy clothes without looking at the price tag? Do it. How about a trip to Hawaii or Aruba? Do it. A week in Vegas and live it up in a deluxe, palatial-size hotel suite on the

Strip? Do it. There was no budget. What budget? There'd be more coming in tomorrow, and more after that, and whatever cash you didn't spend you stashed away in a secret hiding place in your house or in a safe deposit box at the bank where nobody could get at it except you.

Wayne especially relished the power of having money and the freedom that came with spending it. He tipped waiters and bell hops like a big shot and he played the role of generous benefactor to friends who were in a pinch for money and needed help, the way he used to be seemingly all the damn time.

He liked being a have. No matter what anyone said it was way better than being a have-not. It was a good feeling; hey, it *was* a feeling, and that alone sometimes made this thing worth the risk. This wasn't the same boring thing, day after day after day. This was like taking drugs: the money drug. It made your pulse run faster and your heart beat quicker even as it tore up your insides and fried your brain. Some nights you were so wired you couldn't sleep, and some of those nights you didn't want to because of how alive all of this made you feel. And as long as guys kept things outwardly cool and watched what they said and did and who they did business with, there was no reason they couldn't keep getting high on the money drug and feeling these feelings for a long, long while.

That was Wayne's opinion anyhow; Greg was not so sure, not after Foul Ball. The busts in Chicago hit him hard, him and Kathy. They talked a lot about it and sometimes fought. It scared them—the idea of getting caught and thrown in prison. This thing that seemed like such a romp in the beginning had turned into a game in which they could be seriously hurt.

Forgeries were pretty much off the media radar screen when Greg did his first Mantle, but that had changed. Even before Foul Ball, "Sixty Minutes" did a piece on autograph fraud that was the talk of the collecting industry, particularly the crooks in it. Then, in the fall after the Alyinovich indictment, "NYPD Blue" aired an episode in which two detectives investigate an apartment filled with sports collectibles. There, they catch a retired player signing a baseball with the name of Lou Gehrig. The detectives put the collar on the forger and his beautiful blonde accomplice and later bust up their counterfeiting ring.

Such attention—from the media and more significantly, the law—made the Marinos want to get out of the racket. "I tried to stop it," said Greg. "We wanted out of it. But there were all these guys with their orders, pushing and pushing and telling me not to worry."

The strongest and most influential of these pushers was his partner who gave him a sign that said TRUST NO ONE. That was Wayne's motto and it became Greg's, too. He put the sign up in his apartment and the two of them agreed to stay tight and close and not trust anyone save for their closest friends and associates.

Wayne kept after Greg, and others in the racket kept after him too, and maybe everything they told him—how good he was, how smart they were, how tight they were—was just one big fat juicy lie, designed to keep him toking and signing, toking and signing. But what Wayne said ultimately wasn't what kept Greg in the business. Like the others, he was getting high on the money drug and loving it too much to stop.

The secret lives they were leading were built on trust, the trust of people who were practicing the same sort of deceit. "You got all this money," Greg explained. "You can't let the world know that you have this money and how you got it. You gotta spend it with the people you're making it with. You're all making it the same way and so you're all in it together."

Greg was in this thing with his wife, his mother, his father, his brother. Even Big Ricky Weimer was a long-time family friend. But Wayne didn't have this tight group around him the way Greg did. In fact he felt like an outsider around the Marino clan, and he often thought how cool it would be if his best friend, Nate Harrison, could join him in the racket.

Though in his early twenties, Nate resembled a kid in lots of ways—a big, brown-eyed baby-faced kid with thick, dark eyebrows and shoulder-length dark brown hair. He wore T-shirts with the sleeves cut off and beltless blue jeans with the lining of a pocket hanging out. But Nate didn't care or maybe not even notice that the lining was out. His jeans were also a little big around the waist but without a belt to hold them up, he'd simply hitch them up if they were riding too low.

His mom and dad divorced when he was younger, and his father had passed on. But neither of these events explained why he had bailed out of Vista High after his junior year. It was school, you know, the same old boring stuff. "I wasn't into school," Nate said with a shrug. "I just wasn't interested. So I dropped out. To me school was just rehashing the same stuff I knew and had already figured out."

After quitting school he went to work at a 7-Eleven, which he knew really well because that was where he liked to go whenever he cut class or just wanted a place to hang out. What he liked to do more than anything was play video games—*Dungeons and Dragons, Encounter Strike, Ever Quest*—and the 7-Eleven near his Mom's house had an arcade-style console where he could lose himself for hours. "Basically you go into a dungeon and kill stuff," he said, describing the appeal of one game. Real life, especially school life, was pretty dull compared to that.

But, as attractive as it might have been, he realized he couldn't be a gamer his whole life. He needed to make money in order to clear out of his Mom's house and find an apartment, stand on his own, be his own man. Along with video games Nate was into comic books—*Spider Man, Daredevil, Dr. Strange* and his favorite, the *X-Men*—and eventually he started buying and selling them, leaving the comfort of 7-Eleven to run a one-man wholesale business out of his mother's garage. He soon found that you had to adapt to survive in the ever-changing novelty and memorabilia business. When the comic book market tanked, he moved into Beanie Babies, then Pogs, then Magic the Gathering. "I was a fad person. Whatever was in fashion, that's what I sold. Blink, and you'll miss 'em."

One of the things he peddled was baseball cards, and this was how he met the owner of W.W. Sports Cards. "Wayne was always good at decorating his places," said Nate. "It looked good inside. So it was a nice place to hang out." Wholesaling cards and whatever fad happened to be in at the moment, he sometimes dropped by the shop even when he wasn't selling something. "Wayne was cool. He was easy to talk to and he'd talk to me. Him and me have always gotten along. Some people, he's not so friendly to."

When they met, Nate had managed to finally move out of his mom's house and get a place of his own. But after the '94 strike his business crashed along with everyone else's, and he couldn't afford it anymore. So Wayne let him stay in his house for cheap, and they got to know each other even better. When Wayne's son was born, Nate became the child's honorary uncle.

Nate was younger than Wayne and looked up to him as a man who had done things in his life, even if some of those things weren't so smart. Wayne was no gamer, they didn't share that. But they had other things in common: both in the same business, both North County guys, both allergic to school and authority. Nate, who was awkward around girls, admired the ease in which Wayne carried himself in that department. As unfriendly if not downright hostile as he could be around some people, Wayne could turn on the charm with the ladies; he had that bad-boy appeal some of them just love. What each man gave the other, most fundamentally, was respect, which was especially important for Nate, who hated being patronized by older people who thought they knew better. Nate had heard enough of that crap in school. But Wayne wasn't like that: he didn't talk down to him or treat him like a kid who didn't have enough sense to tuck in the pocket lining of his pants. They were peers and friends who saw things the same—some things, anyhow.

Over time, because of their mutual trust and respect, their friendship deepened along with their business relationship. "The card business is the shadiest business in the world," said Nate. "Everybody in it is crooked and dishonest. Dealers bounce checks, don't deliver orders they've promised, lie about prices. That's not the way it was with Wayne. I was always up front with him and he was always up front with me. I told him what I paid for something and how much I needed to make, and he did the same with me."

Nate had faith in Wayne, which was not a thing Wayne was accustomed to. Generally people took one look at his tattoos and jewelry and outlaw biker Fu Manchu—well, they gave him suspicious looks all right, but not their trust. "I love Nate. He's my brother," said Wayne. "And he's loyal. I knew I could count on him. I knew he'd never steal from me. If he lied to me it would only be to protect his family."

Eventually Nate's up-and-down business fortunes took a turn for the better, and he got up enough scratch to move out of Wayne's house and be independent again. But the two remained close, Nate frequently dropping by the house to see the baby or swinging by W.W. Sports Cards where he and Wayne would hang out just like always, even though the new father could no longer be truthful with him. Wayne had thought about clueing Nate in on what was going on—had thought about recruiting him to be part of his family tree—but he had kept his mouth shut until something occurred that forced the issue out into the open.

Along with his wholesaling, Nate had taken over the management of a card shop in Poway. Being in the card and memorabilia business, he knew Greg Marino, who came by the store and sold him a package of items with superstar autographs. Nate casually mentioned this fact to Wayne one day at W.W. Sports Cards, and this was when Wayne decided to deprive his friend of his innocence.

"You know all those autographs you're buying from Greg?"

"Yeah?" said Nate.

"They're fake," said Wayne conclusively.

Nate gave him a puzzled look, so Wayne went on, "The reason I know they're fake is because Greg is forging all my stuff. Everything I sell is fake."

Then Wayne told him the whole story, upping the ante in the process, doing what he had thought about doing for a while and giving Nate a pitch as to why he should forget his nickel-and-dime legitimate business and throw in with him.

As Wayne was talking Nate felt the air rush out of him and he grabbed for breath. It was like a punch to his stomach. He was stunned. Fake? These signatures were fakes? He could not believe what he was hearing except that Wayne kept insisting it was so. He knew Wayne had been selling lots of things lately and doing really well, but he attributed this to his business savvy and good connections, which also explained, at least in Nate's mind, the low prices he was paying for the merchandise he was getting.

Naive? Well, yeah. Guess so. Nate had to cop to that. But another part of him wanted to believe these autographs were genuine because if they were not, what did it say about Greg? And more to the point, what did it say about his best friend?

He felt angry—and betrayed. Wayne was supposedly different from all the rest. He and Nate were honest with each other—or so Nate had believed. Now he wasn't sure what to believe. "I couldn't talk to Wayne for a week," he said. "I came close to calling the sheriff and busting them. And I think I would've except it was Wayne and I couldn't do that to him."

As for Wayne, he backed off a while, then applied more pressure to get Nate to change his mind. In the counterfeit memorabilia business a family tree was a network of business connections, and this was yet another way in which forgeries spread: from one member of a tree to the next. The Marinos had a family tree, people they sold to in addition to Bray. These people in turn had their own family trees. Bray's family tree included Shelly Jaffe, who himself had a family tree, and of course Stan the Man. Nate would be part of Wayne's family tree too, buying everything from Wayne who would maintain his inside position with Greg. But Wayne could still cut good deals for his friend that would guarantee that he'd make money, and lots of it, and this was another reason Wayne wanted to see him come in. What he felt for Nate was not a forged emotion. He genuinely cared for his little bro and hated to see him having so many money struggles, particularly when he no longer needed to.

Nate, poor fella, was still trying to be an honest card and Pogs salesman, and he wasn't ever going to get rich that way. It wasn't nearly as much dangerous fun either.

"Nate's a real moral guy," Wayne said. "I kinda dragged him into it."

He talked about all the money he and Greg were making, how easy it was, and how easy it could be for Nate too. After all, this wasn't a scam in which somebody woke up one morning to find their bank account drained or their life savings stolen. This was a scam that made people feel good. Suppose someone was moved by the aeronautical exploits of Christy McAuliffe or Chuck Yeager or Orville Wright, and wanted to own something signed by one of them. A genuine piece would be expensive, if you could even find one. So instead this person buys a forgery at a modest or even a bargain price, thinking it's authentic. He has this cool signed object to show for his purchase, something that gives him pleasure and that he displays, with pride, in his home or office, and what's the rip-off if he's getting such pleasure from it? If he never learns it's a forgery he'll enjoy it till the day he dies, at which time his children will inherit it or maybe he'll pass it on to a museum or historical society so it can be preserved and displayed for generations to come. What was the harm in that?

Plenty, thought Nate. He continued to resist his friend's sometimes soft, sometimes hard cajoling. Whereas Wayne tended to see every business negotiation as a struggle for raw advantage, Nate was more accepting of the other person's point of view and thus more willing to compromise—or, as Wayne might have put it, give in. But Nate refused to give in until everything fell apart for him all at once.

Practically every penny he had was sunk into Pogs and in the space of a mosquito's lifetime Pogs went from the hottest craze on earth to nothing, zero, zilch. And it busted him flat. His landlord kicked him out of his apartment for failure to pay the rent. Then he lost his shop in Poway because he couldn't pay the bills there either. Some people owed him money but all they could offer were excuses. It was as low as he had ever fallen in his short, mostly frustrating attempt to succeed in business and stand on his own as a man. He felt like he had no other choice, no one else to turn to, so he got in his car and drove over to W.W. Sports Cards to see Wayne.

"Tell me more about this thing," he said to him.

7

Separating old people from their money is a favorite pastime of swindlers, and in sunny Oceanside a low-level operator named Wayne Deloney was running a number on a retired couple with money to spend. Operating under the DBA of Dave Martin and Associates, Deloney had convinced the couple to invest fifty grand of their retirement nest egg into a collection of sports gear signed by Michael, Bird, Magic, all the big basketball names. At first enthusiastic about the opportunity being offered them, the seniors got cold feet and decided to back out of the deal, a development that put a frown on Deloney's face. So what if they were on a fixed income? A deal's a deal, and they had said yes. The Oceanside police finally arrested Deloney after the couple complained that he was harassing them.

Oceanside being located in North County, within the jurisdiction of the San Diego FBI, Tim Fitzsimmons and Jeff McKinney got wind of this and went to see Deloney. Meantime they turned a few of the signed jerseys seized by police over to Anthony West, who told them what they already strongly suspected: Fakes, every one. The agents also suspected the material had come from the pen of Greg Marino, although Deloney, true to his code of honor, would not give up the name of the person who had sold him the memorabilia. But even if he had talked, this hardly constituted evidence to charge Marino or anybody else with a crime. To do that the FBI was going to need a helluva lot more than Wayne Deloney, and the agents knew it.

The Deloney incident occurred in April 1997, a few months after the case had opened. During this time Fitzsimmons and McKinney had been doing a cram course on an industry they knew nothing about, cruising card shows and shops in the area on an informal undercover basis, asking innocent-seeming questions while observing what was being sold and by whom as they figured out how to proceed with the case. "Basically the investigation had to find a way to do three things," said Fitzsimmons. "We had to meet the bad guys, we had to get product from them, and we had to devise a means not to put their fake products back into the marketplace."

Bogus sports memorabilia, like drugs, was largely a cash enterprise—off the books and under the table where the IRS could not track it. Thousands in cash, sometimes tens of thousands, exchanged hands during a single buy, and these buys often occurred in the parking lots of nondescript public places: restaurants, gas stations, convenience stores. The guy with the goods pulled into a lot in his SUV while another guy waited for him beside his vehicle, the goods moving rapidly from one rear compartment to the other, a thick envelope passing even faster between hands—and then off they went, no idle chit-chat, all business, the deal done.

Fitzsimmons and McKinney quickly arrived at the same conclusion: To get in with these guys, to gain their confidence, to make buys and develop evidence against them, Operation Bullpen needed an undercover agent, just as in a drug case.

Fitzsimmons's formal request for a UCA was part of a fifteen-page proposal submitted in June. This proposal, which included an overview of the case and a proposed budget, first came under scrutiny within the San Diego FBI. Legal counsel had to sign off on it, as did the financial manager and the undercover coordinator. The Assistant Special Agent in Charge had the final local say. Nationally, since all undercover ops by field offices require advance approval from Headquarters, the Organized and Racketeering Section of the FBI pushed some paper around on it too. But Headquarters and everybody else gave it a thumbs up, which meant that the next step for Fitzsimmons and McKinney was to find an agent who could fit the undercover scenario they were developing and its unique job requirements.

Neither agent was right for the task—not enough knowledge of the subject area. So they had to find another man—and yes, it had to be a man, a woman would not do. Sports memorabilia was practically an all-male gig. A woman agent posing as a dealer would look out of place and the last thing you wanted was for a UCA to stand out in any way.

This agent also needed to be white. Anthony West told them about the racial makeup of the business but Fitzsimmons and McKinney noticed it themselves: how most of the salespeople standing behind the tables and display cases at the card shows were white and—hey, wait a sec—Asian. There were lots of Asians too: Chinese-Americans and Japanese-Americans as well as Japanese nationals who plied their trade in their native country and the U.S. West's subject lists in fact included some Japanese fraud merchants. The Japanese, it is well known, are as batty about toys and cards and comics as Americans. They play pro baseball in Japan and its most rabid fans follow the game in America and also know stars in other sports such as Michael Jordan. Hollywood celebrities and American pop and rock stars attract huge attention there as well, and you could see ample evidence of all of this by strolling the narrow, crowded aisles of a card show bazaar, with Asian guys behind the tables pledging to buy although they were really interested in selling, and Asian shoppers inspecting a Japanese edition of *Newsweek* with Jordan on the cover or flipping through a CD catalog of Hong Kong martial arts movies or a stack of signed photos of naked Asian pin-up girls.

It was not only Playboy Playmates who appeared at these shows. Lovely, black-haired Asian models dressed in come-hither jean tops, tight short skirts and heels also showed entrepeneurial verve, pushing their products and posing for pictures with guys with goofy grins plastered on their face.

So that was it, then: a UCA of Asian descent who knew Japan and ideally had spent time there. No, this last wasn't ideal; it was vital. The undercover agent could not be an impostor when it came to knowing Japan's people and customs; he had to have eaten the food and enjoyed it with the gusto of a native, know the names of celebrities and sports stars, not just American celebrities and sports stars but Japanese ones too, and gone to see the Yomiuri Giants and maybe some sumo. Yes, sumo: Nothing was more quintessentially Japanese than sumo and no statesider could ever understand why this was so unless he had truly gotten into the culture. For added credibility the UCA had to speak the language, at least some, because any little thing that was not quite right could turn into a big screw-up if one of the subjects being investigated got curious and started asking questions and tried to peel the cover off the scenario. Certainly they would ask questions, that was only natural, and the agent had to respond just as naturally, and the only way he could do this was if he knew his stuff well enough to be able to lie about it.

The agent's scenario would be that he was an American businessman with clients in Japan and the Far East, and because he was selling outside the U.S. this would raise the comfort level of the fraudulent dealers and make them more inclined to do business with him. That was the thinking anyhow. And it made sense, good sense, except there was a problem.

While the overall scenario was a lie, aspects of it had to be on the level. So just as the agent had to genuinely know Japan, this same person had to be an expert on collecting—had to know what a wax box was and an insert card, and why some guys in the hobby look at a '52 Topps Mantle the way other guys look at a Pamela Anderson fold-out. He had to be a collector, and he had to know the business side of the hobby too because how else was he going to be able to bust chops with a bunch of guys in aloha shirts, board shorts and flip-flops who had spent their first allowance on a pack of baseball cards and been collecting them ever since?

And that was the hang-up. The FBI does not hold sports memorabilia classes at its training academy in Quantico, Virginia. Most federal agents, like Fitzsimmons and McKinney, had no knowledge or even much interest in collecting. Nor can this expertise be acquired overnight. A person has to grow up in the hobby or live with it for a long time, and have a passion for it.

Fitzsimmons and McKinney put out the word within the FBI for what they were looking for, finally coming up with a name. Special Agent John Ferreira of the Eugene, Oregon RA was a passionate, lifelong autograph collector who was knowledgeable not only about sports memorabilia but Japan too. What's more, he had once worked with Fitzsimmons in the Honolulu field office. So, in the summer of 1997, anxious to get going on a case that had been dragging along, Fitzsimmons called Eugene to enlist Ferreira as Bullpen's undercover man.

At the time Ferreira was working on an eco-terrorism case—a batch of them, actually, all at once. Relentlessly upbeat and energetic, a multi-tasker extraordinaire, Ferreira was the type who was not happy with one or two things on his plate but only after he had added three or five or seven more. "I'm hyper," he explained. "I like to keep busy. I like having ten things to do at once."

With brown eyes and thick black hair and a mustache speckled with gray, he was carrying a caseload that appeared to have no room in it for a major undercover investigation in another state. His investigations were centered on environmental terrorists in the bucolic, tree-rich lands around Eugene—the burning of a Forest Service vehicle at the Detroit Ranger Station in the Williamette National Forest by the Earth Liberation Front in October 1996; and two days later, another more serious act of arson, the razing of the $5 million Oak Ridge Ranger Station. Although no lives were lost, it was the largest destruction of a federally owned building since Oklahoma City the year before. Ferreira, a domestic eco-terrorism expert, was one of the agents searching for the guilty parties.

As busy as he was, Ferreira had heard about Operation Bullpen and knew why Fitzsimmons was calling. As they got reacquainted, not having spoken to each other for years, Fitzsimmons mentioned how he didn't realize that Ferreira was into this "stuff."

"Oh yeah," he said. "All my life."

This "stuff" was stamps, coins, TV show cards, Beatles cards and of course, baseball cards, shoeboxes full of baseball cards that he had been collecting since he was a boy growing up in his native Honolulu in the sixties and seventies. When he was young practically everything he put his paws on was a potential collectible, and he was no different now that he was in his forties. When he took his family to McDonald's he brought home the Happy Meal toys and tossed them in a drawer, not because he was collecting these toys but because he simply could not bear to throw them away. A burger and fries are gone in a minute. But that little plastic trinket that came with them? Now that's something to hang onto.

Nor did Ferreira believe those Happy Meal toys would become rare and valuable collectibles that he could later sell on eBay; his compulsion to collect, at bottom, had nothing to do with money. It was who he was; he couldn't not do it. And it made him feel good. Two of his most cherished collectibles were signed baseballs given to him by his father—one by Ted Williams, the other by Stan Musial, his dad's favorite player—that he'd never sell. His collection when Fitzsimmons called consisted of about 10,000 autographed items, plus 200,000 to 300,000 baseball cards stored in boxes in the memorabilia room of his house and arranged in alphabetical order according to the player's last name.

"Any star you can name, I can tell you what his signature is worth without looking it up," he said, adding, "I'm not boasting."

His knowledge of prices stemmed from years of autograph hunting, which he loves. On scraps of paper and the backs of used envelopes he would jot down lists of players and celebrities whose autographs he was seeking, these messy columns of red and blue ink being a reflection, in miniature, of a much-commented upon larger trend: how sports has become an arm of the entertainment industry. In one column were Fats Domino, Dom DiMaggio, Sparky Lyle and Luciano Pavarotti. Al Pacino, Annette Funnicello and Art Carney sat at the top of one column across from Bobby Thomson and Enos Slaughter. Steve Martin, George Foster, Sophia Loren and Lou Piniella were in the mix too. Scribbled alongside each name was its autograph price, and when Ferreira managed to bag the cast of "I Love Lucy" or Clem Labine he drew a straight line through it, marking it off his wish list. He had a near-encyclopedic memory for what may seem trivial to others but was not trivial to him, recalling which autographs he had in duplicates (or triplicates or quadruplicates). And when he talked excitedly about the enjoyment collecting autographs gave him, he added a detail that only a person in law enforcement would: "You have a baseball with a star's signature on it and if it's legitimate, the ball probably has his fingerprints on it. There's a part of that guy on the ball."

Ferreira's love of collecting arose partly from his love of sports, which he played with his typically nonstop exuberance and enthusiasm on the FBI softball teams at the various field offices where he has worked. After graduating from the University of Hawaii with a degree in accounting, he joined the Sacramento field office where he worked white collar crime groups. One such group was a ring of Palestinians whose scam was to open an electronics store, establish credit lines with banks, buy merchandise from manufacturers and wholesalers, and sell this merchandise to the public just like a regular business. But eventually these fellows stopped acting regular—not paying for the hundreds of thousands of dollars in gear they had purchased on credit, selling it on the black market for cash, and then declaring bankruptcy or torching their building to defraud the insurance company and collect a big settlement. After leading the investigation of this ring Ferreira learned that the Palestinians had put his name on their own sort of wish list, one that wished him dead.

From Sacramento, Ferreira moved cross-country to the juiciest assignment in the entire criminal investigative division of the FBI, New York City, where national reputations and careers are built. Louis Freeh, the FBI Director during the early years of Bullpen, began his climb up the law enforcement hierarchy as a special agent in New York investigating the Mafia. Ferreira also worked the mob, overseeing the UCAs, wire taps and surveillance of a Brooklyn crew in the Bonanno crime family.

Not being a big city guy at heart, Ferreira was always looking to return to the island life, and when an offer in the late eighties came to transfer to the FBI office in Guam, with the idea he'd eventually be able to get a posting in Honolulu, he grabbed it. Hawaii and Guam share the same ocean but not the same neighborhood; they're about seven hours apart by air. Way, way out there in the blue, blue Pacific, Ferreira encountered something that made him feel like he was back on the Lower East Side: organized crime. The Japanese Yakuza's clannish, hierarchical structure resembles the Mafia in many ways, with some painful differences. When a Mafioso messed up bad, the family killed him. A Yakuza screw-up atoned for his blunder by self-mutilation: chopping off the tip of a finger and presenting it to his boss as penance. Missing tips of fingers was one of the ways (another was their incredible full-body tattoos) that Ferreira and other federal agents identified the Yakuza as they arrived in Guam to do their dirty work.

The Yakuza were investing in casinos and real estate in Guam and the surrounding islands as a means of laundering money. They also manufactured meth and smuggled guns from the U.S. into Japan to sell them illegally. In his investigations of the group, Ferreira frequently worked with Japanese authorities and traveled to Tokyo on TDYs—temporary duty assignments—where he developed a fondness and interest in the country.

Finally receiving his transfer from Guam, he shifted over to the Honolulu field office where, as always, he put his name on a roster for the FBI softball league. There, he met another ballplayer with ability, Tim Fitzsimmons, who was then starting his career with the Bureau. The two worked different cases on the organized crime and drugs squad, both eventually transferring to the West Coast—Fitzsimmons to San Diego, Ferreira to Eugene. They had lost contact over the years but Operation Bullpen was about to bring them back together again.

Ferreira said he'd do it. It was a unique case that required an unusual skill-set for an agent, and he was made to order for it. Shortly after this call he flew down to San Diego for an August 1 meeting at the Carlsbad RA with Fitzsimmons, McKinney, prosecutor Phil Halpern, and Anthony West. He hadn't seen Fitzsimmons in a long while, and it gave the others involved in the investigation a chance to meet and evaluate him. United by their desire to push things ahead more rapidly, and seeing how, because of Ferreira's knowledge of sports memorabilia, he could jump right into the case, they agreed: He was their man.

The plan was for Ferreira to maintain his caseload in Eugene while acting as undercover agent in San Diego one or two weeks a month. Beginning in September, and for every month after that for the next two years, he would fly from the trees to the beach, from the cool wet inland woods to the dry sunny coast, from one state down to the other and back up again.

It was perfect, just perfect. The scenario could not have set up any better. Smart, experienced, full of energy, Ferreira, whose mother was Chinese and his father Portugese, had an ethnic background that matched his cover. He spoke a little pigeon Hawaiian, some Chinese, some Japanese. His Japanese accent was excellent, clearly that of a man who had spent considerable time in the country. Man, he had even been to sumo matches! On top of all this he had dealt with plenty of tough guys before, a lot tougher than these flip-flop mafia guys. And because he was a collector, a bona fide expert, he was fired up about going after the people who were soiling his hobby.

Everything was perfect, absolutely perfect, except for one lousy thing: It wasn't. Ferreira was the right man for the wrong job. And Fitzsimmons, McKinney and Halpern all knew it.

Still full of doubt Nate Harrison got involved slowly in the racket, doing only enough business at first to climb out of debt, pay his bills, get a place of his own again. "I started out light," he recalled. "Then I got greedy, as most people do. I could've made as much money as I wanted to."

As awful as selling fakes made him feel, being broke made him feel worse. And after a period in which everything seemed to go wrong for him and every friend he had except for Wayne had deserted him, he started to feel better about himself again.

Nate had a kid brother he was real close to; they battled each other in video games all the time. But Nate was not about to let him in on the secret. His brother believed everything was the same as it had always been, except that Nate's wholesaling business had picked up and his money situation had improved with it. That was all his brother needed to know, nothing more.

The only person Nate could confide in was Wayne, and vice versa. Wayne could not tell his wife everything he was doing for the same reasons Nate could not tell his brother: The less they knew, the more protected they were. Nate and Wayne grew even closer now that neither of them had anything to hide from the other. As such, the older, more experienced one played Fagin to Nate's Oliver Twist. "Basically," Wayne said, "I taught him everything he knows about autographs." Forgeries, too.

Before, Nate had sold baseball cards and novelties, only dabbling in autographs. Under Wayne's tutelage, Nate steadily shifted out of these less profitable areas into more lucrative realms. Indicative of his trust in him, Wayne told Nate how the operation worked—information he shared with no one else. To the people he was supplying forgeries to, including Stan the Man, Wayne seldom identified Greg by name, saying only that he had a "source," if he said that much. He kept this information private for fear that if he told people the truth, they would try to steal Greg away from him, a fear he did not have with Nate.

At first Wayne didn't tell the Marinos what Nate knew. Worried about the family's reaction if they learned that he had spilled the beans about them to an outsider, Wayne swore Nate to a pact of silence. Nate, not one to rock the boat, said no problem, and he played dumb around Greg and John whenever he had dealings with them.

As they had for more than two years, Wayne and Greg were still working together, still growing their business thanks in large measure to the exemplar books that Wayne had put together. The flimsy black book at the beginning had grown into seven thick black books with some 7,000 exemplars in all, each binder consisting of pages and pages of autographs, with lots of autographs on a single page and more being added all the time. Older autographs of current stars needed to be updated because Greg did not want to mimic a celebrity's sig from the eighties when the celeb could be signing his name with a slightly different twist in the nineties. Many stars had more than one autograph in the albums, a reflection of how their signature had naturally changed over the years. Invariably, as a person's career progresses from newcomer eager and flattered to be asked for an autograph, to famous star who'd rather not be bothered with what he sees as a tiresome task, his obligation to the public, his signature travels on a downward spiral from neat to messy. But messy autographs are a boon to forgers, who generally have an easier time with them than more legible ones.

Now Nate had access to this data base too, and when he compared a genuine exemplar in the black books with the same sig done by Greg on a ball or jersey, in the best cases he saw virtually no difference between the two. Even the bad ones, and there were some of those, weren't completely terrible—maybe a detail or two that Greg could have done better if he had had more time. But even with these Nate knew that very, very few people would ever notice such details or possess the expertise to recognize when a sig was less than perfect.

You didn't necessarily want perfection in a forgery anyway. Less skillful forgers were neat freaks striving to master every detail, and in their careful scrupulousness they became too precise, too exact—and completely wrong. Perfection can sometimes arouse suspicion among trained handwriting analysts, so the best forgers did not want their work to look perfect, they wanted it to look true.

As Greg's skills improved, Wayne needed less and less to check over his work to see if it was right. Also, with the orders cascading in from Stan the Man, there was little time for this.

Stan, Nate learned, was as big a player in this thing as Wayne or Greg, moving tons of product and pushing the California guys hard and contributing ideas that helped them all make more money. For the sig of a dead ballplayer, the most obvious sign that it was bad was to have it appear on a baseball manufactured after the player's death. But genuine vintage balls are hard to find, and expensive when you do, so Wayne created fake vintage ones. First he found old balls with no modern markings or labels and if they had them, he scraped them off. He then devised a red Haiti stamp that he applied to the balls, making them appear as if they were manufactured in an earlier era. (Older balls were made in Haiti, modern balls in Costa Rica.) Stan suggested these balls be signed on the sweet spot to enhance their value, and Greg did as they wished.

Some ballplayers—the living ones, at any rate—resented the fact that many of the autographs they signed for free were later sold by collectors, and they deliberately avoided signing on the sweet spot to decrease the ball's commercial value. Stan and Wayne stayed up to date on the idiosyncrasies of the more prominent stars, and if someone was only signing on a side panel, Greg signed that star's sig on a side panel too.

Stan talked to Wayne, and Wayne talked to Greg, and they all responded to what the marketplace told them. Hall of Famer Duke Snider, for instance, played for the Brooklyn and Los Angeles Dodgers, whose primary team color is blue. So when collectors were looking to buy the Duke's autograph, the ink they wanted it to be written in was blue. But don't ask him to sign the Duke of Flatbush, a nickname he disliked, because he wouldn't do it.

Nate became aware of all these things and so many more, including the need to keep all this new knowledge on the down-low. On Mulberry Drive in San Marcos in the industrial part of town, in a tiny business park just down the block from a 7-Eleven, his office for LNN Enterprises was a picture of shabby anonymity. The business park consisted of two dumpy one-story buildings facing each other across a parking lot with a clump of greenery in the middle. A half-dozen other small businesses had offices there, and Nate's space occupied the middle unit in the building on the south side of the lot. With glass double doors and large front windows, he could pull the blinds down when he needed privacy, but mainly it was used as a warehouse and only a select few members of the flip-flop mafia ever came there.

"My business plan was to develop a big inventory," he said. "Most everybody else bought things to order. One of their customers would place an order with them, they'd go to the Marinos, and the Marinos would fill it for them. But I bought things in volume, warehoused them at the office, and slowly sold them off."

Nate sold strictly wholesale, and his family tree for counterfeit memorabilia grew naturally out of his legitimate business contacts in the past. Not everything he sold was bogus; there was some genuine stuff tossed in there too, pointing up another way in he and Wayne worked together. "If it was real, Wayne said so," said Nate. "If Greg signed it, he told me it was a fake. It was fair on both sides. We didn't play games with each other."

In a business in which everybody figured that everybody else was lying and so you'd have to be an idiot not to lie yourself, Nate and Wayne dealt with each other straight, hashing out a fair price that worked for them both. If it didn't work for both of them, it didn't work—period. No games, no lies, no trying to screw the other guy in the guise of doing him a favor, the way so many other people in the racket operated.

Eventually, though, problems started to develop between them—not problems of personality but of supply and demand. With orders pouring in, just the way Wayne promised they would when he was convincing him to come over, Nate couldn't get all the signed material he needed on a timely basis. Needing to go through Wayne for all his orders, he had to wait until Wayne first processed Stan the Man's stuff through the Marinos. The delays were irritating his customers, who were demanding their goods right away.

"My business kept growing. I was getting new customers, and they wanted more stuff than Wayne could spare the time to get me." Finally Nate went to see Wayne to ask him to step aside as middle-man and let him deal with the Marinos directly.

Wayne listened quietly to Nate's proposition. If somebody else had proposed this idea he might have told him to screw off and cut him out of the supply chain altogether. But this was Nate talking, not somebody else. "Okay," he agreed. "I'll talk to Greg about it. See what he says."

A few days later Wayne brought back the good news: Nate was in. Greg had always liked him and because he and his family had known him and dealt with him for a while, they felt they could trust him. He no longer had to go through Wayne; he could go straight to the source. Nate was stoked. This new arrangement was going to make things a lot easier and more lucrative for him.

Of course, Wayne now stood to lose a substantial piece of change—the money he had been making as the middle between the Marinos and Nate. The two of them talked about it, and Nate agreed to kick back a couple grand a month in earnings to Wayne in exchange for what his friend had done for him.

With Nate moving forward in the racket, Wayne was making changes himself to increase his money-making powers. He moved W.W. Sports Cards to an out-of-the-way address in a grimy industrial park of San Marcos close to the railroad tracks and Highway 78. Nate's shop was practically around the corner and Wayne lived in San Marcos, so this new location was more convenient than the old one. But the real reasons for the shift were to be less visible to the public and to stop selling fakes retail, which he had always disliked. As a wholesaler he dealt only with people he knew. His new address was unlisted; it was safer that way. No more retail customers, no more kids wandering in off the street after school, no more snoops like Anthony West poking around. No one came to W.W. Sports Cards anymore unless he had a reason, and the only people who had a reason were guys in the racket, often dropping in to pick up certs from J. DiMaggio Company.

The J. DiMaggio scam was another of Wayne's ideas, coming about partly due to market pressures and partly due to his desire to make more money. It offended his business instincts to let an opportunity pass him by if there was a way for him to take advantage of it, and authentication was just such an opportunity.

The idea of certs was not new; Anthony Alyinovich had issued them with the fraudulent merchandise he had sold. But particularly after Foul Ball, COAs had become a staple of the autograph industry, both the honest and corrupt sides of it. The public insisted on COAs when they bought signed memorabilia based on the faulty premise that pieces of paper could confer legitimacy on their purchases.

An East Coast authenticator by the name of Donald Frangipani, whose office was on 13th Avenue in Brooklyn and whose letterhead described him as an "examiner of questioned documents," issued certs for Bray and others in the ring. And they liked dealing with Frangipani because when he examined their documents, he okayed everything he saw, even the below-par stuff that came flying off Greg's pen, and there was plenty of that. Stan's Sports Memorabilia, Smokey's and many others also produced paper to cover the fakes they were selling. But Bray knew that much more could be done in this area and what was even better, he knew the man who could do it for him.

Wayne liked to eat at a restaurant in Vista called Monica's, owned by a pleasant middle-aged man named James DiMaggio. Short, with an amiable look about him, his black hair thinning on top and graying in spots, the bespectacled DiMaggio was not normally the type of person who would have attracted Bray's interest. But something about DiMaggio intrigued him, something obvious: his name.

DiMaggio.

James DiMaggio.

Wayne sat in James DiMaggio's restaurant contemplating another DiMaggio, the famous one, turning the two names over in his mind:

Joe DiMaggio. James DiMaggio.

J. DiMaggio. J. DiMaggio.

The name of DiMaggio had instant brand identity, immediately recognizable by sports fans as well as by those who only knew Joe DiMaggio as the lover and husband of Marilyn Monroe. Jim DiMaggio wasn't Joe DiMaggio but he had the same first initial and last name, and it occurred to Wayne that a man who went by the name of J. DiMaggio—for marketing reasons you'd want to play up that famous last name and use only the first initial—could make a lot of money in the authentication business, and one day he approached him about it.

"I need an authenticator and you can make eighty grand cash a year," Bray told him in confidence. "All you have to do is sign your name."

DiMaggio fit the pattern of nearly all the Bullpen crooks: an otherwise law-abiding citizen who felt the pressures surrounding money more keenly than the ones about obeying the law. Those in law enforcement have a term for this slowly corruptive process: "the slippery slope," they call it, and DiMaggio may have felt himself slipping faster and faster downhill and gotten scared about where he was going to eventually land. His restaurant was failing; this may have caused other financial problems. Bray made his pitch two weeks before Monica's shut its doors for the last time, and DiMaggio agreed. They were now partners in the authentication business.

The office of J. DiMaggio Company opened on South Melrose Drive in Vista, with Bray running the show behind the scenes. DiMaggio worked out of his office and at Bray's shop on North Pacific. Having DiMaggio around meant that Wayne no longer needed to use other, potentially less reliable authenticators, and that the guys in the ring had to go through him to get certs. To buy from the Marinos was one fee; to obtain certs from J. DiMaggio Company was another, separate fee.

But would people really believe that DiMaggio was an actual authenticator simply because of his name?* And what about people in the industry? They were going to have questions, no doubt. How did this unknown suddenly pop out of nowhere to start reviewing all this superstar material? Who was he? What were his qualifications? Rival authenticators, especially the crooked ones, might become jealous of all the business he was doing and spread rumors to undercut him. To stop the rumors before they started and to supply a plausible explanation for his entry into the field, an interview was arranged with a well-meaning but completely hoodwinked writer

---

*The FBI later found that yes, Bray's cynical hunch was on the mark. People did tend to place their trust in DiMaggio's certifications simply because of his last name. After DiMaggio started advertising his business, members of the public not involved in the scam sent him autographs to review. He uniformly certified them all.

named John Leptich, who had no idea who DiMaggio really was and who was behind him. For his story he relied on one main source, and the wrong source at that: DiMaggio himself.

Leptich was a stringer for *Beckett Collectibles*, a trade industry magazine popular with collectors. He spoke to DiMaggio in the summer of 1997, and the article appeared in an issue of the magazine a few months later. The piece begins:

> "In baseball history, few names have been more recognized or respected than DiMaggio. And today, one Californian appears to be successfully parlaying the popular moniker with autograph authenticating. The J. DiMaggio Co. of Vista, Calif., recently entered the ever-increasing world of signature authenticators. While the surname and first initial are well known, the individual who founded the business is relatively obscure."

Since it would not do for the man entering the ever-increasing world of signature authenticators to only have a background in breakfast, lunch and dinner, DiMaggio and Bray, but mostly Bray, invented a new bio for him. And Leptich faithfully wrote down every phony word of it. He continues,

> "Unlike any of his previous business ventures, DiMaggio determined it was time to put his familiar last name to work. 'Yes, the fact that DiMaggio is my name helps me a lot,' he says. 'Joe is my father's first cousin. I haven't seen him for over forty years. To my knowledge, he doesn't know about this business.'"

If you're going to tell a fish story, why not make it a whopper? Jim did not just possess the famous DiMaggio name, he was related to the great man himself! The article went on to say that his years of collecting had "provided him with an inventory unlike many others," which was true. With access to the black books, DiMaggio had at his fingertips one of the best and biggest exemplar collections in the country, albeit one being used for criminal purposes. The magazine included a photo of him talking on the phone with books in the background—if you want to portray a person as scholarly and serious, always put books in the background of the shot—and a copy of J. DiMaggio Company's "Document of Authentication."

DiMaggio was not an authentic authenticator but he acted like one, carrying around a spiral-bound notebook in which he dutifully recorded a short description of the signed item and its six-digit code number corresponding with the DOA he had issued. While such a system suggested scientific methodology, much as the books in the photo conveyed an image of intellectual rigor, it was not all hokum. He did evidently look at every piece he certified even if most every one was fake. One reason for this was that it probably made him feel better about what he was doing. He was not just a crook making easy money and not caring how he did it; he was doing something real, he was working, and his notebooks proved it.

Keeping the notebooks also protected him against the law. If ever confronted about his activities he could point to his meticulous record-keeping as evidence of honest intent—that he was not just issuing blanket approvals for obvious fakes but conducting an actual business.

Another reason for inspecting every piece, although his judgment on each was preordained, was that many of these balls and bats and jerseys were cool to look at. They were not antiques but they were like antiques. And the signatures were not real but they were like real.

Every J. DiMaggio Company DOA contained his signature and the company seal, signifying that the autograph was genuine "within the strict guidelines of our established exemplars," as DiMaggio told the reporter, who dutifully wrote it down. On the back of every DOA was a disclaimer stating that the opinion rendered was just that—an opinion—and not an absolute guarantee of authenticity, a reminder, DiMaggio said, that authentication was an imperfect science and that even the most conscientious examiners made mistakes.

A disclaimer of this sort was an essential part of the authentication dodge, a self-protection clause for swindlers. An authenticator's approval was only an opinion, not a warranty, and since buyers were advised of this fact, DiMaggio could not be held legally responsible for saying a thing was true when it was actually false. He was off the hook.

The article could not have been more perfect if DiMaggio and Bray had written it themselves. But the reporter did not rely solely on DiMaggio for his information; he called up one of J. DiMaggio Company's best customers to get his opinion.

"I trust [DiMaggio] better than others I know who have the same type of service," said Nate Harrison, who was in on the whole thing and laying it on thick. "Jim's pretty strict. I've had stuff that he didn't pass. This guy has collected a long time and knows what he's doing."

Nate, who was a crook, was vouching for another crook, and their lies were being published in a national magazine. It was sweet, very sweet. And Wayne, who remained out of view while pulling the strings on the scam, could feel good for another reason too: His student was learning the ways of the teacher.

9

Jim DiMaggio only dealt with Wayne at the start, no one else. The last thing on earth he wanted was to meet other guys in the racket or have them see his face, so if any of them showed up at W.W. Sports Cards when he was there he retreated into a back room and closed the door until they left. His fears soon melted away, though, and he started dealing face-to-face with the guys who were flooding him with cash.

One of those people was of course Nate, who was paying J. DiMaggio Company about five thousand a month to certify all the stuff he was selling. Having been handed the keys to the magic kingdom by his pal Wayne, Nate became a member of the inner circle with direct access to the Marino forgery factory. His nickname was "Nate the Skate," a joking reference to both his slacker's approach to the business and his non-confrontational personality. He got along well with Greg, the man everybody wanted to get along with. "I liked dealing with Nate," said Greg. "He never argued about prices or anything else. If I didn't feel like signing, I'd tell him and he'd say okay. He didn't try to wheel and deal. He never rushed me, never pushed."

Nate spent one day a week attending to the affairs of LNN Enterprises; the other six he hung out and played video games. Entering the racket had granted him a life of leisure at the ripe old age of twenty-five. The high school dropout had it made; he was skating.

In the children's story *The Gingerbread Man*, the title character is a big, soft doughy gingerbread man who runs away from a succession of animals trying to catch him until he meets a fox. The clever fox tricks him and eats him. Being a little soft and doughy himself, Greg good-naturedly accepted the nickname of the Gingerbread Man, while Gloria Marino, who herself possessed a fair bit of shrewdness, hung the tag of the Fox on Wayne.

More nicknames within the inner circle: Tricky Dick Laughlin and the two Rickys, Big Ricky Weimer and Little Ricky Mitchell. Little Ricky wasn't that little (five-feet-nine inches tall), but the others needed something to call him to distinguish him from the bigger and chunkier Weimer. Hence, his nickname.

Little Ricky joined the inner circle about the same time as Nate the Skate, and he brought his own distinct qualities to the party. Boyishly good looking with blue eyes, brown hair and the trim, well-groomed appearance of a young suburban professional, he immediately became a figure of suspicion for Wayne. Unlike Wayne and Nate, who were blood brothers, Wayne and Little Ricky were uneasy allies. Born and raised in small-town Ohio, Little Ricky was smooth, clean-shaven, no jewelry, no tattoos. A sports fan and a real collector. He was college-educated (University of Akron, B.A. in business), and as a salesman for the Prudential Company, he wore a suit and tie while on the job. Bray would sooner die than wear a standard business suit, and he jumped on Little Ricky as soon as he heard he had entered the racket.

This occurred after Little Ricky's first trip to Vegas, his first time selling fakes, which he had done with Greg's blessing. This was why Wayne came on so strong with him, because Little Ricky was Greg's close friend and therefore, in Wayne's view, a potential rival, somebody who had to be watched.

While managing a card shop in Poway, Rick had met Greg the same way Wayne did: through business. Actually it was John Marino who rumbled into the shop first, carrying the faded portfolio bag full of Angelo Marino's lithographs. Only by this time they were being signed by famous sports stars. Rick bought some pieces for the shop and some for his private collection and soon came to know Greg, who was also pushing his father's lithos and other signed things. While doing business together Greg and Rick became friends, chummy enough for Greg to invite him over to his apartment in Escondido one afternoon.

When Rick entered he noticed all these pens everywhere, more pens than he'd seen in any one place except at an office supply store: Sharpies (extra fine blue, extra fine black, fine point black, medium metallic), Bics (permanent grip blue, round stic blue), Accountants (fine point blue, fine point black), Vis a Vis (permanent fine point blue), Sanfords (gold coat extra fine metallic, gold coat slim tip metallic, gold coat bold metallic), Unipaints (fine line gold, medium line gold), Broad Lines (liquid silver, liquid gold), and old fountain pens that resembled antiques. His curiosity sparked, he asked Greg what he did with all of them.

Smiling, Greg said, "I don't normally like people seeing me do this," and he promptly forged, on a *Sports Illustrated*, the autograph of the star featured on that week's cover. It happened so fast Rick wasn't sure what he saw. Laughing, Greg did it again on a second SI cover. This time Rick got it—and it blew him away.

"It occurred to me that everything in my room, everything on my walls, everything I had bought and collected from the Marinos was fake," he recalled. He had bought thousands of dollars of stuff from them, believing, he says, that it was authentic. Now he suddenly knew different. It was a moment not unlike what Nate Harrison had experienced when he first learned the truth about what Wayne was selling, but Rick reacted somewhat differently. Returning home, he decided to rid himself of every Marino piece he owned, stripping his walls and bookcases and cabinets and throwing everything into boxes in the garage. "I was done," he said.

Not done with the Marinos, mind you, just done with being gullible and stupid. If somebody was going to get ripped off, it wasn't going to be him.

The next Friday, Rick and his manager at Prudential met a client in Riverside County, after which they kept heading east for a boys' weekend in Las Vegas. In the trunk of Rick's car was some of the phony signed memorabilia that had been taking up space in his garage.

That night he threw away some money at the blackjack tables, rising the next morning with the idea of making back everything he had lost. Hotels all around Vegas have gift shops, souvenir shops and memorabilia shops that cater to the tourists looking for the perfect thing to bring home after their gambling vacations. Being unusual conversation pieces and having some celebrity glamour attached to them, autographed material—signed Rat Pack photos, guitars inscribed by the Rolling Stones, anything and everything touched by Elvis Presley or Marilyn Monroe, the usual big-name sports stuff—was often just the right thing. That morning and afternoon Rick went calling on these shops. Looking clean and crisp and dressed casually but nice, he had that small-town Midwest charm working for him that was ideal for conning people. But none of the shop owners he talked to could be described as innocent; most seemed to know the score as well as Rick now did. Few asked questions and the ones who did barely listened to his answer, perhaps recognizing, correctly, that his reply would be evasive anyway.

Was it deceitful to sell a person a fake if the buyer knew what he was getting though neither party spoke the truth aloud? What they talked about, what they could talk about, was how beautiful these pieces were: Beautiful frame, beautiful Shaquille O'Neal jersey, beautiful sig. Beautiful, and a total lie.

If only gambling were as easy as selling fakes. After selling out and making a few thousand bucks, that night Mitchell left everything he made on the blackjack tables.

When he returned to San Diego he knew he had a decision to make: "Do I sell forgeries or do I sit across the dining room table from people and try to sell them life insurance?" Before he could come up with an answer his phone rang. On the line was a man he'd never seen or met. It was Wayne Bray, and it was not a social call.

Before leaving for Vegas Rick had told Greg what he intended to do there, and asked if he had any problems with it. The easy-going Marino said no, just stay away from Smokey's, which was his client, and Rick had obligingly gone to other shops and hotels around the Strip. The man on the phone was much less hang-loose about Mitchell's activities. Hang-loose was not a phrase to be applied to Bray at any time, but especially when talking to a person who might be entertaining thoughts about stealing Greg away from him.

Wayne knew that Rick and Greg were good friends. He also knew, because Greg had told him, that Rick had gone to Vegas to sell bad stuff with the possibility of selling more in the future. His message, bluntly delivered, was to tell Mitchell what he could and could not do in the business, should he continue to sell Greg Marino products.

For Wayne, this was pure business, how he played the game. For Rick, it was unlike any business call he had ever received in his life. "He came off very harsh," he said. "It was very intimidating. I was scared to death of the guy."

Mitchell's opinion of Bray did not change much after they met, although it was not Wayne's looks per se and certainly not his size that was intimidating about him. It was his attitude. Wayne talked at times with this bored, I-don't-give-a-crap air, but he clearly did. This was no game to him, this was serious, and he was playing it for all it was worth. This was a big thing, maybe the only big thing he'd ever have in his life except for his wife and kids, and he sure as hell wasn't going to let some junior insurance agent mess it up for him.

And yet for all his passion Wayne also appeared deeply cynical, as if walled off within himself to what he was doing and the effect it had on people. There was no other word for it. The guy was a...*criminal*.

But you know what? And this was what was so wild about all of this: So was the young suburban professional with the good family background and higher education. He was entering Crooksville too, full speed ahead.

Mitchell does not consider himself a judgmental person—"I accept everybody for who they are. I don't judge people by their cover"—nor does he put himself on a pedestal above others. But he could not help but look around at some of the guys he had met selling fakes—the tattooed, menacing Bray; Greg, the sweet-hearted pot-smoker; Nate, the slacker—

and compare himself to them. Another was a smoothie out of Laguna Niguel named Laith Neesan: "a con man, a drifter and a forger," in the assessment of Mitchell, who marveled at how Laith could fool people, including Mitchell. A true con man can take your money even when you know you are being hustled; Neesan had that kind of ability. He'd order a Babe Ruth-signed baseball from Rick, promising to pay him as soon as the guy he was selling it to paid him. Then Laith would tell the other guy he needed his grand or whatever up-front before he could deliver the ball. So then Neesan would disappear with both the ball and the money while Mitchell and the other guy would end up only with a stupid look on their faces.

Nobody would see Neesan for a while until he'd sail through town again, arriving as mysteriously as he had left, offer a reasonable excuse coupled with an apology for what had happened before, and somehow, amazingly, even though Mitchell knew that Neesan was going to try to screw him and Neesan knew that Mitchell knew this, Laith would work the same con on him again.

Good boys who try hard and play by the rules get rewarded in the end, don't they? Rick may have thought so at one time. But Laith* and a whole bunch of other people, including all the shop owners Rick had sold to who maintained a respectable front but were as guilty as anybody else, weren't playing by the rules and they were making tons more dough than he was selling life insurance. "When you see all these people, who are half the person you are, making all this money…" he said, not finishing his thought. It hurt. It didn't seem right, it didn't seem fair, and he felt he deserved better.

With Wayne around, Rick knew he couldn't go a certain way in the racket, but he didn't really want to go that way anyway. "My whole thing was to fly under the radar if I could. Not attract the attention of law enforcement like the bigger players. I never pushed it hard like some of the others did. I never advertised, I never sold on eBay."

After their first uncomfortable conversation he and Wayne got along fine, no problems. Rick respected the boundaries laid out for him, and Wayne came to realize that despite his friendship with Greg, Mitchell represented no threat to his dominance. "Wayne knew I had a niche in the business he didn't," said Mitchell.

Per his plan to keep his activities as inconspicuous as possible, he never dealt directly with photo houses or sports gear manufacturers, instead running his orders through Nate who, for a fee, supplied him with the blanks he needed. Most everything Rick sold was immaculately framed and

---

*Neesan, a small-time player in the ring, "distributed hundreds of thousands of dollars of counterfeit memorabilia," according to FBI documents in the case.

packaged, and his framer, the man who made these pieces look so nice, had a shop in San Diego not far away from him. Mitchell threw so much business his way that the two became friends and often escaped to Vegas together on guys-only weekends. The framer almost certainly knew that the autographed pieces he was prettying up were phony. But he never asked, and Rick never told. It was better that way.

Mitchell's primary business turf was Vegas, which was also his primary playground. He went there a couple times a month, often with his framer buddy, loading up the car with fakes neither could discuss truthfully, driving up on Friday night and bunking at the Ritz, Rick's favorite hotel. The weekends followed a predictable pattern: selling counterfeits by day, roaming the blackjack tables at night. The cash he made in fakes he used to gamble with, so even when he lost it was like he didn't lose because he wasn't playing with his own money. It was like free money. And there was plenty more where that came from.

"Suddenly the biggest forger in the country was living in my backyard," he said in an awestruck tone. Not only that, the biggest forger in the country was his good friend. The result of this—for Rick, for all of them—was that it opened up a whole new realm of forbidden pleasures, gambling being only one of them. Rick had certainly gambled in the past but all this free money flying around gave him the wherewithal to do it like never before. And since he was already breaking the law, why not live it up and go all the way? As messed up as it was on one level, on another level it was pretty damned cool. In his case he got to be a whole new person, Little Ricky, who was not bound by the conventions that tethered Rick Mitchell.

One of his Vegas clients who spent lots of money with him owned just the coolest car: a red, two-seater Ferrari 308 with a fuel-injected V-8 and five-speed rear wheel drive, custom black leather seats with red trim and a black Targa top. It was the spitting image of what Tom Selleck drove in "Magnum P.I." Some nights the client would pull it out of his garage, and he and Rick would go out on the town together.

Little Ricky Mitchell, former Ohio schoolboy, cruising through the neon paradise in Tom Selleck's car on an evening so warm they could have been naked and not felt the chill. Who says crime doesn't pay?

When he got back to San Diego the party kept going, at least when he was over at Greg's place. Some days Kathy was off somewhere and it'd just be a bunch of guys doing what guys do—smoking, drinking, talking loud, music blasting, the game on the tube. It was sort of like when they were all boys, collecting and trading baseball cards. Only now they were buying and selling forgeries.

In the center of everything was Greg, still in his boxers, no shirt, big gut, smoking and signing. Sometimes he did his forging while still in bed, half-covered by a sheet, using a pillow instead of his usual couch cushion to support his arm. Rick always called ahead to see if Greg needed something—fast food, drinks or whatever—and then stopped and picked it up on his way over. Everybody played errand boy for Greg and did him favors, not just Rick. They kept him well-stocked in the best sensemilla. He was the guy putting cash under their mattresses, and they wanted to keep him happy.

One of the ways Rick endeared himself to Greg was by introducing him to Marty the Money Man, who had a real last name but nobody used it. In Marty's business it was probably better not to use your real name anyhow. He was their bookie and an honest-to-God character. In his early seventies with a big white Santa Claus beard, he claimed to have acted as the business manager for one of the Rat Pack, and it was possible Marty was telling the truth because he had that sort of old-time Rat Pack style. He drove a long black Mercedes and dated two busty blonde twins who were half his age. Pictures of them in bikinis he kept inside his golf cart. Only one was actually his girlfriend but Marty said he did them both and who cared anyhow? It was just an old man having some laughs.

Greg, John, Wayne and some others came to Marty on Little Ricky's recommendation, and the Money Man adored him for this. Waging ten to fifteen thousand dollar bets on a football game was not uncommon for the group. They spent a lot and they were good for what they bet, paying in full and on time, and no bookie could ask for more.

"The way it worked was that everyone called an offshore number that was answered offshore," said Mitchell. "But it connected to Marty in Rancho Santa Fe. He took the bets. My arrangement with him was when I got up a thousand bucks, he had to pay me off. But when I got down a thousand I had to pay him. The week was considered over after 'Monday Night Football.'"

It is legal to call offshore and place gambling bets, but it is not legal for the exchanges of money to take place on American soil. As with so many other criminal statutes, the guys did not always observe the niceties of this law.

Mitchell loved the competitiveness of gambling, the challenge of it, the emotional high when you went on a run. Every hot streak ended sooner or later, that was a given. But how do you know when the end has come? That was the unknowable thing—how high was high? It always seemed possible in the midst of a streak to keep it going and maybe get a little more of what was coming to you. But you could only get that if you stayed in the game, if you kept playing despite the risk.

It was the same with selling fakes. They were all riding a hot streak but how could they know where the top of it was? You think if you get a little bit more, you'll stop. Then you get that little bit more and you think, "Well, a little more won't hurt." And so you keep going, knowing you should stop but not wanting to at the same time.

But, as Little Ricky saw it, there was a chance, a strong chance, he'd never get caught. The others maybe, but not him because he had a plan. His plan was to make only enough. That was all: enough. Enough to pay for his gambling jones and then some but not enough to make the law notice—or for that matter, his wife.

Only those in the racket knew about the Little Ricky side of him. His wife truly knew nothing and suspected nothing and he danced a careful dance to keep her thinking everything was fine, everything was normal. Rick Mitchell was selling sports memorabilia and doing very well at it, and that was all she knew and that was all he told her. She had a demanding job as an elementary school teacher, and she had neither inclination nor reason to pry into her husband's affairs. Certainly she did not conceive of him as a criminal and nothing he did around her made her think different. So far as she knew he was a good man and a good husband and a good provider and since he kept the books for the couple and paid the bills, she did not know how much money on his side was coming in or going out. Much of his illegal business was cash and off the books anyhow.

She supported his frequent trips to Vegas because, in fact, he ran an honest side business selling unsigned memorabilia to sports bars and theme restaurants. There was a legitimate reason for him to be away so much.

Rick did not lie to his wife unless you consider not disclosing the whole truth a kind of lie. When he told her he was going over to Greg Marino's, he was. And he did. He just happened to omit certain pertinent facts about the nature of his business there. She was ignorant of the truth and if his plan succeeded, she'd forever remain that way. And this was Little Ricky's biggest gamble: to keep his secret life hidden even as the FBI was making covert preparations to blow it apart.

10

Since John Ferreira's cover was to be a businessman, he obviously needed a place to do his business, and with Ferreira away in Oregon before returning to California to begin his duties as undercover agent, the job of finding an office for him fell to Jeff McKinney.

For this assignment McKinney himself went undercover, posing as a businessman when he spoke to the property manager of a three-story office building on El Camino Real in Oceanside. At the junction of Interstate 5 and Highway 78, Oceanside was the ideal site for the office because it gave Ferreira easy access north or south along the coast and inland into the Bray-Marino lair of San Marcos and Escondido. It was also only a few minutes away from the Carlsbad RA. Friendly and with a comfortable air about him, dressed in an establishment suit and tie, the agent aroused no suspicion as he explained that he was looking to rent an office with an adjoining storage space. The property manager showed him two offices next to each other on the bottom floor of the building, which fit the bill perfectly. McKinney signed the lease; rent for the spaces was $770 a month.

The property manager no doubt felt good about the arrangement because while Suite 100 was ready for occupancy, Suite 101 was a disaster. The carpeting was ripped out and it had barely workable plumbing. But McKinney told the manager this was not a problem; the room would be used to store supplies only. Maybe they'd install a phone line, that was all.

El Camino Real is a broad, traffic-heavy boulevard, but a small quiet side street led into a parking lot in back of the building. The other tenants paid little heed to the plainclothes technicians pulling into the lot to wire Ferreira's office and set up the monitoring room. Tucked back into the recesses of the building, the two suites were truly basement offices—bland, anonymous, cold. A slender rectangular window separated 101's dark green door from 100's dark green door. Brown mini-blinds covered the windows and together with the solid green doors and white concrete walls of the building, the cool remoteness of the setting was striking. Well into late morning, shadows spread across the area darkening the entrances to the offices.

"Suite 101 was the monitoring room, where we put our video and recording equipment," said McKinney. "That's where I was a lot of the time when John met with a subject. I was also there for security in case something went wrong. We had hidden cameras and microphones in Suite 100 and John could activate them from his side."

When he returned to San Diego in late August Ferreira assisted in the preparations, coming up with the name for his company: The Nihon Trading Company. "Nihon" means Japan in Japanese.

His knowledge of Japanese culture and sports came in handy in many other ways, including the set-up of Suite 100 which had to look like the office of an actual shipping operator. To create this look the FBI casually arranged international shipping labels and packing materials on a table set against the wall in the small front room. A couple of boxes, also studiously casual, sat in one corner. Dominating one wall was a Michael Jordan poster with his forged signature that Upper Deck had supplied. But the best touches came from Ferreira's personal collection: Japanese posters of Ichiro Suzuki and Hideki Matsui, who were then unknown to American sports fans. Ferreira had seen the two stars play in Japan, and realizing that once they came to the States they'd make an impact on the American game, he had collected posters and other stuff on them that were displayed around the office.

For another touch of verisimilitude, the agent recorded two greetings on his phone message: the first in Japanese, the second in English.

If the undercover investigation was a kind of theater piece and Ferreira its lead actor, Suite 100 was the stage. It had to provide a believable setting in which the flip-flop mafia would feel comfortable enough to sell their products and talk candidly. Both the front shipping room and an even smaller back office, where Ferreira put his desk, were wired for sound and pictures. The only place a person didn't have to worry about being taped was the bathroom.*

Once Ferreira made a buy from a subject, the plan was for either McKinney or Fitzsimmons to pick up the goods at the Nihon Trading Company, or for Ferreira to take them over to the apartment in Oceanside

---

* *The San Diego FBI used digital recording equipment, but since the language of investigators remains rooted in the analog age, with agents still using terms such as "tapes" and "taping" subjects, these terms will be used in the book.*

where he was staying while on the job. His fellow agents would meet him there and shuttle the goods to an evidence warehouse near the FBI's Aero Drive office in San Diego.

In order to protect his cover Ferreira stayed well away from the FBI offices in Carlsbad and Aero Drive. Only twice during the entire investigation did he venture near Aero Drive, on both occasions meeting at a coffee shop in the area to brief the Special Agent in Charge on the case. Investigators did not want to take the risk of him being accidentally spotted going in or out of an FBI facility and thus blow his cover. Even within the FBI his identity was closely held information.

When Ferreira arrived in town from Eugene, Fitzsimmons picked him up at the airport and drove him to the lot where his undercover vehicle was parked. This was a dark blue, 6-series BMW that had passed the 100,000-mile mark—not a clunker exactly but no showroom model either. It had been seized in another investigation and the government was recycling it for use in this one. On the drive the agents would discuss the undercover plan for the week, Fitzsimmons then peeling off for Aero Drive while Ferreira headed north in his Beemer to assume the role of John Freitas, owner of the Nihon Trading Company.

Not being from San Diego or a California resident, Ferreira had to create and document a new identity. Any personal papers associating him with John Ferreira—FBI IDs, driver's license, credit cards—remained in Eugene, as did his FBI-issue handgun. "I never carried a gun in San Diego," he said. "If I was carrying a gun and I had been stopped by police for some reason with only my John Freitas identification, I would have been arrested."

But why would an autograph dealer need a gun anyhow? John Freitas was a businessman. Instead he packed a cell phone.

Under his assumed name Ferreira applied for and received a business license, California driver's license, car registration, credit cards and checking account. Though the government supplied and monitored the funds in his bank account, the account was not linked in any material way to the FBI. For all the bank knew, he was who he said he was: John Freitas. He may have shown the bank clerk who set up his account his two business cards: his Nihon Trading Company card with his local contact info and a second card for his other, equally phony business, Broadway Investments of Guam and Saipan. For this business, supposedly his main source of income, his job title noted on the card was "Private Investments/Project Specialist," a deliberately vague title that Ferreira had made up.

His cover needed to be specific, and yet not so specific that someone with a suspicious frame of mind could check on the details. Ferreira served as a project specialist, whatever that was, for resort developments in Guam and

Saipan where he had worked for the FBI. Many of the memorabilia boys vacationed in Hawaii but their knowledge of Guam and Saipan was surely slim, and almost certainly they'd never go to either place to see if what Ferreira was saying was really true.

"I know about real estate so I can talk about that," said Ferreira. "And I could talk about a project being built near the Saipan airport as one of my projects. But I didn't work for a company. I worked for myself, so it was impossible for them to call a company and check on me if they wanted to. I made up stuff about everything."

His Broadway Investments business card carried two phone numbers: an 808 Hawaii number and a 671 Guam number. Both of these were real but fake—real in the sense that they were actual Hawaii and Guam numbers, fake in that the calls were rerouted to a dedicated phone line that had been set up in the Eugene FBI. When the flip-flop mafia called Ferreira, they would think he was on the sunny sands of Honolulu when in reality he was in Oregon probably getting rained on.

Even as these preparations were moving ahead, worries about Ferreira's suitability as Bullpen's undercover agent had surfaced among the investigative team. In Operation Bullpen's organizational structure, Phil Halpern worked most closely with Fitzsimmons, and McKinney acted as the primary contact for Ferreira. So it made sense that when Halpern had doubts about the choice of Ferreira as UCA, he expressed them to Fitzsimmons.

"This was a major investigation, a Group One undercover proposal," said Halpern, recalling his concerns at the time. "And this was his first and only time he'd ever been undercover."

A Group One investigation signifies a case of national import, designated within the FBI as a top priority. Headquarters had reviewed and approved the investigation, and was kicking in federal dollars to help make it happen. But after meeting Ferreira at the sit-down in Carlsbad on August 1, the AUSA was skeptical he could handle such a major assignment.

"He was dedicated, enthusiastic. But he did not have it," Halpern went on. "You give a kid a glove and put him in right field in Yankee Stadium and he's not going to do the job even though he's enthusiastic."

The prosecutor's objections centered on the fact that in Sacramento, New York, Guam and Oregon, Ferreira had acted only as a case agent for the FBI, never an undercover agent, which had different responsibilities, different skills and a far different outlook. The case agent was the manager or chief executive of an investigation, while the undercover agent was the one who got down and dirty with the crooks, moving around with them in their element.

"It takes a specific type of person to fall into a criminal milieu," said Halpern. "John did not have it. He was too nice of a guy. He was not cut out to be a crook."

Fitzsimmons needed to listen to Halpern because Halpern was an aggressive, experienced prosecutor—colleagues described him as "tenacious," "a bulldog," "he doesn't let his agents rest"—who had handled high-profile federal sports cases before. A native of Long Island with a Rutgers law degree and studies in criminology at Cambridge, he had worked as a Hudson County, New Jersey prosecutor until transferring to the United States Attorney's Office in San Diego in the mid-eighties. Not long after beginning his new post he got a call from a border inspector at the busy Tecate port-of-entry. The inspector had stopped the car of a muscular British-born weightlifter named Tony Fitton, who was trying to smuggle in drugs though the official wasn't sure what kind of drugs they were. So he called the prosecutor's office, and Halpern asked him to read the labels over the phone. "The agent started reading these labels, and I heard something like 'Tes-trone,' 'Tes-trone Kyponate,' 'Anadrool,' and so on." Halpern recognized these barely pronounceable drugs to be anabolic steroids, and ordered the inspector to arrest Fitton. Officials uncovered more than two thousand boxes of steroids in his car—"enough to supply half the football teams in the U.S."—and Fitton became the focus of Halpern's first federal steroid smuggling prosecution, also the first in the country. The Brit later fled to beat the rap but authorities stayed on his case and he ultimately went to prison.

From this beginning Halpern became, in the words of a muscle magazine, "the steroid smugglers' worst nightmare," for a time taking on nine of ten federal steroid smuggling prosecutions in the U.S. and advising on the others he was not directly involved in. In the early days of steroids, smugglers stupidly stashed the goods under their seats or in the trunk of their car where inspectors easily found them. Over the years their techniques became more sophisticated, with the drugs being hidden inside wheel wells, fake gas tanks and elaborate, electronically controlled compartments built within the vehicle specifically for smuggling. When Fitton was busted the government had not yet designated the most powerful steroids as controlled substances, and having them in your possession was not a federal felony. But the drugs had to be declared upon entry into America, and failing to do so was a violation of the law. Since then the government has toughened the laws on steroids, and those caught smuggling them across the border are treated much the same as if they were bringing in cocaine.

Still, smugglers remained as determined as they were resourceful. One ring busted by Halpern traveled on dirt bikes and dune buggies across the Mexican desert into the Imperial Valley. Smugglers routinely hired Mexican nationals to transport the drugs but the prosecutor also sometimes encountered mules of a different kind: petite blondes and brunettes. Perhaps not into steroids themselves, they slept with the guys who were, and hid vials and syringes in their bras.

The biggest steroid ring prosecuted by Halpern was Laboratories Milano of Mexico, which manufactured counterfeit steroids for distribution in America. His most celebrated case was that of David Jenkins, a one-time golden boy of English track who won an Olympic silver medal for Great Britain but who became involved in a $400 million black market steroid operation in the United States. Halpern indicted Jenkins and thirty of his associates in 1987.

Although steroid prosecutions made him a natural fit for the Bullpen case, Halpern realized the differences between contraband drugs and contraband autographs. Legally speaking, forgery—defined as "the making, drawing or altering of a document with the intent to defraud; a signature made without the person knowing or consenting to it"—was a somewhat murkier proposition. Unlike with illegal drugs, possession of a forgery was not a crime. Selling one forgery or even one hundred forgeries was not necessarily a crime either, because the seller may be honestly unaware of the true nature of his products. It is possible, or at least arguable by a skilled defense attorney, that the seller was taken in by the same grifters who were swindling the public at large. What Halpern and the FBI looked at most closely was sales volume: If a dealer was selling large numbers of autographs he almost certainly knew they were fake because legitimate Alis and Jordans and Mantles simply do not exist in the marketplace in such quantities and at such low prices.

But how do you prove it in court? Even the experts find it hard sometimes to tell the difference between an authentic signature and a top-drawer counterfeit. Due to the heavy volume of autograph requests they receive, Hollywood stars and athletes have long used surrogates—secretaries, clubhouse attendants, family members—to sign fan mail on their behalf. Shaquille O'Neal was rumored to hold pool parties at his mansion in which his friends signed things for him. Some celebrity surrogate signers are so expert that their fake autograph is a virtual match for their boss's real one.

With all this legitimate confusion in the marketplace, what was to prevent a dealer from being honestly confused? A bogus dealer may sell thousands upon thousands of fraudulent items but what if he claimed he didn't know they were fake? That he thought they were legitimate? What did investigators do then? How did they prove he was lying?

"The intent to defraud" was essential in defining forgery and the sale of forged material as criminal acts. Intent implies awareness, which was what Halpern and the FBI needed to prove if a lying dealer ever took the stand claiming ignorance. Their best and strongest evidence, irrefutable really, had to come out of the mouths of the crooks themselves, secretly captured on tape.

And this was why Halpern was having such trouble with the choice of Ferreira. He didn't think Bullpen's undercover agent could get those vital admissions because he was such a non-crook himself. In a criminal world of double talk, Ferreira, an accounting major in college, was a straight shooter. He had never cheated on his wife with a stripper girlfriend. He had never hooked up with girls from porno movies and had sex with them and shot videos of it. He had never rented a limo and banged whores or partied with them in a luxury hotel. He didn't take drugs and never had, didn't gamble, didn't drink so much as a lite beer, and seldom swore. In the commission of his duties as an undercover agent Ferreira could not break the law, so it's not as if he was expected to engage in licentious or criminal behavior. Nevertheless he had to win the confidence of guys who were doing such things, and he had to become or seem to become one of them to get them to relax around him and open up.

Anthony West noticed how friendly Ferreira was at the August 1 meeting and thought how strange it was. "It was hard to believe he was an FBI agent," said West. "He was so down to earth."

Down to earth, personable, decent, friendly. These were all traits to describe John Ferreira the human being and he, for one, saw no reason to be any different when he assumed the role of John Freitas. Which brought up another of the concerns about him: his charm school approach to the job. His undercover strategy was not to get down and dirty with the crooks but to be what he was—a nice guy—and deal with them in a cordial, businesslike fashion, and win them over that way. Ferreira believed strongly that if he tried to be someone other than who he was, the memorabilia boys would see right through him and spot him as an impostor.

"My approach was to be nice to them. Be friendly and be friends with them. Be helpful. Whoever I can help, I help." He added that Fitzsimmons had different ideas on how he should act: "Tim would say, to be an undercover agent, you need to act like a jerk. Tim wanted me to be more of a criminal."

Fitzsimmons shared some of Halpern's concerns about Ferreira, as did McKinney. It was true: Ferreira was untested, untrained, uncertified. He had not been the first choice to be Bullpen's UCA; that agent had passed on the job. Also true: His personality and approach were highly unusual for undercover work. "John was not the smooth talking type of undercover agent, not the type you typically see as an undercover agent," Fitzsimmons admitted. "He never felt comfortable doing it. But his role in the case was so unique, and it fit him so well."

McKinney agreed, saying, "Choosing the UCA was a balancing act between undercover expertise and area expertise—knowledge of collecting. John had none of the former and lots of the latter. He was definitely not a smooth talker but even a smooth talking UCA, if he didn't know the area, it wouldn't work.

"Being an undercover agent takes unique skills," McKinney added. "You're basically living a lie and you've got to be able to lie with a straight face. Being a good UCA requires fast thinking on your feet and you've got to do what pops into your mind."

If the UCA doesn't say and do the right thing in the moment, it can blow his cover and wreck the case. A case agent, in contrast, can examine a problem and figure out what needs to be done without the same urgency. McKinney described himself as a case agent type, a managerial personality who likes "to contemplate, ponder a problem." Asked what category Ferreira fit into, he replied, "He's a case agent type."

Before an agent can go undercover for the FBI, he or she must undergo specific training at Quantico and be undercover-certified. Ferreira had not taken the training course and the FBI had not certified him to conduct undercover work. Nevertheless, Headquarters approved him as UCA because of the unique nature of the investigation and how well he fit the scenario that had been developed for it. Also, while the memorabilia boys may have had many unpleasant vices, a propensity for violence was not among them. Ferreira was not dealing with hardcore drug or organized crime figures, and his life was not in danger.

Unable to take the FBI's undercover training course because of the length of time it would have required him to be away from San Diego, Ferreira did later fly to Washington D.C. for interviews to determine his suitability to be an undercover agent. Alas, Headquarters concluded that no, he was not fit to go undercover. But Ferreira said this rejection had nothing to do with his ability to handle the job. Instead, the brass was worried about him spreading himself too thin by taking on a demanding undercover investigation on top of his eco-terrorism cases in Eugene. "They felt I had too much on my platter," he said.

Ferreira's first official day posing as John Freitas was September 2, 1997. Nice guys finish last, said Leo Durocher. But do they make good undercover agents? It was time to find out.

11

Located north of the railroad tracks and Highway 78 in the industrial section of San Marcos, the Balboa Industrial Park consists of two two-story buildings in front and some smaller ones in back. The two-story buildings are identical in appearance and color with fading white exterior siding and light brown roof trim. A narrow asphalt parking strip runs parallel with the street along the front of the buildings.

The building to the east, 133 North Pacific, has six office units—three down, three up. The three units on top open onto a wooden open-air walkway that extends the length of the upper floor and is covered by a flat-topped roof. Wooden stairs connect this walkway with the ground floor of the building, which is partly below street level. Cars parked on the asphalt strip block this lower floor from view, creating the impression of a building that is not two stories but one. From the street it appears the first floor is sinking into the ground and it is only a matter of time before it takes the second down with it.

A leafy palm tree with a squat thick trunk rises out of a small decorative area for shrubs in front. Unlike the building, which seems to be collapsing in on itself, the tree appears solidly anchored into the ground and in no danger of going anywhere but up. To the left of the palm tree is a flagpole with an American flag, the edges of the stripes starting to shred from exposure to the warm coastal winds and sun. Opposite the flag on the far right of the building are the steps leading to the upper walkway, and the first space at the top of those steps was Suite D, the office of W.W. Sports Cards. Its door was open, and on this day in late fall Special Agent John Ferreira was standing on the walkway peering in.*

To avoid confusion, Ferreira's real name will be used, not his undercover name.

The man Ferreira had come to see was not in his office. He was standing over by the Balboa Industrial Park sign between the two front buildings, smoking a cigarette. The agent's blue BMW was parked on the asphalt strip. Bray did not notice it although even if he had, it would not have caused him any alarm. Cars and trucks frequently came and went during the day.

What would have alarmed him, though, if he had looked that way, was the appearance of a stranger at his shop. The owner of W.W. Sports Cards did not like strangers nosing around, certainly not ones looking with such avid curiosity at an open cardboard box of signed Jackie Robinson and Roberto Clemente baseballs sitting within view of the door.

A trailer truck belched exhaust as it rumbled down North Pacific en route to making a delivery at another industrial park across the street from where Bray was standing. One of the businesses there was a custom motorcycle garage, and this may have been where Bray bought the racing pipes that he installed on his souped-up Harley Sportster 883. When in the mood for fun he fired up the Sportster or his almost brand-new Cobra Mustang convertible, both of which fit his fast car guy's need for speed better than his Toyota Land Cruiser, his work vehicle that doubled as the family car.

His wife usually drove the Land Cruiser, but its rear compartment was perfect for hauling illegal merchandise and Bray often used it on the job. Today it was parked on the strip not far from the government-issue Beemer.

Along with W.W. Sports Cards, 133 North Pacific contained offices for a sheet metal operator, a dragster mechanic and a small start-up company developing a method to treat the water used in chemical manufacturing processes. Another unit belonged to a cabinetmaker who stored lumber there. A few of the guys at the site referred to Wayne as "the Cancer Man," a knock on his pack-a-day habit and his tendency to throw the butts on the ground outside the building after he was done smoking. If one of them asked Bray what he did for a living, he might have said, "Sports memorabilia," but if the questioner expected a more elaborate answer he inevitably met with disappointment. Wayne was hardly the gabby type when it came to discussing his line of work, which may have been why one person who occasionally crossed paths with him at North Pacific described him as "somewhat shady. I don't want to say gangster-ish, but you know…"

Bray's office did not have his company name or even a letter outside the door identifying it as Suite D. The men in the industrial park thought this was a strange way to run a business, and it contributed to the mysteries surrounding the Cancer Man.

Other random events seemingly unrelated to him added to the puzzlement. A car mechanic who worked in one of the rear buildings recalls seeing a man in a parked car taking pictures of 133 North Pacific from across the street. The mechanic approached the man, asking who he was and what he was doing there. The man said, "We're in law enforcement." "If you're in law enforcement, show me your badge," said the mechanic, at which point the man started up his car and drove off. The incident struck the mechanic as curious and he mentioned it to the other guys in his shop, not suspecting that the man in the car was an FBI agent who was watching the comings and goings at unmarked Suite D.

This being fall in the coastal southern California desert, it was warm enough for Bray to wear a short sleeve Hawaiian shirt that revealed the tattoos on his arms. As he sometimes did, he left the top buttons of his shirt undone, casually showing off a piece of his suntanned chest and a thick gold chain. On his right wrist was a gold band and perhaps a silver one on his left, and he wore an eye-catching diamond wedding ring and possibly one or two other diamond rings as well. He loved bling, especially diamond bling, which went along with his fondness for expensive, showy Rolex watches.

As another truck rumbled down North Pacific, the cars speeding by on Highway 78 emitted a kind of constant background hum. Nearby a train blew its warning whistle as it slowed to pass through a railroad crossing. If Bray seemed composed on the surface, in reality he was churning on the inside. Smoking gave him something to do, an outlet for his nervous grinding energy. The pressures on him had made his stomach churn constantly, and the banging inside his head had gotten worse, if that was possible. He popped pills daily to make the banging stop. He wasn't sleeping worth a damn, either.

Still, as bad as dealing fakes made him feel on a physical and moral level, on a profit-making level it could not have been sweeter. This was no way to live—or the only way to live. Even in his wild meth days he had never been on a run like this that took so much out of him and yet gave so much back. The business was going like gangbusters and yet it was also tearing him up, making him nervous and jumpier than usual. After all, he trafficked in fakes that appeared true but were actually false. Reality could be like that too: shiny and polished on the outside but rotten at the core. Bray knew from hard experience that a person can't always trust the surface appearance of things, no matter how rosy things looked.

But business was good, of this there could be no doubt, and if one needed proof all one had to do was scan the Stan's Sports Memorabilia catalog. Created by Wayne, Stan and Greg, the eight-page catalog resembled a fantasy novel in that some of it was true and based on fact but mostly it was made up, a work of the imagination. Featuring 2,400 products in thirty-three different categories, prices ranged from a low of ten bucks (a Rico Petrocelli baseball) to a high of $2,500 (a Mantle Yankees jersey with the autographs of Mantle and other members of the 500 Home Run Club). Most everything was forged and although some of Stan's customers surely knew this, many did not. Naively believing that what they were buying was real, they participated in the fiction too, thinking they could pay next to nothing to own a piece of stardust.

The range of products was breathtaking, the largest and most varied in the racket, featuring phony signed merchandise for everybody from Hank Aaron to Frank Zappa. Baseball had the most personalities listed and predictably, since he was Greg's signature creation, Mantle claimed the most individual products with twenty-four, including eight 500 Home Run Club items. Because these items featured the sigs of the elite group of major leaguers who have hit 500 or more home runs in their career, collectors considered them to be very rare—and they were, except at Stan's Sports Memorabilia, where they could be produced on demand.

Besides the Home Run Club, the catalog offered a host of combo and team-signed items, the Yankee championship clubs being the most requested in the team-signed category. These pieces were time-consuming and challenging; Greg had to squeeze more than thirty sigs on a single 8x10 photo. But he didn't mind doing it because it was the Yankees.

Movie and TV celebs—Tom Cruise, Cameron Diaz, Leonardo DiCaprio, Nicole Kidman, Whoopi Goldberg, Spike Lee, Jay Leno, David Letterman, Oprah Winfrey—took up nearly two pages of the catalog. But even more impressive was the wildly eclectic music mix: Mariah Carey, Harry Connick Jr., Melissa Etheridge, Michael Jackson, Mick Jagger, Elton John, Whitney Houston, Cyndi Lauper, Madonna, Bette Midler, Prince, Frank Sinatra, Bruce Springsteen, Barbra Streisand, Randy Travis, Eddie Van Halen, Frank Zappa and bands such as the Carpenters, Eagles, Kiss, Nirvana, and Pink Floyd. Group or cast shots fetched the highest celebrity prices. Whereas individual 8x10s of Ringo Starr, George Harrison, Paul McCartney and John Lennon were fairly affordable, a signed black and white picture of them together as the Beatles cost $2,100. [These are 1997 prices, after Lennon's death and before Harrison's.] Another popular category was movie and TV posters, such as "Rainman," "A League of Their Own," "ER," "Friends," and "Star Trek." People bought them thinking they were cast-signed but really they were just Greg-signed.

Other popular products were astronauts and presidents, usually group photos with combo sigs. The Apollo 11 astronauts—Neil Armstrong and Buzz Aldrin on the moon—were a big item. Other favorites were the five presidents (they were all alive then)—Richard Nixon, Gerald Ford, Jimmy Carter, Ronald Reagan and George H.W. Bush—when they appeared together at the opening of the Nixon presidential library. Reagan by himself also drew considerable interest.

Based on the variety of signatures they offered and the speed and quality in which they delivered them, the Bray-Marino-Fitzgerald partnership was tops in a competitive field, first among many. But something else set them apart from virtually every other forgery ring in the country, for they had staked out a terrain that others feared to tread: the kingdom of the dead.

Beginning with Mickey Mantle, they had discovered that in the graceless world of popular culture, death was often good for a celebrity's career. And with their competitors mainly forging living personalities, this left the market wide open for them. Again, this came about largely because of Bray. "He was one of the people most responsible in the United States for the proliferation of cuts," Phil Halpern would say years later in discussing Bray's impact on the autograph marketplace. "He practically invented cuts, and if he didn't invent them he took them to a whole new level. Before Bray and the Marinos, cuts practically did not exist. After them, cuts were everywhere."

A "cut" in the language of collectors is a piece of paper with a star's autograph on it. On page one of the Stan's Sports Memorabilia catalog was a category called "Vintage Cuts," vintage being a euphemism for dead. A vintage cut, then, is paper signed by a dead celebrity or sports star. Below is the complete listing for Vintage Cuts as it appeared in the catalog, with the name of the star and its price next to it:

Berlin, Irving 299
Bogart, Humphrey 1200
Cagney, James 300
Chaplin, Charlie 399
Clemente, Roberto 350
Cobb, Ty 600
Cooper, Gary 299
Dean, James 1500
Disney, Walt 895
Flynn, Errol 425
Foxx, Jimmy 350
Gable, Clark 399
Garland, Judy 499
Gehrig, Lou 700
Gershwin, George 795
Greenberg, Hank 225
Harlow, Jean 899
Hemingway, Ernest 895
Hendrix, Jimi 599
Hitchcock, Alfred 1495
Holly, Buddy 1495
Hornsby, Rogers 199
Houdini, Harry 895
Johnson, Walter 650
Jolson, Al 140
Joplin, Janis 599
Karloff, Boris 375
King, Martin Luther, Jr. 795
Laurel & Hardy combo 675
Lazzeri, Tony 275
Lee, Bruce 350
Lombard, Carole 299
Lombardi, Vince 225
Lugosi, Bela 299
Mansfield, Jayne 175
Marx, Chico 125
Marx, Groucho 225
Marx, Zeppo 125
Mathewson, Christy 1200
Miller, Glenn 199

Monroe, Marilyn 1200
Moon, Keith 350
Morrison, Jim 599
Ott, Mel 350
Paige, Satchel 249
Presley, Elvis 850
Reeves, George 399
Robinson, Jackie 350
Ruth, Babe 700
Speaker, Tris 199

Stewart, Jimmy
(with Harvey sketch) 225
Thorpe, Jim 499
Tracey, Spencer 299
Valens, Ritchie 1495
Wagner, Honus 450
Williams, Hank Sr. 399
Wizard of Oz (4 sigs) 899
Young, Cy 600

At the bottom of the list was a label that read: ALL AUTOGRAPHS ARE GUARANTEED AUTHENTIC. LIFETIME GUARANTEE. Stan's products came with a money-back guarantee if returned within fourteen days, and every piece was backed by a certificate of authenticity, often issued by none other than the J. DiMaggio Company.

No other forger was bold enough or foolish enough to offer so many dead celebs and with such lively flourishes. The Jimmy Stewart autograph, for example, came with a sketch of Harvey the Rabbit from the classic Stewart movie. The sig and the sketch were the work of Greg Marino, the amateur cartoonist. His Alfred Hitchcock included a line drawing of Hitch's famous profile similar to what was used on his old television program.

Some of the dead celebs on the vintage list were sold on 8x10s as well as cuts. Some not on the cuts list—Sammy Davis Jr., Ben Hogan, Liberace, Jackie Kennedy Onassis, Sugar Ray Robinson—went out mainly on 8x10s, but if Stan received an order for one or all of these stars or anyone else for that matter, Greg and Wayne supplied it. Some of the cuts Greg did, such as any of the dead presidents, did not appear in the catalog because they were so rare and unusual that to advertise them would be like telling the world, flat-out, that you were selling frauds and you didn't care who knew it. But if an order came through for a Jack Kennedy or a Teddy Roosevelt or heck, even an Abraham Lincoln, Greg simply dashed it off and thought no more about it because something equally preposterous was sure to follow.

The chief reason the gang went into the dead celeb business was simple: It paid. But there was another important reason. Authentic vintage sports gear, particularly baseballs, was hard to come by. Signed baseballs represented a big part of the business, with nearly five hundred products featured in the catalog. Cases of new balls could be purchased easily, not so with old ones. Even Big Ricky Weimer, with all his sources eager to sell him old gear he could overpay them for, could not come close to supplying all the quantities needed. Nor was Bray's idea of rubbing the markings off older balls and putting a fake Haiti stamp on them a complete answer. This technique worked for stars still alive in the 1960s and 1970s but what about the Big Kahuna of collecting, Babe Ruth, who died in 1948? What could they do about him?

The gang focused its energies on Ruth because Ruth memorabilia is among the most valuable in all of collecting.* Bray had collected dozens of Ruth exemplars in the black books and Greg had pushed himself to get the sig right despite encountering early problems. "I wasn't very good at Ruth at first. You had to get the *B* and the *R*. The *R* was real hard to get. But I got real good at it in the end. I could do it in my sleep now. The same with Gehrig."

Besides the sig itself, the challenge in doing Ruth or any dead celeb of the past was in making sure the materials used—pen, ink, baseball—predated his death and were authentic to his time. If not, the forgery could be exposed. To avoid this, said Wayne, "I kept Greg in a steady supply of pens from the old days, the ones they actually used," though he was hardly alone in this regard. While browsing an antique store in Escondido, Little Ricky stumbled onto a case of World War II-era, military-issue blue-black ink at a cost of two bucks per pint. Two bucks! When you were in business with Greg Marino a discovery of this kind translated into earnings of tens of thousands of dollars. On another of his shopping excursions Little Ricky found a pair of Babe Ruth-brand underpants made in the 1920s; Greg signed the box the undies came in.

Marino enjoyed using the blue-black ink because of its near-magical properties: "It started fading from black to blue when it touched the page. It looked like a faded blue in color after a minute or so on the page." And this fading instantly gave it the look of age, what they were seeking to create.

Greg mixed some vintage inks to produce different shades, but mostly he relied on the old pens supplied by Wayne and the others, whipping out forgery after forgery with a vintage Parker Duofold Streamline or a Vacumatic Golden Pearl. When the ink ran dry he opened one of Little Ricky's blue-black ink bottles, dipped in the nib of his pen, and let the ink rise up into the empty bladder inside the pen much like filling an eye dropper.

With the pens and ink irrefutably genuine, the boys still faced the issue of finding legitimate pre-1948 baseballs or, if this was not possible, devising illegitimate ones. Greg gave credit to Little Ricky for inventing

---

* *Prices for Ruth memorabilia vary widely, though they're always high. In the late nineties a Ruth-signed ball sold for a record $55,000 at an auction. In his investigations Tim Fitzsimmons saw a Ruth ball with a price tag of $10,000. Then there was the Ruth-Roger Maris-Mark McGwire combo-signed ball that Fitzsimmons saw in 1999 after McGwire broke the single-season home run record. Its asking price was $500,000, and it almost certainly was a Greg Marino forgery.*

what Marino laughingly called "the science of dipping"—the practice of shellacking baseballs in order to disguise their true age so they could be sold as authentic Babe Ruth artifacts.

"First you get a ball, any old leather baseball," explained Mitchell. "But you have to be sure there are no identifying markings on it, and no label. So we'd go down to Play It Again Sports and look through this basket of old balls they had and find a few that were right for what we needed. Each one cost maybe five bucks. Then we'd bring them back and wash them with soap and water and turn them over to Greg, who'd sign them with a fountain pen from that era. But they still looked so fake it was unbelievable. They looked just awful—these old, worn, washed baseballs with Ruth's signature on them. Something more had to be done."

That something more was "dipping," a job often done by John Marino, the utility man of the operation. In Ruth's time people shellacked valuable baseballs as a means of preserving them, mounting them on a trophy-style wooden plaque. The crew did much the same thing, coating the ball, in Greg's colorful phrase, "like a candy apple." Since dipping could get messy, it was "a garage operation" handled by John at their parents' house. One technique was to drive a nail or screw into the seams of the ball, careful not to form too large of a hole. Then, holding the ball by the nail, John dipped it into a gallon can of orange-rust shellac similar in color to what the old-timers used. Once the ball was fully coated it was left to hang-dry with the nail still in it. The nail came out after the ball had dried.

Another technique was to use what came to be called "the dipper," more commonly known as vice grips. The vice grips allowed them to immerse the ball in the shellac without using a nail.

Still, even after dipping, something vital about these balls was missing, something that had to be there: the smell of antiquity. Tucked away and forgotten in an attic for generations, only to be uncovered in recent times, baseballs this old must have a certain musty smell attached to them. But these balls didn't smell like that; all they smelled of was shellac. "They didn't smell old, and they certainly didn't smell like they'd been sitting around for seventy years since the time of Babe Ruth," Mitchell continued. "So we'd buy a big bag of mothballs and stick the mothballs in a plastic trash bag with the baseball. We'd let the ball sit in the bag for a few days or whatever and that would make it smell old."

Another way they duplicated the smell of age was to forego the mothballs altogether and stick the baseball in a bag of dog food. After a day or two in the bag they'd pull it out and let it cure in the sun a while. When the process was over it was hard to say exactly what the ball smelled like except that it fooled people and that was all that mattered.

"People didn't know what it smelled like, but it smelled old to them," said Mitchell. "It stinks and it smells old, and that convinced them it was legitimate."

The innocence of people, their longing to believe in the authenticity of the memorabilia they were investing in—plus their own greed in many cases, the thought that they were getting a steal on an ordinarily super-expensive Babe Ruth-signed baseball—led some to pay thousands or even tens of thousands for used balls dipped in shellac and aged in Purina.

Given how stinking hard it was to reproduce authentic-looking antique baseballs, it is easy to see the appeal of cuts. They were far simpler and faster to do with no messy dipping required. "A cut would take as long as it takes to write your name," said Marino. "That's how long it took me. I'd do a hundred in an hour if there were orders. But usually I didn't need to do that many. Typically I'd maybe do forty or fifty cuts in a day."

The public only paid seven hundred dollars for a Ruth cut, but it was still a highly profitable undertaking given that the raw materials for it could be found at any thrift store. John and Greg typically handled this chore, shopping at the Goodwill in town or wherever else they could find old books. The books they bought predated World War II and sometimes World War I. Typically books published in this era had four or five blank pages in the front and back, which the Marinos tore out. These books with the ripped-out pages then got tossed into the garage with the mountains of blank memorabilia waiting to be signed, but unlike the memorabilia, they were headed for the trash. Sadly, on some pickup days the Marinos' garbage can overflowed with the works of long-forgotten authors who surely deserved a better fate. Feeling guilty about throwing away so many books, John once returned a bunch to the thrift store where he had bought them, absent their blank pages. (After the takedown the media erroneously reported that John had ripped the pages from old library books; he felt offended by this, telling investigators he would never do such a thing.)

Besides being more plentiful, old books had an advantage over old baseballs in that they did not need to be stored in mothballs to achieve the smell of age. Sitting untouched on shelves for years, their pages pressed together as people swept by them in search of the latest thing, when finally opened up again they truly belonged to a time that was no more. The paper smelled old and looked old and was of a thicker stock than what is used in books today. Often the right edge of the page was ragged, per the custom of the day, and time had turned its color from white to yellowish or light brown.

"I did two sigs per page," said Greg, "never more. Then we cut the page in half with scissors or a razor blade. A cut would be about the size of an old-time 3x5 index card. Mostly I used old ink pens from the thirties and other eras but I did pencil cuts too. With pencil you couldn't detect how old it was."

In Ruth's time the staple of collecting was the 3x5 index card; fans mailed it to celebrities requesting their signature. In the modern era index cards have fallen out of favor, as collectors much prefer autographs on photos or balls and jerseys. But the collecting public understood that Ruth, a willing and prolific signer, and other celebrities of that era autographed lots of these 3x5 cards, which provided a logical rationale for all the phony paper flooding the market from the Bray-Marino enterprise.

The public seldom bought a cut as a piece of paper; nearly always it came packaged in a nice frame with a picture or pictures of the star whose autograph had been forged. A framed cut of Ruth with a signed photo sold for $2,900 retail, the same price as a framed photo of the Beatles with cuts of John, Paul, George and Ringo. Whatever the price, what sold these pieces every time was presentation. Put a corrupt thing in a pretty package and people will view it more favorably than a genuine thing in a plain package.

But, really, there was no reason to suspect any of these items based on how they looked. They were perfect, or as close to perfect as criminally possible: signature, ink, pen, paper, presentation. All the parts added up, every one, to create an illusion that made the living feel more connected to the dead and gave the dead a presence in the halls of the living. The living generally paid happily for these beautifully packaged cuts and the dead did not care. But it wasn't without risk. Nothing Bray and the gang did was without risk. But nobody ever got rich without taking risks, and they were willing to risk it and keep risking it because the payoff was so incredibly high.

Dropping his Winston Light to the pavement and crushing it with his shoe, Wayne turned to go back to his office, approaching the wooden stairway of the building that seemed to be sinking into the ground. When he reached the bottom of the steps he saw Ferreira at the top, sensing immediately that this man had been peering into his shop with the door open.

"Who are you?" he said warily.

Turning away from the unmarked office with its open box of forged baseballs, Ferreira had seen Bray coming and met him at the top of the stairs. "Hi," he said, extending his hand in a friendly, outgoing way. "I'm John Freitas. I'm—"

"Who?"

"John Frei—"

"Who?" said Bray, interrupting again, ignoring the visitor's outstretched hand. "What do you want?"

Dressed casually in long pants and a sports shirt, Ferreira wore hidden body microphones and a black fanny pack with a concealed recording unit about the size of a cigarette pack inside it. His strategy was to be friendly, upbeat, a guy you wanted to be in business with, but Bray made it clear he wanted nothing to do with him. Every time Ferreira tried to say something, Bray cut him off and didn't let him get a word in.

Still, the agent stayed cool, stayed in character, finally getting the chance to explain how he was looking to buy autographed memorabilia for his business, the Nihon Trading Company. "The door to your office was open. I kept calling and calling to see if anyone was in. But," he added reassuringly, "I never went in."

Beginning his assignment in September, Ferreira had spent two weeks in San Diego before flying back to Eugene. He had come back the following month and returned home again. Now it was early November and he was starting what constituted his third undercover stint as John Freitas. Basically his job early on was to go around to card shops and shows in the area, meeting people, making contacts, all the while assessing who was crooked and who was not. He conducted this search as methodically as he did his autograph collecting: ripping the page out of the phone book with the listings for "Baseball Cards and Sports Memorabilia" and marking out any of the shops he visited that appeared legitimate. Any shop suspected of selling dirty goods, he circled on the page. Those were the ones he wanted to look into more thoroughly.

W.W. Sports Cards had two listings on the page, both circled. Neither address, however, was for the shop on North Pacific, which was unlisted. Unmoved by the agent's smiling reassurances, Bray heatedly demanded to know how Ferreira had found his shop.

"I got it from the phone book," he said.

"It's not in the phone book," said Bray testily.

Not missing a beat the UCA responded that he had just been to another shop in the area, and the guy there had told him to go see Wayne Bray on North Pacific over by the railroad tracks. This was a lie, obviously, but the game had begun in earnest and each man was playing it to the fullest, lying to the other about his real purpose in being there.

Ferreira managed to get inside the shop but never sat down, remaining cordial though Bray's clear desire was for him to be gone as fast as possible. The agent left after only a few uncomfortable minutes, heading back down the stairway to his car, leaving Bray alone in his office with the door now firmly closed.

Despite the lies they were telling, each man fairly accurately assessed the other. "He thought I was a cop," said Ferreira, who was almost correct. Bray thought he was the law, all right, but not a cop. He waited until the BMW had safely passed out of sight before picking up his phone and punching in a familiar number.

"Greg," he said. "The fucking FBI was just at my office."

12

In a voice palpable with rage and scorn and defiance he poured out the story of what had happened: "I knew he was an FBI agent as soon as he walked in the door. He was wearing a stupid fanny pack that all those FBI guys wear. He was way too interested in what I was doing. He said some bullshit story about how he was buying for the Japanese. It was all bullshit."

Greg heard his partner out but he wasn't convinced. The FBI? Maybe, maybe not. He wasn't a worrier by nature, unlike Wayne who tended to see FBI agents hiding under every bush, and not nearly as serious or dramatic. But he agreed to keep an eye on this guy, whoever he was, and after hanging up Greg went back to the order he was working on and the sweet-smelling reefer burning in the ashtray.

Greg was at his apartment on Beaumont Glen, which was where he worked part of the time. As a party and forgery pad it possessed definite advantages because he could smoke pot freely and happily away from the disapproving gaze of his mother. Gloria and Angelo opposed their sons' drug use and Greg, sensitive to this, never lit up in their presence. Others in the racket also had to be on their best behavior when they were around Gloria at her house, so they preferred Greg's place where they could get high and the atmosphere was more relaxed.

For some time though, Greg's main base of operations had shifted over to his parents' house on Smokewood Place. This was where Gloria, Angelo and John lived, as did John's children part of the time. Smokewood Place was a small, quiet, keyhole-shaped court in a residential neighborhood filled with other "wood" streets: Glenwood, Heatherwood, Lochwood. On the weekends and after school kids rode bikes and skateboards along the sidewalks and broad flat streets. The homes were all one- and two-story tract homes, their front lawns turned dark green by automatic sprinklers and chemical fertilizers. Some houses in the neighborhood had security alarm signs out front, though almost no crime to speak of ever occurred there, at least not of the breaking-and-entering variety. The Marino home (they were renting) was at the end of the court and had a small driveway and two-car garage. The front door was set back on the right side of the house and tucked slightly into the side yard, facing away from the street. A short concrete path curved along the front lawn past a small hexagonal kitchen window. A large palm tree stood to the left of the garage; to the right of the garage was a postage stamp lawn with a leafy tree in the center.

On some days John could be spotted playing basketball at a hoop on the street. Gloria was in the kitchen making lasagne, and Angelo had his easel and paints set up and was seeking to evoke, on canvas, the athletic power and grace of a Derek Jeter or Jack Nicklaus. Meanwhile Greg sat in the living room watching TV or at the kitchen table next to the hexagonal window, cranking out the material that gave his brother steady spending money and allowed his parents to comfortably retire.

After years of spinning out sigs of Keith Moon and Wally Moon and Keith Richards and Richard Nixon and Richard Gere and Rosey Grier and Teddy Roosevelt and Ted Williams and Rosie O'Donnell and Roberto Clemente, so many names all running together in a kind of hallucinogenic stream it was impossible to keep track of them all, Greg had evolved into a craftsman of the first rank. His early awkwardness was gone; forging had truly become second nature to him. He could glance at an exemplar in one of the black books and his hand could immediately produce a high quality replica of the signature he was looking at. "I got into a flow," he said. "I could look at an autograph, and I could do it exact. I could see where he [the signer] started the pen, and I could see where he ended it. It didn't matter how hard it was. I could do it. I mean, I did a million autographs. And when I say a million, I mean a million. Not tens of thousands, not hundreds of thousands. A million."

Some weeks Greg only worked a couple of days—"Autograph Days," he called them—making sure to get all his orders done by Thursday so he and John could get down to the Bada Bing and play. But Autograph Days were intense, starting basically from the time he got out of bed (or even while he was still in bed) and lasting until he crashed that night. He'd take a short break around noon and if he was over at his mom's, she'd fix lunch for him. Some days if he was at his apartment Gloria would even drive lunch or dinner over to him. When Kathy was home she also fixed meals for him so he could keep going, keep his strength up, and keep making money for them all.

Kathy was part of the Smokewood Place scene too, helping out in a variety of ways: going on pickups and drop-offs, dealing with clients over the phone and taking their orders, and handling setups. In the early days Wayne had done all the setups for Greg, but after things got going she took over the job from him. Wayne coached her on his techniques and she rapidly became adept at this process, unpacking the balls from the boxes, unwrapping the plastic around the balls, taking them out of their egg carton containers and setting them up in the living room with the sweet spot showing so Greg and his smoking Sharpie could come down the line and sign with no wasted motion. Bam! Bam! Bam!

Wayne soon started paying her to do his setups for him. So did Nate after he joined the inner circle and started moving his big orders through. On some orders all she had to do was unpack the balls and put them in a basket next to the living room couch so that Greg could sign while watching the Yankees game on the box. This was the way he preferred to sign balls because he could use a couch cushion to prop up his arm and avoid writer's cramp. When a basket was filled with signed balls Kathy cleared it away and replaced it with a fresh basket of unsigned ones, delivering a snack tray and a drink for Greg at the same time. During a nine-inning game he could polish off three cases or nearly four hundred balls.

Signing bats represented a separate challenge. Like balls, they are awkward to hold and the writing surface is unusual. In the early nineties, as part of an autograph deal, a videotape was made of Joe DiMaggio actually signing bats at the Louisville Slugger factory. Greg got hold of this tape and watched it with a close eye, observing how the great DiMaggio's techniques differed from his. In fact they were very similar. The bats were lined up for Joe much the same way Kathy lined them up across the living room sofa and chairs—all in a row and slightly lower down "so Joe could come right down and sign, sign, sign," said Greg admiringly.

Once an order was done Kathy would call Wayne or Nate or one of the others who had access to the house to tell them to come by and pick it up. Or, what was more likely, Wayne and Nate would have already called the house two or three times asking if their order was done and could they pick it up today? Once space was cleared in the living room, John moved the next order of blanks in from the garage. Cold blank memorabilia waiting to be turned into warm lovely cash often filled up the garage with no room to park a vehicle.

For their customers not allowed to visit the house, Kathy and John, or Kathy and Angelo, or Angelo and Gloria, or Gloria and John—whatever the combination as long as it did not include Greg, who was excused from the job—drove their finished orders to the parking lot of a Hungry Hunter or some other meeting place where they would make the exchange of signed goods for cash. The customers usually placed additional orders at these meets, supplying the Marinos with more blanks to fill up their garage.

As dysfunctional as they might seem in a conventional view, the Marinos were strongly bonded and loyal to one another, and as the center of a national counterfeiting network they were absurdly effective. Everybody had a job to do and everybody did it. If business demanded it they could turn an order in a day—pick up the blanks in the morning, take them back home, unload and unpack them and lay them out in the living room, pack them all up again after Greg had finished with them, load them back into the car and deliver them to a client waiting anxiously outside a Petco store. Then as the sun was setting and the wispy clouds in the west were turning pink and orange, they'd return home and sit down to a family dinner, another long but satisfying day at the forgery factory having come to an end.

But gradually, as they got busier and the operation kept growing with seemingly no end in sight, Kathy, for one, grew disillusioned with the whole rotten business. More of a worrier than her husband, her feelings, her fears, had grown more intense over the past two years as the realization set in strongly that this was no game. When Greg first started forging he had just lost his job at the Welk and they needed the money. Now they had plenty of money, enough for her to quit her job at the bank and stop worrying about bills and fly off to Tahoe and Cabo whenever they got the urge. To be part of the early excitement, to help her husband, to share in what her in-laws were doing, and of course to make money, she had willfully joined the family business. But forgeries had since moved from being "a fluky thing" into an all-consuming activity that was chewing up their lives. "We thought it was a one-time thing but it kept going on," she said unhappily.

Torn up by what they were doing, the one-time California party girl sought the counsel of her church pastor. "I went to Pastor Richard at Calvary Chapel and I told him everything," she said. "I asked him what to do."

Kathy went to see him because she had no one to confide in besides her husband and his family. Her friends and her other family in the area had no clue what was going on behind the door of her apartment and Gloria and Angelo's house, and this was how they were going to remain: clueless and safe. Telling them about her activities would only shift the burden of what she was feeling onto them, forcing them to confront the same hard choices she was struggling with.

The pastor, she said, "thought a long time before he said anything. Then he said, 'I guess you need to turn them in.'"

"But it's my family," she responded, pleading with him. "I'd be turning in my own family."

The pastor insisted it was the right thing to do, and Kathy agreed with him. It was the right thing to do—morally, spiritually and legally. But she couldn't do it. How could she betray the man she loved most in life? How can that ever be the right thing?

"I couldn't do it. I couldn't turn Greg in. About then I turned it over to God and asked Him to decide for me. It was too much for me alone. This was when I started to pull myself away and not be so active in it."

As she steadily pulled away, Greg's mother and brother stepped forward to take over her duties, and the beat went on. Her more limited role in the racket led to greater involvement with John's three young children, all of whom needed attention with both their parents struggling with drugs and rehab. Kathy and Gloria often went over to John's ex-wife's house to make sure the kids were being taken care of, and Kathy made herself useful by driving them to swim lessons or soccer practice or wherever they needed to go. But the choice she had made—and not made—was always present in their lives with the phone ringing off the hook and guys coming over to their apartment to beg and wheedle and cajole for a piece of her husband's time. Sometimes she just hated the crazy machinery of what they had created, and she tried to stick a monkey wrench in it. "Dealers would call and I'd try to be as mean as possible to them. 'No, no,' I'd tell them, 'we're not doing it anymore. Leave us alone.' I even had our number changed. But they'd get hold of Greg anyway and he'd fill their order."

The whole thing seemed unstoppable and yet one trip to the police would have stopped it. She knew for certain that she should make that trip, but she knew with even greater certainty that she would not and could not. Her inability to make the thing stop added to her impatience with the never-ending calls, the never-ending line of guys pestering her husband. She wished they would all go away and she knew, at some point, they all would. She just didn't know how or when. That would be decided by God, she felt. There'd be a knock at the door and that would be it. It'd be over.

Early in the afternoon on Tuesday, November 4, there was a knock at the door of the Smokewood Place house, and it was Kathy who answered it. Standing outside was undercover agent John Ferreira.

Kathy knew this wasn't right. This simply wasn't done. People did not just drop over to their house to ask about autographed memorabilia, and certainly not people they didn't know. She called out to her husband to let him know that someone was at the door. Then, just as she had mostly withdrawn from the racket in general, she stepped aside as Greg appeared.

As Ferreira began to explain why he was there, Greg cut him off. "Who are you?" he said loudly. "Who the hell are you?" This was the day after Wayne had called to warn him about an FBI agent in their midst. Now this same man, wearing the same black fanny pack that Wayne had talked about, was standing outside his front door giving him a rap about how he was buying for the Japanese and all that. No longer able to dismiss his friend's concerns as idle paranoia, Greg grew furious. "What are you doing here?" he went on. "How do you know about us?"

Big, bearded Greg Marino—kick-the-shit-out-of-you big—moved aggressively outside towards the agent, getting right up in his face, forcing Ferreira to step back to create some distance between the two of them. In bits and pieces the agent managed to say that he had been at a memorabilia shop in downtown San Diego and seen a couple of signed photos on sale. On the wall below the photos was the business card for Front Page Art. Being in the autograph business, Ferreira said he decided to call on the address listed on the card to see if there were any more signed photos for sale.

"You're full of shit," said Greg, starting to yell. "Tell me who you are. Tell me who you are."

The agent had in fact spotted the photos and Angelo's card at the shop and as soon as he saw them he knew he had a plausible reason for visiting the Marinos. When he discussed his plan with McKinney and Fitzsimmons, McKinney in particular had worried about how the family would react to a stranger dropping by their house. But Ferreira, who was eager to make contact with the family, felt certain he could handle it. So McKinney and Fitzsimmons had agreed to let him have his way: the direct approach.

Ferreira was alone, without backup, which wasn't unusual. McKinney or Fitzsimmons frequently covered him at the Nihon Trading Company; away from the office he operated on his own. The day before at W.W. Sports Cards, he had been by himself. Surprisingly perhaps, this encounter did not trigger much concern among the investigators. They felt that Ferreira may have rattled Bray a little, given him something to think about, put some extra pressure on him—and none of that was bad. Of course, the FBI did not know about Wayne's subsequent warning to Greg about an undercover agent in the neighborhood.

As soon as Greg started yelling, his brother came running out of the house, followed by Angelo and Gloria who shut the door behind them. John started crowding around Ferreira and yelling at him and getting in his face too. Both the brothers were bigger than Ferreira, and both were using their size to bully him and to some degree they were succeeding because Greg started to pat him down, aggressively but clumsily putting his hands on his shirt and checking his pockets.

Ferreira was in a T-shirt and shorts—perfect garb for this lovely sunny November day and the casual image he wished to project to his subjects. But his lack of clothing gave him fewer places to hide his recording gear and made it easier for Greg to search him. Greg was looking for something—badge, gun, recording unit—that might expose him as a law enforcement officer. Staying in character, Ferreira tried to be accommodating—to a point. He obligingly opened the front pocket of his fanny pack to let Greg see what was inside, folding its flap back over the rear compartment.

"I kept my pack around my waist all the time, unzipping the front compartment and folding back the flap," recalled Ferrierra. "This covered the rear compartment where the recorder was hidden, and Greg missed it. He didn't look there."

While covering up the rear pouch Ferreira pulled his wallet out of the front one, diverting Greg's attention. Ferreira handed over his driver's license to show that he really was John Freitas and look, there was his picture to prove it. The name on his license matched the name on his credit cards, which Greg also inspected. Even Ferreira's wallet, being Japanese made, added credence to his tale about buying memorabilia for Japanese clients.

Greg handed back the license and credit cards. He remained skeptical about the agent's stated identity and intentions, but things grew calmer. The brothers stopped yelling and backed off, and the threat of the incident turning physical melted away. Knowing that the contents of the rear pouch was safe, Ferreira relaxed a little too. He may have even felt a sense of joy. His cover was still intact, and his quick thinking had rescued the investigation from disaster.

A brief, uneasy conversation ensued. While the brothers stood sullenly aside, Ferreira spoke with their father, expressing interest in acquiring material related to Hideo Nomo, the Japanese-born pitcher then starring for the Los Angeles Dodgers. Angelo, who painted baseballs with Nomo's likeness on them, said this was a possibility, and gave Ferreira his card for Front Page Art. It read, "Experienced in Creating Exciting Illustrations for Major League Sports." The card listed Angelo as artist; its president was Greg Marino.

Ferreira asked about prices, and Kathy said their computer had crashed so they couldn't supply him with a price list for Angelo's lithos. The agent said he'd be interested in seeing it when it became available. He politely thanked them for their time and despite the misunderstanding, hoped they could do some business in the future. He said he'd call them soon.

Then the agent returned to his car, and the Marinos retreated uneasily inside their home. This was a troubling moment for the family, Kathy especially. If the man at the door was FBI, it meant they were under investigation. And if they were being investigated they could be arrested at some point and sent to prison. Her fears were being realized. The knock at the door was coming. The only questions were how and when.

13

Ferreira called Fitzsimmons and McKinney from the road to tell them what had happened, and both agents expressed surprise at how the Marino brothers had reacted. But both also had good words for how Ferreira had handled himself in a tough situation. He had faced his first real undercover test and passed it.

When he returned to the Nihon Trading Company, while his memory was still fresh, Ferreira did what he did after every meet with a subject: wrote up a 302. Federal Document 302, as it is formally known, requires a short synopsis of what occurs during a meet: who the subjects are, who says what, what time the agent turns the recorder on, what time he turns it off. As a case agent who had overseen numerous undercover ops, Ferreira knew that keeping up with his paperwork was an essential if unromantic part of being a UCA. If you didn't watch out the government buried you in forms, and so he diligently finished his 302 on the Smokewood Place incident.

Reading Ferreira's 302 and listening to the tape of his shouting match with the Marinos caused further reflection and assessment among his colleagues. In the words of Fitzsimmons, "We got puckered. With drug undercover work you're puckered on a daily basis. The danger is always there, and things happen you can't anticipate. But because the Marinos were not a threat for violence, we had no reason to suspect anything like that would happen."

In a sense the confrontation confirmed his original hunch when he opened the case—that these guys weren't pushovers, and they weren't going down easy. For months the FBI had conducted surveillance of the Marino house with an agent sitting in a car in the neighborhood watching as Wayne and Nate and some of the other guys pulled up and went inside. But as often as not they stayed put, ordering in pizza and watching the ballgame for the rest of the afternoon until the frustrated and bored agent had no choice but to call off the surveillance and report back to the office.

Those times the Marinos did leave the house, surveillance noted that they frequently "dry-cleaned" themselves, using different streets and routes to and from their meets. This suggested they were aware of the possibility they were being watched and were taking steps to avoid it.

Then there were the times Greg and John came barreling out of the house, climbed into their vehicle and sped off to downtown Escondido or some other neighboring town to—of all places—a thrift store. The agent discretely followed them inside as they browsed the used books section. Used books? The Marinos hardly seemed the type to be fans of classic literature. But there they were, loading up their arms with old books, carrying them up to the register, throwing them into the back of their vehicle, and speeding back home.

Fitzsimmons had a good idea what they were doing with those books, but he couldn't be sure, not completely. And now throw in another thing they could no longer take for granted: how the Marinos—and Bray, for that matter—would react if pushed. They might push back.

The confrontation also caught McKinney off guard, though he had anticipated the brothers weren't like going to like it when Ferreira showed up. Still, that was undercover work for you; it always came with surprises. "You're always revising plans in undercover work," he said philosophically. "You come up with the best plan. If it works you go through with it. If it doesn't, you do something different and roll with it."

Adapt to the changes and roll on—these were the hallmarks of successful undercover ops—and this was what the team planned to do, now that Ferreira had cleverly arranged to do some business with Angelo. A few days later, as he had promised to do, Ferreira followed up with a call to Smokewood Place to discuss the Nomo balls painted by Angelo. He spoke to a nervous-sounding John Marino who, anxious to get rid of him, said the family was thinking about getting out of the art business and going back to New York. Not so easily put off, the agent tried again a couple more times and finally reached Angelo, who said sure, he'd be willing to sell him some balls. Ferreira explained that he was seeing some clients in Japan and he'd be back in town again in December. They set a time and date for a meeting, and Angelo agreeably said he'd deliver the balls personally to Ferreira at the Nihon Trading Company and bring his wife with him.

This was a real coup. After the case had nearly blown up in their faces, investigators were back onto their original plan of establishing business relations with the family. And if things went well with the father, perhaps, over time, Ferreira could patch things up with his sons too. What's more, they were going to get their first long look, on their own turf, at one of the most powerful players in the racket, Gloria Marino.

"Greg," observed Ferreira, "was the main spokesperson for the family. He was in control. He was the boss." Despite playing the tough guy his brother was clearly in a secondary role, taking orders from Greg and following his lead. Kathy seemed to be a peripheral presence, as did Angelo who, said Ferreira, "was passive. His attitude was: Let my sons do it." This stood in sharp contrast to his more outspoken wife who clearly occupied a central place in the family hierarchy.

"She was pretty aggressive," said Ferreira. "It looked to me like she ran the family."

The agent's first impressions were on the mark because after Greg, Gloria was the most dominant figure in the family—and the family business. Wife, mother, grandmother, she was, like her husband, in her sixties, a New Yorker grafted onto California soil. A traditional homemaker for much of her married life, she cooked the meals for her family and tended to the house. She had a strong mother's pride and love for her three grown children, chatting frequently on the long distance phone with her daughter Andrea and worrying about John's and Greg's drug use. She had supported Angelo and his art dreams throughout their marriage, and she was a caring grandmother to John's young children. About five-feet-four inches tall, tending a little to the plumpish side, with brown eyes and brown hair and a round face with dark eyebrows, she chain-smoked Virginia Slim Longs, which gave her voice a raspy quality. The hoarseness of her smoker's voice plus her strong New York accent made her an unmistakable presence in the forgery factory.

"Was there a mother in 'Good Fellas'?" said Bray. "Well, imagine the mother of an Italian hit man. That's Gloria."

You knew it when Boss Gloria was saying something to you, and you paid attention when she did. As much as Wayne might have wished to, it was impossible for him or anyone else to avoid her when they came to Smokewood Place to do business. She lived there and unless she was out on a memorabilia run, she was nearly always around. You had to deal with her and stay on her good side because she had a big hammer at her disposal—the power to cut off access to her son—and she was not afraid to use it.

Shelly Jaffe never met Gloria in person and spoke to her only once on the phone. But the call left a lasting impression on him: "She was a nut, a little crazy. All she could talk about was how great her son was."

In the early days of the racket Gloria knew what her son was doing but mostly stayed out of it. Then Greg came to her with a plea for help. "I asked her to come in," he said. "See, I was getting cheated all the time. Guys were short-counting me, not paying the full amount on things. My prices were too cheap, and I was so busy I didn't have the time to keep track of everything."

A former grocery store accountant who had handled the bookkeeping for her husband's beauty shops in Long Island and California, Gloria had a good head for money. She also had the backbone to say no to the parade of whiners loading up Greg's answering machine begging him to sign. These were his friends, not hers, and she immediately established her priorities: Family first, and everybody else not even close. If somebody had a problem with that, well, they could take their business to one of the discount hacks.

Gloria changed the rules of the game, gaining and wielding power in a racket dominated by men. Before she came in, they'd plead with Greg to move their orders to the front of the line because the sooner they got their stuff from him, the sooner they could turn it around to their clients. Now it was Gloria who largely determined who got served, and when, and her decisions were based less on loyalty and friendship and more on dollars and cents. Sorry, fellas, it's not personal. Just business.

She increased prices. Higher prices meant more money for the family, and they were a more effective way to ration Greg's precious time. Their clients could have a piece of her son but only if they paid more dearly for it. Upon learning that other rings steered away from forging dead people, whereas it was one of her son's specialties, she created a two-tier pricing structure for cuts: "Regular" for living celebrities and "Premium" for dead ones. For Regular she charged seven dollars per item, keeping her in line with their rivals' prices. But the cost for Premium cuts rose to fifteen dollars per, exploiting the Marinos' dominance of this segment of the marketplace.

Cuts were typical of the way Greg had handled his business until his mother cleaned things up: "Lots of them I'd do for free. It was like no big deal for me. Guys were always knocking on my door begging me to sign. I'd get calls on my machine every day. 'Here,' I'd say, 'here's ten more. Just get outta here.' I'd do it so they'd get out of my house and leave me alone."

Gloria, raspy-voiced, chain-smoking, tough-minded Gloria, stopped the giveaways and started counting everything that came into the house, including and especially money. No more short-counting, no more cheating, no more slipping things past her overly busy, frequently stoned son. Predictably, this ticked many of the boys off. Further irritating them, Boss Gloria imposed strict new rules on who could pay by check and who had to come up with cash. Since checks can be traced, only a trusted few were allowed to pay by check and even with these people, Gloria stated her preference clearly:

greenbacks, glorious greenbacks. However a person paid, check or cash, the money always went straight to her. You put it in her welcoming palms, and with a cigarette dangling from the side of her mouth, she counted the bills on the spot to be sure the amount was correct.

"I hated the mother as a person," said Nate Harrison. "But just about everybody did. Even the FBI. I stayed away from her and gave her the money and that was it."

"She was always nice to me," said Wayne. "Whenever I'd come over she'd always ask me, 'Can I get you some coffee?'" His strategy was to stay on her good side. If he had a beef about some aspect of her system he took it up with Greg or John, not her. In a fair fight Bray could chop the knees off any of his competitors in the racket, but it wasn't a fair fight with Gloria and it never would be. How do you chop the knees off a guy's...*mother?* Better to work within the system and try to get along with her personally.

Little Ricky's approach was a mix of Nate's and Wayne's: stay on her good side while staying away from her. "I dealt directly with Greg a lot of the time and mostly went around Gloria. But sometimes I'd have a big deal with one of my Vegas clients and throw it through the system." On these deals he paid higher prices for his goods because he was buying them through Gloria rather than on the sly from Greg (an arrangement she would have stopped had she had known about it). Still, this served as a kind of insurance policy for the ex-insurance salesman, showing Gloria that he was greasing her palms just like everyone else. Thus he stayed on her good side, where everyone wanted to be.

Before Gloria, doing business with Greg was a freewheeling, let's-get-high party. Once she came onto the scene that way of doing business died a quick death.

"Gloria created a system," said Mitchell. "Before her, there was no system. You'd go over to Greg's place and it'd be a bunch of guys trading and drinking and goofing off, much more laid-back and fun. She changed everything. She turned it into a business. Suddenly all the big accounts had to go through her. Nobody could deal directly with Greg, now they had to go through her. She counted everything. There were no more freebies. Prices went up. You dropped stuff off, you didn't come into the house so much anymore. Gloria would inventory everything, and then you'd pick it up the next day and pay her. Needless to say, nobody liked this."

Gloria split the family money three ways: one-third to her and Angelo, one-third to Greg and Kathy, one-third to John. But even John occasionally griped about this arrangement because B.G. (Before Gloria) he had more spending money than he did A.G. (After Gloria). He and his brother both burned up piles of cash indulging their considerable appetites for fun, and controlling the money may have been Mom's attempt to modify their behavior. It's hard to make money, even illegal money, and Gloria's one clear, deeply felt desire, the underlying reason for all the changes she instituted and partly why she got into the racket in the first place, was to keep more of the money the Marinos made within the family and put it to more productive purposes, namely their dream house in the hills.

The house was the thing, the big thing, the object of all their aspirations. First the Marinos looked around for an existing home in the area that was big enough for all of them—Mom, Dad, Greg, Kathy, John and his children. But they couldn't find anything they liked, so their thoughts turned to buying land and building a custom home. This led Kathy and Angelo to go on shopping jaunts for real estate, one day driving high up on Mountain Meadows Road into the chaparral-thick, boulder-filled hillsides of northeast Escondido. Climbing past a golf course development known as Hidden Meadows, they reached aptly-named Alps Way, a tight, steep, windy mountain road in which the homes, what homes there were, were set well back from the pavement and obscured by tall fences and greenery. The lot they had come to see was nearly the last one on Alps Way before the road met a dead-end.

When Kathy and Angelo stepped out to look around, it was love at first sight: a five-acre slice of paradise on top of the world. Looking south from what would be their backyard, they could see in the far distance a sliver of Escondido, which means "hidden valley" in Spanish. From this remote perch the city was truly a tiny, hidden valley, for as far as the eye could see, there were only pristine chaparral hills and rocky outcroppings under a vast broad bowl of pale blue sky.

After this discovery the rest of the family traveled the long windy road up into the hills and joined the fantasy, excitedly imagining what it would be like to live there. The house would be big as a castle, and inside would be a spacious central living room—a great room—and an equally spacious kitchen with an island and walk-in pantry and super-deluxe stove and refrigerator, everything top-of-the-line. They'd have all the latest furnishings and beautiful cabinetry and hardwood floors that gleamed and master bedrooms with walk-in closets you could lose yourself in and giant bathrooms with Jacuzzis like they had in Vegas. Every bedroom would open up to its own private Santa Fe-style patio with burnt-orange and red flagstones and there'd be outdoor fireplaces and when you sat outside at night in the redwood hot tub you'd be able to see shooting stars flashing across the sky. There'd be gardens aplenty and land to grow grapes and possibly make their own wine, just like in Sicily where the family traced its roots. Best of all, though, they'd be together. That was an essential part of their dream: all of them living together under one roof, one big, happy, forgery-creating family.

But it takes money to realize your dreams, especially if they're real estate dreams, and this was, finally, why Gloria had gotten into this thing and taken control. She had dreams too. She wanted nothing less for herself and her loved ones than what other families had and what she had once possessed: a piece of the rock, a slice of the American dream. She wanted it and damn it, she was going to get it.

On the day of their meet with Ferreira, she and Angelo drove to Nihon in their white Caddy and parked in the small lot behind the building. They walked down the concrete path past the box hedges and knocked on the dark green door of Suite 100. Ferreira opened it and enthusiastically invited them in.

Since Suite 100 was wired for sound and pictures, the agent did not need to wear a body wire. Even so, he was aware of the location of the hidden camera and microphones. Although this was not a drug investigation where the people buying and selling the drugs should be caught doing it on camera, he subtly tried to get Gloria and Angelo into the right positions so their faces could be seen and their voices distinctly heard. In the next room McKinney operated the monitoring equipment and watched intently.

Pleased to be making a sale, Angelo—"a nice man," in Ferreira's words—chatted pleasantly about his art. He left most of the talking to his wife whose casual but pointed questions centered on Ferreira and his business overseas. As a hidden eye watched her, her eyes traveled around the room observing the packing supplies on the front tables, the boxes in the corner, the posters of Ichiro and Matsui. But what fascinated her most was the Michael Jordan poster with the Jordan forgery on it. She went up to it and inspected it closely as if to see whether the signature was her son's work or not.

Each of the four Nomo balls carried a likeness of the pitcher but not one of them had a forgery on it. Angelo turned the balls over to Ferreira, and Ferreira paid him six hundred dollars in cash. Then the couple said goodbye and left, and that was the last time Bullpen's UCA ever saw them.

What might have been a big moment in the case turned out to be a dud. Gloria and Angelo made no admissions, no incriminating statements, saying nothing that would have indicated they were anything but a nice elderly retired couple selling painted baseballs.

Furthermore, the FBI's plan to establish business ties with the Marinos failed miserably too. At Smokewood Place Kathy had said she couldn't give the family's price list to Ferreira because their computer had crashed. In truth, the Marinos didn't own a computer. And she never called Ferreira.

This was true for Greg and John too. They didn't return Ferreira's calls and finally he stopped calling. The agent never went back to Smokewood Place, with or without backup.

Similarly, he never again ventured up the wooden steps at W.W. Sports Cards to see Wayne Bray. Bray and the Marinos shut him out completely, and the agent's failure to penetrate the inner circle would haunt the investigation almost until the very end.

14

It was a small community of crooks and news traveled fast around it, especially news of possible FBI undercover activity. Interestingly, the man who had caused all this nervous chatter knew that people were talking about him.

"Everyone knew what happened at the Marinos because they told everybody," said Ferreira. "And I could understand why they were suspicious. Here I was, hitting on all these guys, not just one guy but all of them. So they're thinking, 'What's going on here?' What I'd tell them was that I was dealing with everybody because I'm looking for the best price. Whoever gives me the best price, I'll deal with him."

One of the guys Ferreira was hitting on was a stocky, dark-haired, forty-one-year-old named Carmen Lombardo, known to everyone as Chip. His nickname reflected his personality: chipper, quick with a joke, easy to laugh—except when the agent uttered the f-word around him. Outgoing Chip clammed up at that point, preferring a more delicate term—"secondaries"—when talking about forgeries. Chip's company was called Home Field Advantage, and his business card doubled as a refrigerator magnet. On the card was an outline of a football, inside of which was his contact info: phone, address, e-mail, website. Some of the autographs Chip sold on his site, realautographs.com, were real. Many were not. Equipped with a phone, computer and Internet connection, he ran Home Field Advantage out of his townhouse on Portofino Drive in Del Mar close to the famous race track where the Marino brothers, Bray and others in the ring occasionally came to throw money around and play the ponies.

Chip knew and did business with Jon Hall, who was also a Ferreira subject. In his fifties, a genial, soft-spoken father of a policeman, Hall ran a card shop in Del Mar not far from the track and Chip's place. Hall bought fakes directly from the Marinos and sold them at his shop. Whenever John Marino made a delivery to Del Mar Sports Cards he refused to come inside, calling ahead on his cell so that Hall would meet him outside in the parking lot. There, they made the swift exchange of forged goods for cash—Hall carrying the stuff back into his shop and Marino tearing off again, perhaps to put some money down on a horse he liked in the fifth. It was during one of these parking lot deals at the Flower Hill Mall with its white Spanish-style architecture that Marino relayed the news about the encounter with Ferreira to Hall, who later passed it on to Chip.

Suspicious as they were, their suspicions were all they had to go on. Even the Marinos and Bray did not know for sure about this mysterious new stranger, for what would have established him conclusively as a federal agent did not occur. There were no busts, no arrests, no seizures. It was crooked business as usual. If this guy was the law, how come nobody had been popped?

This was the FBI's strategy, of course, and why fellows like Chip and Jon Hall kept selling to Ferreira despite their qualms about him. The FBI did not have enough evidence to bust anyone at this stage but even if it had, it would have been reluctant to do so because its goal was to explore the conspiracy in its entirety, follow all the various strands of the web wherever they might lead. So the investigative team was willing to bide its time, an approach that allowed Ferreira to keep making buys and waving money at people.

The agent called Chip for the first time in September, and Chip paid his first visit to Nihon the next month. "From the very start," said the agent, "Chip kept pushing me to buy more," and why not? Selling fakes was a cutthroat business and you'd have to be a fool to walk away from some guy throwing money at you, knowing that if you did, one of your competitors would be happy to take it. Chip was no fool, and he cultivated the agent's friendship for reasons that had nothing to do with friendship. He wanted to reach deep inside Ferreira's wallet, and Ferreira sought evidence that Chip was dealing frauds and knew it. That being said, "We became buddies," said the agent, who hung out with Chip a lot: touring the Hall of Champions sports museum in Balboa Park, watching "Monday Night Football" at a sports bar, lunching at Mikko in Old Town Carlsbad. Both Chip and Ferreira liked Japanese food, and Mikko was the perfect place for the agent to showcase his knowledge of Japan, and he poured it on with true stories of watching sumo matches in Tokyo, a sport that fascinated Chip because it was so foreign to America.

After lunch, if he didn't have another meet to go to, the agent drove back to Nihon or the Village North Apartments in Oceanside. There, he'd write up a 302, change tapes and stash the merchandise Chip had sold him until Fitzsimmons or McKinney could pick it up. A cluster of faded orange and pink stucco three-story buildings grouped around a central swimming pool and Jacuzzi, the Village North served as the FBI's safe house, where Fitzsimmons and McKinney could come and go without worrying about running into the crooks. Next to the pool was a laundry room with coin-operated washing machines and dryers, and from the laundry room up a flight of steps was Ferreira's undercover flophouse. To say it was furnished in a Spartan manner would be to render an injustice to Sparta; early college student more accurately describes its humble furnishings and décor. When setting up the one-bedroom apartment over the summer the FBI had provided a dumpy couch, coffee table, lamp and TV that looked like they had come from one of the thrift stores being raided by the Marino brothers for old books. Thinking it looked a little sparse even by government standards, Fitzsimmons brought a spare kitchen table and chairs over from his house so Ferreira would have a place to sit and eat his meals.

His bed was a mattress and box springs placed on the floor—no bed frame. Ferreira didn't have a problem with this except that his bedroom looked out on I-5 with its traffic thundering by in both directions day and night. After nights of tossing and turning and getting no sleep, he finally abandoned the mattress for the couch in the front room where the freeway sounds were more muffled and he could at least get some rest.

"I didn't complain about the apartment because I knew what the budget was and I know how thrifty undercover ops can be," said Ferreira. "Having a nice undercover place only matters if you're bringing the bad guys over, which I wasn't doing." When Chip suggested coming over to see him, the agent would say, "Aw, it's a nothing place," and propose meeting at Mikko or some other spot. Since, according to his cover, Ferreira spent most of his time overseas on business, it was reasonable for him to stay in a nothing sort of place while in the area, and nobody pushed him on it.

In the first few first months of the investigation, Ferreira continually tried to put at ease guys who were highly suspicious of him. He made the most progress with Chip whose tongue, as Ferreira kept oiling him up with thousands and thousands of dollars in business, began to loosen slightly. The agent listened carefully and recorded every word for Chip was a pioneer of sorts, one of the first members of the Bullpen ring to exploit the emerging new medium of the Internet.

It is no accident that the early, wild days of the Internet coincided with the rise of the Bullpen network. Excitement over the seemingly limitless possibilities of this new medium and the Gold Rush mentality it spawned sent the financial markets into a tizzy, the greatest bull run in history. These were high times. A spirit of risk, of anything goes, was in the air, and it was as true for collecting as it was for investing. Like high tech stocks, the prices for autographed memorabilia surged upward in extraordinary, record-setting runs, and people from all walks of life put their money down and climbed aboard for the ride.

In September 1995, when the Bray-Marino partnership was kicking fully into gear, a young, ponytailed computer programmer named Pierre Omidyar launched a new website called AuctionWeb. Its name suggested its purpose: an online auction site for people to buy and sell things. In those days the Internet was still the province mainly of college students and techies, and Omidyar figured the principal users of his site would be techies like himself buying and selling computer gear. What he found was that although techies did indeed use the site, so did another group of people: collectors.

On its Labor Day launch not a single visitor clicked onto AuctionWeb. Traffic picked up a little after Omidyar, working alone in his Silicon Valley townhouse in the now-legendary tale of how he parlayed his idea into riches, spread the word about the site through online chat rooms and message boards. In a couple of weeks AuctionWeb was hosting nearly twenty non-computer auctions, the largest category of these being "Antiques and Collectibles," which included the following items:

Autographed Marky Mark poster. Bid: $400.

Autographed Elizabeth Taylor photo. Bid: $200.

Autographed Michael Jackson poster. Bid: $400.

There is no way to know whether these autographs were real or fake. What is certain though is that signed celebrity and sports memorabilia was sold on AuctionWeb from its inception and contributed to its phenomenal growth. Two years after it launch, in January 1997, the same month Tim Fitzsimmons was launching Operation Bullpen, one of the biggest bursts of activity in company history occurred when the site auctioned a football autographed by Vince Lombardi and other Green Bay Packer greats in the weeks before the Super Bowl. The auction generated huge publicity, and that January AuctionWeb recorded more than one million hits, then a record for a single month. It also hosted 200,000 auctions that January, al-

The Big Three of baseball collecting consists of Mantle, DiMaggio and at left, Ted Williams. Greg Marino's forgery of Ted ran the *d* together with the *W*, just the way Williams did it.

Greg Marino studied films of Joe DiMaggio signing autographs to see how he did it. Though experts do not consider his DiMaggio forgery as perfectly rendered as his Mantle, it still fooled people and that was all that mattered.

From left, Dennis Rodman, Michael Jordan and Scottie Pippen, and their bogus sigs. Michael signed the *M* in his name like a 23, his number for the Bulls, and so did all the crafty individuals who forged it.

Father and son teamed up on this Bret Favre lithograph: Greg spun out the forgery (under Favre's right arm, somewhat obscured by the dark background), and Angelo painted the painting. Angelo's signature is in white in the lower left corner.

The brilliant, scheming mastermind of the enterprise, Wayne Bray, as seen in an interview with ESPN after his creation came crashing down.

Stan Fitzgerald, posed here with his wife Donna and pitcher Greg Maddux in an ad for Stan's Sports Memorabilia, used his connections with unwitting sports stars to give a legitimate cover for the millions of dollars in fakes he sold.

This picture, taken by a hidden FBI surveillance camera inside the Marino home, shows the bearded Greg Marino seated at the kitchen table and signing a forgery. Behind him is his mother Gloria, the financial brains of the family business.

At left, a J. DiMaggio Company "Document of Authentication," for a bogus Lou Gehrig cut. Invited to join the scam because of his famous last name, DiMaggio issued tens of thousands of phony certs similar to this one.

Little Ricky Mitchell and others hunted for vintage pre-1948 bottles of ink for Greg to use for his Babe Ruth forgeries.

The gang invented a technique called "dipping"—coating a baseball with shellac similar to what people did in Ruth's time to preserve valuable old balls. On top of the can is a shellacked ball with a Ruth forgery on it.

The flip-flop mafia created and distributed countless numbers of fake-signed Ruth balls that sold for thousands and sometimes tens of thousands of dollars apiece to unwitting fans.

Individually, the forgeries of John, Paul, George and Ringo sold for modest sums. But together as the Beatles, they were like gold.

A dishonest cut of Honest Abe, signed by Greg Marino. Cuts were easy and cheap to do, and the raw material for them could be found by simply tearing out the blank pages in the back of old books.

For combo-signed forgeries such as this one to be successful (bearing the sigs of all five presidents), the buying public must believe that all these famous figures got together and autographed this one photo, carefully placing their sigs in all the right places, and that this photo and others like it were widely available at low prices.

These Sosa and McGwire fakes, produced right after the famous 1998 home run chase, were likely the handiwork of Mike Moses of Universal Authentic Memorabilia. Moses's McGwire was good enough to fool a national magazine, which put a copy of the forgery on its cover, thinking it was the real thing.

From left: Tim Fitzsimmons, John Ferreira, Mark McGwire and Jeff McKinney. This shot was taken during the 1999 season when the three FBI agents and Phil Halpern visited Dodger Stadium before a game between McGwire's Cardinals and the Dodgers. The purpose of their visit was to enlist McGwire's participation in a FBI ruse to catch a dubious authenticator. The business aspect of the meeting over, Halpern snapped this souvenir photo.

During phase two of Operation Bullpen, this rare photo—showing Muhammad Ali in an exhibition match with the Japanese wrestler Antonio Inoki—became a crucial piece of evidence in the investigation of former heavyweight boxer Chuck Wepner and two associates, John Olson and Brian Ginsberg. The Ali sig was done by Olson, one of nearly 10,000 Ali forgeries he did in his career.

In a comic exchange during phase two, investigators sent this photo to two forgers, pretending not to know who was in the picture with DiMaggio. The forgers knew the man's identity, though, and signed his and DiMaggio's name. Thus, the FBI bagged a forged autograph of J. Edgar Hoover.

Mystery surrounds the author of the forged Mother Teresa photographs. Marino does not recall signing any Mother Teresa photos, though this sig appears similar to the one on the baseball below. Shawn Jackson, a forger busted in phase two, said that he once had a copy of Mother Teresa's autobiography and contemplated signing her name to it, but just couldn't bring himself to do it.

A close-up of one of the most famous forgeries of all time, by Greg Marino. Note the letters "mc" at the end of her signature, which stand for Missionaries of Charity, her religious order. This was a detail only handwriting experts and professional forgers would have known about.

most as many as occurred in the entire previous year, with the fast-growing Antiques and Collectibles category leading the charge.

Because its prices were not firmly set or agreed upon, varying widely based on the condition of the object, a star's popularity and other hard-to-quantify factors, autographed memorabilia was considered to be an ideal product for online bidding and selling. In the old days collectors searched garage sales and swap meets for ancient, neglected treasures; increasingly, they were looking online.

In the fall of that year, when Ferreira was coming on as Bullpen's UCA, the site dumped its old handle and took the name of eBay. In describing his motives for founding eBay, Omidyar said, "I wanted to do something different, to give the individual the power to be a producer as well as a consumer." To do this he changed the rules about what it meant to be an auctioneer. In fact, eBay was not an auctioneer at all; it was only an electronic platform, a virtual marketplace for buyers and sellers to connect with one another without a third party regulating or overseeing their transactions. Aware of the possible abuses in this more direct form of commerce, Omidyar established for eBay users what he called "community values," based on five governing principles. The first and most important of these principles—"We believe people are basically good"—reflected both the founder's idealism and how his company operated in its early years of explosive growth. Of course, Chip Lombardo and his associates did not follow the honor system, and by exploiting Omidyar's Utopian vision they did nothing less than revolutionize the ancient practice of forgery and usher in a new era in the sale and distribution of counterfeit merchandise.

As old as the written word, the origins of forgery as a criminal practice date back to the great library of Alexandria whose patrons paid royal sums for the manuscripts of Sophocles, Aeschylus and other superstar Greek playwrights of the day. Such manuscripts were not easy to come by, however, and certain less than scrupulous individuals decided that if they could produce documents that appeared genuine in most respects but were in fact fake, the library's patrons, if they did not know better, might buy them. Thus, a lively counterfeit trade was born on the shores of the Mediterranean more than 2,300 years ago.

Through the days of the early Greeks when forgers inserted spurious passages into Homer to promote a specific city or region, a form of ancient tourist boosterism, and into the Middle Ages when Pope Innocent III published a set of rules on how to decipher a forgery and the Catholic Church executed three clerics for producing phony papal bulls to push their own religious agenda, forgery remained essentially unchanged. It was a literary crime intended to fool the educated elite, including those in the church who were among the privileged few in society who could read and write. Similarly, forgers themselves belonged to this educated class because they had to be able to read and write to craft the documents they were passing off as authentic.

Even as literacy became more widespread in society, the pattern held. Forgery was a thing done on paper, typically by one scheming man whose work was intended to defraud, and often lighten the pockets of, those members of the educated public who cherished the written word. Forgers were typically literary people (or literary hangers-on) who read poems, plays, novels and works of history, just like those they cheated.

One of the most famous forgers of all time, William Henry Ireland, was the son of an 18th century engraver who worked in the printing trade and who longed to own a letter written by William Shakespeare. So Ireland faked a Shakespeare letter for his father, moving on from there to produce his own faux-Shakespearean canon until a sharp-witted authenticator, Edward Malone, exposed him as a fraud. Noting how Ireland's manuscript contained a number of different watermarks indicating paper of varying ages, Malone challenged him to explain why his Shakespeare folio appeared on such a hodgepodge of foolscap. Ireland could not produce a satisfactory answer, and his ruse came to an inglorious end.

One of the most prolific old-time forgers was Denis Vrain-Lucas, who churned out thousands of letters purportedly written by the likes of Alexander the Great, Attila the Hun and Joan of Arc. One of his letters was from Pascal to Isaac Newton in which the philosopher claims to have discovered the law of gravity. Being French, Vrain-Lucas evidently wished for one of his countrymen to receive the credit for one of science's greatest discoveries, not a Brit like Sir Isaac. He was exposed when someone calculated that Newton would have been only ten years old when he received this letter, a tad too young to be exchanging scientific correspondence with one of the world's most brilliant minds.

George de Luna Byron fooled people with both his tongue and pen, posing as the illegitimate son of Lord Byron while forging letters by him as well as Keats and Shelly. The scam worked for a time because Byron was definitely a player when it came to the ladies, so it was conceivable he had fathered a child out of wedlock. And as his ostensible son, it was conceivable that de Luna would have had access to his late father's private papers. Conceivable alas, but not true.

One of the first great American forgers, Robert Spring, ran a rare book shop in 1850s Philadelphia, using it as a cover to spin out lots of rare but phony letters from George Washington. Joseph Cosey, another great Yankee forger, authored hundreds of manuscripts by Washington, Ben Franklin,

Abraham Lincoln and prominent literary figures of the time. Cosey's Lincoln is considered without peer, the master work of a dishonest master.

An Ivy League graduate who was dubbed "the Baron" for his haughty, aristocratic manner, Charles Weisberg was another in the long line of educated scoundrels who forged for fun and profit. Posing as royalty was just an act, a way to trick people into believing in his Washington and Lincoln forgeries. When a box with the letters of Francis Hopkinson, one of the signers of the Declaration of Independence, was found in a New England basement, historians hailed it as a major find until it was revealed to be the work of the Baron. He later went to prison for forgery and died an ignoble death there in 1946.

Perhaps the most sensational literary forgery of recent times occurred in the 1970s when Clifford Irving crafted a letter from Howard Hughes saying that he had received permission from the reclusive billionaire to write his autobiography in cooperation with him. Irving's claims proved false, as was a will alleged to have been written by Hughes in which he bequeathed a portion of his fortune to a Utah gas station owner named Melvin Dummar. The Mormon Will, as it was called, was said to be Hughes's thank you to Dummar for helping him out one night on the desert when he was stranded. The will was bogus, and Melvin never got the millions he hoped for.

As gifted as he was corrupt, an anti-religious miscreant named Mark Hoffman created elaborately forged documents designed to undermine and embarrass the Mormon Church. He committed murder and was sent to prison. In the early eighties the publication of diaries allegedly written by Adolph Hitler during World War II fooled some historians who proclaimed them genuine. The sinister motive behind this fraud was to rehabilitate the dictator's image in the eyes of the public. The most attention-getting forgeries often have political motives—witness the tricked-up typewritten form intended to cast doubt on George W. Bush's National Guard service and damage his presidential re-election chances.

While, for political, economic and religious reasons, sensational frauds of this type will no doubt continue to occur, they represent only a tiny percentage of the forgeries being done today. The racket has changed, mirroring changes in society at large. Television mainly shapes popular taste today. A celebrity is basically someone who appears on the box in your living room at home; these include TV stars, movie stars, rock stars and pro athletes. The stars of the written word have steadily lost their luster and their works are less valued. Shifting with the marketplace, forgers have abandoned Emily Dickinson for Elizabeth Taylor and Michael Jackson.

Since Hollywood stars and pro athletes never write letters, why bother forging them? Long declining in interest, letter writing suffered a death blow with the advent of e-mail, another aspect of the Internet revolution. Writing letters belonged to the past, a slower way of life, and most forgers in turn shifted from the long form to the short: autographs. They worked with a pen as always, but now they only had to deal with two words—a person's name—as opposed to a whole bunch of them cluttering up a page or two and arranged in salutations and sentences and paragraphs with punctuation marks that nobody understood how to use correctly anyway. For forgers, all the much remarked-upon trends of modern life—the busy pace, more distractions causing shorter attention spans, the decline of reading and print, the rising influence of TV, video games, DVDs, iPods and other forms of electronic entertainment and learning, and the cult of celebrity, the desire among so many to connect with those beautiful golden faces beaming out from the box at home—combined with a trend in collecting: cheap, commonly available, mass-produced flats and bulkies. Applying Tom Cruise's or Kobe Bryant's or Bill Clinton's sig to a baseball was the perfect formula for forgery in the modern age.

And so this was what Greg Marino and Chip Lombardo and Mike Lopez and so many others never targeted by the FBI did. They produced forgeries on a historically unprecedented scale by using modern methods of mass distribution. As brilliant as they were criminally, one cannot describe this new breed of forgers as part of the educational elite. They belonged to a different class of folks who bypassed the old, limited audience for literary forgeries and sold their products across the mainstream of society to people very much like themselves—people who loved movies and TV, enjoyed sports and most importantly, had money to spend on autographed knickknacks related to these pastimes. And beginning in the mid-nineties, this new criminal wave found an exciting new way to reach consumers through the online flea market (so the critics derided it in its early days) dreamed up by the well-meaning Pierre Omidyar.

Counterfeiters no longer needed to bring their wares to a central source or buyer, as they did in Alexandria. They could now sell around the world to anyone with a computer, an online hookup and a credit card. In olden times, since the market forgers were trying to reach was limited, so was the relative quantity of their output. It made no sense to churn out huge quantities of fakes because there was only so much they could earn from them anyway. Besides, it takes considerable craft to reproduce a letter or manuscript. So many details need to be right, and getting the details right takes time. With the coming of eBay, counterfeiters had a fast and easy way to reach people who were seldom expert about what they were buying. Some people bought autographs over the Net without seeing the actual autograph on screen, relying on a description of it provided by sellers whose goodness was on hold at that moment.

Internet auctions offered an advantage even over television as a method of mass distribution because on the home shopping channels, the crooks still had to pass their material through a central source. Selling on eBay eliminated this go-between, helping them move mind-boggling amounts of product through devices such as a Dutch auction. In a Dutch auction, sellers put up for bid a quantity of identical items—say, fifty Tiger Woods–signed golf balls—all at the same time. The top fifty bidders then claim their dubious prizes.

When sellers auctioned items on eBay they had three basic options: set no limits on the transaction; establish a minimum bid below which they will not sell; or place what is called "a reserve," a minimum bid known only to the seller. When a bid hits this reserve level, the auction is considered official and a sale can take place. Bogus dealers used all three methods to defraud people. Knowing that what they were selling was essentially worthless and they couldn't lose money whatever the price, they didn't set minimum bids. This approach helped them unload material to people who thought they were getting a bargain but were just getting screwed. Realizing, however, that selling a signed Tiger Woods Titleist for pennies is equivalent to saying it's bogus, many fraudulent dealers set a minimum bid purely for the sake of appearance. Others set up a reserve auction establishing a low minimum bid, but because this number was secret they avoided attracting suspicion.

The anonymity of the Internet, a blessing in so many ways, was the richest of blessings for the Bullpen ring. In real life a person who uses an alias may indicate a shady operator; in the virtual world an alias is part of the culture, how things are done. The memorabilia boys used a variety of fictitious screen names, often multiple ones at the same time, abandoning one screen name and adopting another if they received complaints. They dealt directly with their customers but never in person; everything was done anonymously. Just sell the thing, get the money and sell some more.

While doing the eBay hustle Chip Lombardo also peddled fakes the old-fashioned way, and in early December he rolled out of his Del Mar townhouse and drove north on I-5 en route to a meeting with a client. Turning east on Highway 78, he traveled for a few miles before getting off at an exit that took him to the Pacific Coast shopping plaza in Oceanside. His destination was the warehouse-sized Sports Authority sporting goods store. Between the Sports Authority and a Statler Bros. supermarket was a small lot tucked away from the larger shopping center lot where most of the cars parked. Chip parked his Toyota pickup in this smaller lot, got out, locked the door and hurried into the store.

The biggest merchandise area was Sportswear in the center section. To the right of Sportswear were Shoes, Golf, Team Sports; to the left, Skiing and Outdoor Sports. Anxious to make his meeting on time, Chip grabbed an empty shopping cart in the front and pushed it down the left aisle as store loudspeakers played soft rock music interspersed with occasional in-house promos.

A cluster of a dozen or so poles and hoops marked the beginning of Basketball. Here, Chip turned left down the aisle and encountered shelves and shelves of basketballs in an array of colors—black, light brown, dark brown, orange and white, red, white and blue—and brands: Spalding Official WNBA, Wilson Supreme, Wilson NCAA Final Four, Nike 500, Nike 1000, NBA Game Ball, NBA Indoor/Outdoor, NBA Ultimate, NBA All-Court. Each ball was packed tightly into a square box, its label turned outward so it was facing the aisle.

Chip filled his cart with several of the NBA-endorsed brand and steered it back down the aisle past Outdoor Sports and Skiing to the register. From there he pushed the cart outside along the sidewalk and back to his truck. Quickly loading the balls in, he jumped in the cab and shut the door, glancing around to see if there was anything suspicious going on. All was clear, so he popped open the glove box and pulled out a trusty black Sharpie. Then he put a ball on his lap and signed Michael Jordan's name to it.

It was that fast; it took only an instant. Done with one ball, he set it aside and picked up another and signed it. Then another. And another. That was when he looked around the lot again and noticed a man in a car watching him.

The man was an FBI surveillance agent who had been tailing him since Portofino Drive. And the agent's efforts had produced an unexpected dividend: actually witnessing a subject in the act of forgery. Trouble was, he'd been burned.

Chip instantly threw his Sharpie and everything else down, fired up his Toyota, backed up and peeled out heading straight for a freight alley that ran along the perimeter of the shopping center. Whatever that truck had under the hood, Chip demanded all of it. Turning right at the alley he put the pedal down and flew out of the shopping center as FBI cell phones started beeping all over the place.

The first to beep was McKinney's at the Carlsbad RA. "We've been burned," the embarrassed surveillance agent told him. "What do you want me to do?"

"Oh shit," McKinney muttered, saying he'd get back to him.

The next cell to go off belonged to Fitzsimmons, and it was McKinney telling him about the blow-up. Fitzsimmons immediately got with Ferreira, who was at the Nihon Trading Company, while McKinney called a second surveillance unit to tell it not to lose track of their subject who was still careening wildly around the streets of Oceanside.

Chip had no idea about this second unit. Finally he pulled into the back of an Albertson's, hopped out of his truck, tossed the balls with their fake Jordan sigs into a dumpster, hopped back in and careened off again. The FBI later picked up the balls as evidence.

The biggest problem wasn't the blown surveillance, though. What the FBI feared most was that Chip, once he settled down and began to think more clearly, might connect the surveillance to the man who had placed the order for the Jordan balls just so his colleagues could tag along with Chip to see what he did. "Chip is buying stuff for John," recounted McKinney, "and if Chip connects the surveillance to John, we're screwed. If this guy goes home and starts calling people, he could screw the investigation."

After hastily talking it over with McKinney and Fitzsimmons, Ferreira called Chip on his cell to rag on him about not making their planned meeting. "Where are you, man?" he said. "I'm here waiting for you. I gotta catch a flight."

This was not a lie; the agent was scheduled to leave town that day. Only it was back to Oregon, not Japan as Chip thought.

"Something's going on," said Chip, wheeling around in his truck, the panic evident in his voice. "I don't know what it is. I'm not gonna make it today. Talk to you when you get back," and he clicked off, leaving the FBI to ponder its next move.

Over the next few days the agents talked about what to do, even considering whether or not to come forward and reveal the investigation to Chip. If he had already figured it out, it wouldn't be revealing anything anyway, and they might be able to persuade him to flip—to come over to their side and work with them on an undercover basis. But the agents decided against this, instead opting to do "some damage control," as McKinney put it.

"Remember, John was supposedly leaving for Japan that day," said McKinney. "So we had an FBI agent in Tokyo buy a postcard of some sumo wrestlers and FedEx it to John in Eugene. John addressed it and wrote a brief note to Chip, stuck it in an envelope and sent it back to the agent in Japan who mailed it from there. Then we did the same thing with a box of chocolate macadamia nuts from Hawaii. A Honolulu agent bought a box and expressed it to John, who enclosed a note saying, 'Merry Christmas,

Chip. Great doing business with you. Looking forward to seeing you when I return. Sincerely, John.' Then John put the note in the box and sent it back to Hawaii where the agent mailed it."

As sly as this gambit was, the investigators could only guess how the recipient of all this holiday cheer was responding. Was Chip buying it, or had he connected the dots and made Ferreira as an FBI agent?

The answer came after the first of the year when Ferreira returned to San Diego and called Chip to do some more business. Chip said not a word about the incident, telling Ferreira he'd be happy to get together. Friendly and chipper and full of charming mischief as always, he thanked the agent for the macadamia nuts and the postcard, saying how much he'd love to go to Japan some day and see a sumo match.

15

On January 16, 1998, a white Cadillac wound its way across Escondido to the Palomar Savings and Loan on West Grand Street. After finding a space in the lot in back, Gloria Marino turned off the ignition, taking a quick nervous puff on her cigarette before stubbing it out in an ashtray crowded with butts. A leather briefcase was on the seat beside her. Dressed nice and respectable, like a person with money, she wrapped her fingers around its handle and slid out the door.

Across the lot she made the long walk to the rear entrance of the savings and loan, a squat three-story building that somewhat resembles a bank vault. The rear lobby consisted of two soft plush chairs and a small table. To the right was a row of teller's windows. But Gloria needed more than a teller for the transaction she was about to do, and when a clerk greeted her she asked to speak to a manager.

The manager soon appeared and, smiling and gracious, escorted her to a private conference room on the left of the lobby opposite the teller windows. They entered and shut the door. The manager took a seat behind her desk and Gloria sat down across from her, unloosening her tight grip on the briefcase to set it on the floor at her feet. Her hands were slightly trembling, and she folded them in her lap so the manager wouldn't notice.

The manager asked what she could do for her, and Gloria explained the purpose of her visit. Her family was buying a five-acre parcel of land on Alps Way in the hills. The purchase price was $123,000. Today she wished to make a payment of slightly more than half that amount to the escrow company handling the sale of the property. What she needed from Palomar Savings and Loan, then, was a check for $63,000. Upon receiving this, she'd drive it over to the escrow company whose office was in a shopping center a few blocks away.

Fine, said the manager. What funds are you going to use? Gloria said she'd first like to withdraw $13,000 from her savings account.

Excellent. And the rest of the amount?

In reply Gloria reached down for the briefcase and placed it on the desk. She clicked it open. Inside was $50,000 in cash.

The manager's face betrayed no emotions even as her heart surely started to race. When a person brings lots of cash into a bank, the staff at the bank tends to think: drugs. These stacks of fifties and hundreds did not come from the drug trade, but how Gloria got them was just as illegal, and so she said not a word on the subject. Nor did the manager ask. The manager did say that Gloria would need to fill out some forms to complete the transaction—strictly routine—and stood to go get them. Left alone in the room, Gloria took a calming breath and waited.

The manager returned shortly with the forms and Gloria dutifully filled them out, listing her occupation as a "retired bookkeeper." Meanwhile the manager silently counted the bills to make sure they added up to the amount claimed. They did, since the retired bookkeeper had counted them that morning.

With the forms complete, the manager presented Gloria with the $63,000 check as requested. Gloria thanked her and placed it in her purse, picked up her now-empty briefcase and made polite small talk as the manager led her out of the office to the rear door. Stepping into the warm, restorative sunshine, she paused to light a Virginia Slims Long and took several long, satisfying pulls from it. Then, not quite finished for the day yet, she got back in her Caddy and drove over to Escondido Escrow to deposit the check.

The next week she returned to Palomar Savings and Loan to withdraw more funds and get another check, this one for $60,000. She again drove it over to the escrow company and deposited it, thus completing the purchase of the property. As soon as the land cleared title, it was theirs.

As Gloria was moving forward on her dreams, her sons and their cohorts were living a kind of dream life too. That month San Diego was hosting Super Bowl XXXII, and Greg, John, Wayne, Nate, Little Ricky and another guy rented a limousine for an all-day and all-night party of football, booze, drugs and girls. The limo picked them up at their respective houses in the morning and ferried them down to Qualcomm Stadium where they held a tailgate party under balmy blue Pacific skies. Finally the game started, and they claimed their Gold Club seats costing $1,500 apiece. It was Broncos against the Packers, and they all had major money riding on the outcome. After the game they wandered back out to the lot where their limo was still waiting for them, ready to take them wherever they wished. Nobody wished for it to be home. They spent the rest of the night and a good chunk of the morning on a barnstorming tour of the local titty bars. Since they were men with Benjamins to burn, they had lots more fun with the girls than they ever did watching the boys play football.

As originally conceived, the Bullpen investigation was to proceed like a drug case, with the UCA initially buying from lower-down dealers and gradually working his way up the food chain to the people in charge. But the people in charge of the nation's biggest forgery ring wanted nothing to do with Ferreira, forcing him to work lesser lights like Chip Lombardo and Mike Bowler, an amiable, fortyish dealer who, like his buddy Chip, sold hundreds of thousands of dollars in fakes, primarily over the Internet. It was Chip who introduced Mike to John, and early in January the three of them went to see Tiger Woods play at the Mercedes championship at La Costa. Bowler had of course heard all the rumors about the owner of the Nihon Trading Company, and the tournament was his first chance to check him out in person. It was also a chance for the three of them, all genuine sports fans, to check out the most exciting player in golf.

They went to La Costa on Wednesday to see Tiger during a practice round, before official play began, and hundreds of other fans had the same idea, pressing and pushing and crowding up against the gallery ropes to get close to him. Mike, Chip and John all wanted Tiger's autograph but tight security prevented them from approaching him. Nevertheless Ferreira, an experienced autograph hunter, noticed that a small opening occurred at the end of each hole as Tiger was crossing from the green to the next tee. Looking ahead and moving fast, the agent scrambled ahead of the crowd and thrust a pen and tournament ticket at his quarry as Tiger walked towards him. Tiger stopped, dashed off his sig, returned the pen and ticket to Ferreira and then stepped onto the teeing ground, the gallery ropes springing up around him an instant later.

To be that close to greatness, however brief, was thrilling, and a *San Diego Union-Tribune* photographer, also looking ahead and moving fast, got the shot of Tiger signing the autograph for a fan. It appeared on the front page of the next day's sports section with the headline, "Walking the Walk." In the picture with Tiger was Ferreira wearing his black fanny pack.

Now having your picture appear in the paper in the midst of an investigation might not ordinarily be considered good undercover form, but Ferreira's head was turned in the photo and his face was not showing, so it was hard to recognize him unless you knew it was him. But even if one of the crooks did recognize him, so what? He was out watching Tiger play and collecting his autograph, which fit his cover perfectly. Getting a fresh in-person star sig was like gold in the racket because it could then be forged with the assurance that this was how the star was signing at that moment. And Ferreira had showed skill and cunning to bag Tiger, which both Chip and Mike failed to do.

Another bogus dealer being courted by the agent was Jack Morgenstern. Ferreira found out about him when Morgenstern placed an ad in the paper listing autographs for sale. Ferreira called the number in the ad and Morgenstern answered, saying he had more than $500,000 in sports memorabilia for sale. Within days Ferreira was sitting at the kitchen table of his house gazing at some of it.

With longer, pushed-back hair, Jack had a chunky, medium-sized build similar to Chip's, but without the latter's outgoing personality. "He was not into the hobby," said Ferreira with clear distaste. "Everything was about money for him." Spread out across the table was an array of signed merchandise he was selling—some of it real, some not. Ferreira could tell the real from the fake because "the garbage he wanted to sell. The real stuff he wanted to keep."

The agent spent five hundred bucks that day on a bunch of garbage. He followed that order with another for a grand, and Jack started walking down the same path being traveled by the others: letting his love of money override his suspicions. In time he trusted Ferreira enough to give him a tour of his suburban San Diego home where he stored his half-million dollar pile of garbage.

While doing business with Jack, Ferreira intentionally let it slip that he was also doing business with Chip, which pissed Jack off. "Jack got mad because I was buying stuff from Chip, and he saw that as taking money out of his pocket." Jack wanted Ferreira to spend all his money with him, which was what Jon Hall wanted too. Since Hall bought directly from the Marinos, he promised Ferreira lower prices than Chip who obtained his Marino products through Hall and other second hand sources.

"You have to play these guys and I played them," said Ferreira with satisfaction. "I was playing everybody against everybody else."

But this play had a serious purpose, for it helped to drive down the prices he was paying for things. If Chip hadn't spotted the FBI surveillance and actually delivered those forged Michael Jordan basketballs, he would have charged the agent a couple hundred bucks per ball for them. Due to competition and his desire to keep one of his best customers happy and coming back for more, Chip eventually lowered his price on Jordan basketballs to sixty bucks per. (Retail for a signed Jordan basketball was six hundred to eight hundred at the time.) Paying less for forgeries meant that Ferreira could make more buys and collect more evidence.*

So round and round they went—John playing Jack against Chip, and Chip against Jon, and Jon against Mike, and Mike against Jack—with the agent buying everything in sight. Early in the spring of '98 he and Chip went to an exhibition game between a touring squad of the New York Yankees and the San Diego State University baseball team. During the game, which was held at the university's field, a foul ball landed in the stands near where Ferreira and Chip were sitting, and the agent excitedly jumped up to grab it and just missed it. When he sat down again he realized that the mikes attached to his chest had accidentally popped off. Sneaking a glance over at Chip, who noticed nothing amiss, Ferreira excused himself to take a pee. In the privacy of a restroom toilet stall he reattached the mikes under his shirt and then hustled back to his seat to watch the rest of the game.

Even as he worked the outer edges of the ring Ferreira had in his sights a much bigger player in the racket: Dave Tabb, the king of celebrity autograph fugazzis. Just past thirty, a heavyweight packed into a middleweight's body with light brown hair, light green eyes and Don Johnson-style whiskers on a soft white chin, Tabb cut quite a figure in the racket, dressing in casual but expensive finery, driving a Ferrari and other luxury automobiles and stashing his always-thick money roll in the visor above the steering wheel. The name of his company was Hollywood Dreams, and he was moving millions of dollars in counterfeits through an arrangement with AMC Theatres to sell signed memorabilia in the lobbies of its movie theaters. Every moviegoer in the U.S. who went to an AMC theater with a razzle-dazzle Hollywood Dreams display was potentially his patsy.

The pursuit of Hollywood Dave by the FBI began in earnest soon after Ferreira entered the case. On a Friday night in September he visited a theater in Carlsbad with a Hollywood Dreams display in the lobby. On sale were perhaps five hundred signed pieces: celebrity 8x10s, movie posters, other trinkets. Acting innocent, the agent approached a young sales clerk, Jess, and began to chat him up.**

"I said to him, 'Wow, this is neat stuff. How do I get involved?'" Eager to court a new prospect, Jess gave the agent his Hollywood Dreams business

---

* *Ferreira spent about $200,000 during the investigation to acquire forged memorabilia, according to the FBI.*
** *The FBI did not name Jess as a conspirator in the scam. Only his first name will be used.*

card featuring an illustration of Darth Vader and Jack Nicholson in sunglasses. The card listed the company's address as Hollywood but its actual location was a Santa Ana industrial park. The Hollywood number was just for show. On the back of the card Jess wrote his Santa Ana phone number and told Ferreira to give him a call, which the agent did, shortly thereafter, placing an order for some hard to obtain Jordan and Mantle items (hard to obtain if genuine, that is). A few days later Jess appeared at the Nihon Trading Company to deliver the order in full, and with the hidden cameras and microphones recording their every word, the agent and the kid engaged in a verbal minuet of evasions, partial truths and lies—the agent gently but aggressively seeking to elicit information about the kid's boss, and the kid firmly but politely deflecting the agent's advances, not wanting to reveal much of anything to his questioner.

Jess said his boss was too busy to take on any more clients and preferred for his sales staff to handle new customers. Ferreira knew this was a lie but he didn't push it, wondering privately how much the kid knew about the scam in which he was engaged.

Ferreira also dealt with another eager Hollywood Dreams employee, Melanie, who filled a series of big orders from him. As he had with Jess, when she came by Nihon to deliver the stuff Ferreira quizzed her about her boss and when he could meet him. Melanie danced away from the questions but, not wishing to offend a cashed-up customer clearly in the mood to spend, she dropped a thank you note in the mail to him after one of their meets. Accompanying this note was the twelve-page Hollywood Dreams inventory list consisting of about six hundred items—two-thirds movie and television celebrities, the rest sports. In her note Melanie explained that for orders of a thousand dollars or more, Ferreira would receive wholesale pricing, a considerable savings over retail. The agent had told her he was about to go to Japan on business and her note concluded with a cheery "Have a great trip!"

Receiving the price list was a good sign for the FBI, a sign that Ferreira was getting closer to his intended target. He was developing a relationship with two of Tabb's employees, both of whom liked him and wanted to keep doing business with him, and although he had yet to lay eyes on their boss, he felt confident it was only a matter of time.

Then the media got involved and everything went screwy.

Late in 1997, a local TV news reporter named Marti Emerald aired two "Troubleshooter" reports on Tabb, outing him as a suspected dealer of counterfeits. Appearing "60 Minutes"-style at the front door of Tabb's company with a hand-held camera following close behind, she swept dramatically through the receptionist area into his office and confronted him with a bogus Tony Gwynn-signed ball that had been purchased at a Hollywood Dreams display.

Wearing a green and black short sleeve shirt and sitting at his desk with a "Batman and Robin" movie poster on the wall behind him, Tabb appeared nervous on camera. "I would never need to have an autograph that is not authentic at our booth. If you have this autograph," he went on as the camera moved in for a close-up of his stubbly chin, "it was not our autograph, which means it must've come in trade."

Bogus autograph dealers tell as many stories as Scheherezade, and "it came in trade" is one of their favorites. The dealers did not themselves knowingly produce the forgery or have it produced for them; rather, they unwittingly bought or traded for it. This tale has timeless appeal because it allows the crooks to cast themselves as victims who were ripped off in the scam just like consumers.

The Channel 10 reports were followed by a rash of complaints from outraged viewers who had bought things from Hollywood Dreams and now felt burned. Spurred into action, the California state attorney general's office swiftly launched a raid of Tabb's suddenly very popular South Village Way office, confiscating hundreds of pieces of counterfeit memorabilia.

Like Marti Emerald, the attorney general's office knew nothing about Operation Bullpen which, after all, was a secret investigation. Nor did the state realize that one of its expert witnesses in the case, Jim Bellino, who was brought in to assess whether or not the stuff being sold by Hollywood Dreams was fake, was himself a target of the FBI. Based in Orange County, Bellino's main business was selling billiards equipment, but on the side he ran an authentication company, Forensic Document Services, which certified tons of Marino forgeries and bogus material.

"Bellino was first singled out by the Chicago FBI," said Fitzsimmons. "Not only that, HBO's 'Real Sports' had done a piece on him identifying some of the forgeries authenticated by his firm. But after that piece ran he just switched authenticators. It wasn't clear if this new authenticator was being duped or if he was in on it too. In any case Bellino was one of the reasons the state was able to obtain a warrant on Tabb."

It was a case of one dubious operator informing on another and with an unintentional assist from law enforcement, possibly helping to drive him out of the racket. In a further twist, some of the autographs sold by Tabb were authenticated by Bellino, which meant, in effect, he was ratting out his own stuff.

Chip Lombardo and Mike Bowler later introduced Bellino to Ferreira, who would make him a target of his investigation. But for now the FBI was more concerned with Tabb, who had been busted once before for selling bogus memorabilia at a restaurant chain in southern California. In a foreshadowing of the state raid, local police had trooped through his office, cited him and walked away with 1,200 counterfeit items.

Was the king of Hollywood fugazzis going to stay in the racket, or get out? The FBI had no way of knowing. It could only wait and see if one of its prime subjects, a guy it had spent a lot of time and money cultivating, was about to go up in smoke.

To hear Dave Tabb tell it, he never wanted to sell fakes. "I had no intention of getting into forged stuff," he said. "I was dealing in real stuff. I remember I put on this charity event once and Samuel L. Jackson came up to me after he saw his autographed picture on sale. 'Damn,' he said, 'it's real. Ain't that a trip.'"

A gifted salesman and weaver of words, Tabb has been in business for himself since he was a teenager selling food and gift items at the Orange County Fairgrounds. He loved collecting, so it was natural for him to start putting on trade and collectibles shows. He soon found a niche for himself as a promoter, organizing in the early nineties one of the largest memorabilia shows of its time in southern California. The *Los Angeles Times* put his picture on the front page of its business section. Then in his early twenties, he was a boy wonder, a comer in the surprisingly lucrative field of collectibles.

Thinking big, he leased a 32,000-square foot warehouse space on Glenwood Street in Santa Ana with the idea of hosting events that would attract and feature celebrities. A place needs to be nice for the Hollywood crowd to come to Santa Ana, and this one was. "The Rolls Royce of warehouses," as he described it. "Totally plush. Thirty-two TVs, satellite dish, air conditioning, carpeting." Samuel L. Jackson, Arnold Schwarzenegger and the cast of "Friends" were among those who made star turns at these events, and the Rolls Royce of warehouses became known in the industry as a happening spot, the place to hold your charity or business event. Its go-go owner partied with the likes of Dennis Rodman and the Mighty Ducks hockey team, and to celebrate his birthday one year he rented out the Twin Palms in Newport Beach, dancing the night away with friends and clients to a nineteen-piece swing orchestra.

In many ways Tabb appeared to be the picture of upper-aspiring Orange County contentment: nice home, nice wife, new vehicles, thriving business. It was all pretty terrific for him until the '94 baseball strike and labor fights in hockey and basketball gutted the hobby. "Collecting was awful, nobody was buying, and the warehouse started going downhill," he said. "It was costing $20,000 a month to operate but I was only bringing in $10,000 a month. My car was repossessed. I was in credit card debt and there were lawsuits because of it."

In a deep hole that was getting deeper every day, Tabb turned to selling forgeries: "How did I feel about selling stuff I knew was bad? If you could put words to it, it's hard. It's impossible to describe. You're struggling to pay the bills. You've got people to pay, a payroll to meet. You can't get rid of your overhead. And you keep telling yourself, 'You're not gonna do this anymore. You're gonna find a new supplier. You're gonna get out of it.'"

But he didn't. Instead he said sayonara to the events business and his money-draining warehouse and moved his digs into a bland, boxy industrial park in Santa Ana. The one-time boy wonder of collectibles had become a big-time seller of fakes.

The police raid in '97 was a minor irritation: "They cited me for operating without a business license. I paid the fine and got a license." And resumed doing business.

For Tabb, a former child actor, Hollywood Dreams was a dream venture. Selling celebrity memorabilia made him again part of show business, admittedly on the distant fringes of it, but still, his business was essentially the business of dreams, the same as the movies. When the lights come up in a theater and dull reality descends on the audience, they want to take a piece of that dream home with them, keep it as their own. This, in essence, was the service he felt he provided at Hollywood Dreams—that is, until all the bad publicity and the attorney general's raid ended Tabb's relationship with AMC. All his merchandise was pulled out of its theaters, and he and his company plunged into yet another cash crisis.

At that point, he resolved to get out of autographs. "I was done with the autograph business. I was going straight and I had gotten another job in a totally different field. I was finished." What drew him back in, he says, were Jess and Melanie telling him about this buyer they had on the line who had done tens of thousands of dollars in business with them and was looking to place another huge order with the company if he could just meet the owner. This, says Tabb, was news to him. "I didn't even know who Ferreira was. I had no flipping idea Jess was doing all this business with him. Then I hear about this thirty thousand dollar deal he's offering. So I'm thinking to myself, 'I'm getting out of this business and why are you pulling me back in?'"

Whether the FBI pulled him back in or he voluntarily jumped, Tabb agreed to meet Ferreira at an Angels game at Edison Field in the opening month of the '98 season. Melanie came along and handled the introductions, though the game was just a pretext for getting together, a neutral place for the two principals to size each other up. The meet represented a victory for Ferreira, who had worked seven months to be able to shake Tabb's hand. Another victory came at the end of the evening when his subject agreed to eliminate the intermediaries—no more Jess or Melanie—and deal one-on-one with him.

From then on, said Tabb about Ferreira, "every time I met with him he gave me $5,000 to $10,000 in business." [In the meantime the FBI had told the state attorney general's office about its investigation, and the state withdrew from its pursuit of Tabb.] To the agent's frustration, however, the king of Hollywood fugazzis had mastered the art of saying a lot while saying nothing. If he had any remorse over the crap he was selling, it did not show in his facial expressions or gestures and certainly not in what he said. He gave nothing away—nothing incriminating anyhow. His words were like good movie dialog: all subtext, nothing on the nose. Everything was implied and under the surface, nothing overtly stated.

"If you like it," he told Ferreira, referring to an autographed piece, "buy it. If you don't like it, don't buy it." Adding, "Unless you personally see a thing signed, you never know."

Nothing more than that, never more than that. That was all the agent could get out of him. If Ferreira remained in character, playing the upbeat, dependable businessman, Tabb stayed true to his role too: the polished talker, willing to deal fakes but not willing to admit to it. "It was very difficult to get the f-word out of him," said Ferreira. "It was like pulling teeth."

Ferreira never actually got the f-word out of Tabb, a point conceded by Fitzsimmons. "Tabb was a salesman. He could talk your head off but he wouldn't make admissions." Adding that Tabb "never incriminated himself by what he said, rather by what he did. What he sold to John and for how much showed as clearly as words that he knew what he was doing."

Tabb knew precisely what he was doing, but he wouldn't talk about it to Ferreira. One reason for this was his feeling bordering on a clear conviction that Ferreira was the heat. "I knew right away he was a cop or an undercover agent," he said. "He was too goody-goody. It was too important for him to talk to me. All he cared about was meeting me. He wanted to shake the hand of the man he was doing business with. That's what he told my employees in order to get to me."

Tabb kept his visits with Ferreira limited, especially when they occurred in the unfriendly confines of the Nihon Trading Company. "His office was sterile, blander than bland. There were no personal pictures of him or his family. It looked like no one was really working out of it." And whenever they had lunch together, the agent "was always going to the bathroom. I had a feeling he was in there changing tapes, which was what he was doing. I should have felt him up."

Such thoughts crossed Tabb's mind but they remained only that: passing thoughts. He never reached across the table to feel for the microphones under Ferreira's Hawaiian shirt or surprise him in the men's room to see what he was doing in there. And while he kept taking Ferreira's money—$10,000 in checks and cash in one deal in July outside the Benihana in Anaheim—no visible law enforcement action ever occurred. Which made him disregard his feelings and keep doing business with him.

"Ferreira's style was business-like. You need to put on a show when you're undercover, and you need to be willing to tell people to buzz off and walk away so that they're crazy for your business. Ferreira never did that. He never cut anything off. He just kept spending more money with me. To be a good undercover agent you really must become [like] your subject," Tabb went on. "You must be willing to embarrass yourself if necessary. If the subject wants to go to a strip club, you go to a strip club. If he wants to talk about sex, you talk about sex. If he wants to get drunk, talk about pussy, you do it with him. And that's your favorite thing. Ferreira wasn't like that. His manner was real straight."

The investigation's problem with Ferreira, though, was not one of style but of substance. He was simply not delivering the admissions that the government needed to bring cases against the ring—and nobody was more ticked about this than Phil Halpern. "Months and months passed," said the AUSA, "and John pissed away all kinds of opportunities."

Ferreira had been on the case for nearly a year, and there had been no breakthroughs. Big breakthroughs were more TV than real life, but you needed to make progress and where was it? The lack of results confirmed Halpern's initial misgivings that Ferreira was not cut out to be the UCA for a Group One case. It was vital to have a dealer admit, on tape, that he had knowingly sold forgeries—and not just once but that he had done it in the past too, because he (or his lawyer) might argue that that one time was a freak occurrence and the rest of his dealings were above board. But Ferreira had not gotten Tabb to admit to dealing forgeries even once, let alone that he was doing it routinely.

It was mostly the same with Chip and the other guys, too. While collecting piles of circumstantial evidence against them, Ferreira was still having trouble getting them to say incriminating things. And sometimes he'd even let them say exculpatory things on tape making it sound as if they weren't really criminals engaged in criminal acts.

Frustrated as well by the lack of results, Fitzsimmons and McKinney talked frequently with Ferreira, coaching him on different ways to approach the subjects to get them to open up. Be bolder, more direct, less of a nice guy. Use the f-word more blatantly. Ever the team player, Ferreira listened to their suggestions and tried gamely to incorporate them into his undercover approach, even though the tough guy act went against his nature.

"They wanted me to be more of a criminal," he said. "It would be nice to hear the subjects say, 'This is a forgery.' But it's hard to get them to say that."

Maybe it was hard, but nobody on the investigative team cared about that. What they cared about was admissions—and they weren't getting them.

"This is no good," Halpern would say in exasperation after listening to one of Ferreira's undercover tapes. "He's got to say this, and he's not saying it. He said the exact opposite of what he was supposed to say. What are we doing here?"

As investigators struggled to answer that question, events in baseball were about to send the forgery racket spinning off into crazy new heights.

16

On July 29, one day after Mark McGwire hit his forty-fifth home run of the 1998 season, *USA Today* carried a front-page article on the astounding number of fake McGwire autographs being sold in the St. Louis area. The article, headlined "Bogus McGwire Autographs Hit Missouri," described how the Missouri state attorney general, acting on complaints by McGwire and others, had launched an investigation into counterfeit memorabilia, seizing phony goods in shops in St. Louis and tracing some of the fakes back to dealers in other states.

Less than a week later, *Tuff Stuff,* a leading sports card and collectibles magazine, featured the brawny Cardinals slugger on the cover of its latest issue. The picture showed him following through on yet another home run swing, his massive thighs and upper body twisting with his bat in hand. Near his right shoulder on the cover, in bold print, it read: "62?" the headline being posed as a question because in early August it was still in doubt whether McGwire would break the single season home run mark, "baseball's sexiest record," as the magazine put it. Across Big Mac's right arm in the picture was a facsimile of his autograph which, to the embarrassment of the magazine's editors, turned out to be one of those fakes McGwire and the Missouri attorney general were so unhappy about.

"Some of these autographs are ridiculous," McGwire told a reporter. "I just can't believe a person would knowingly sell something that is as phony as what I've seen. This stuff isn't even close." It was especially galling for McGwire because he had not done a paid signing for more than a decade and had rejected offers to market memorabilia in his name, signing only for free at the ballpark or for people he knew.*

---

* His attitude has since changed. After retiring from baseball in 2001, McGwire signed an autograph deal with a company.

To publicize his unhappiness with the liberties being taken in his name, McGwire submitted to a test conducted by Krause publications in a hotel before a game between the Cards and Milwaukee Brewers. Wearing a ball cap and casual shirt, he sat at a table as the publisher's representative placed six photos in front of him. All six bore his signature. The test was to see if McGwire could tell which sigs were from his hand and which were from somebody else's.

It turned out to be not much of a challenge. Bing, bing, bing, bing, bing—instantly he tossed five aside as rank phonies. Only one was legitimate, he said. Although this one, it was revealed, came from McGwire's business agent who had supplied it for the test without his client's knowledge. The other five had been purchased from mail order firms selling signed memorabilia. The big man expressed disappointment at this news because it suggested to him that fakes were all over the place and multiplying like rabbits, an assessment shared by FBI and Justice Department investigators working secretly across the county in San Diego.

"Tens of thousands of different counterfeit autographs done by scores of different forgers across the country," Phil Halpern said about the frenzy that occurred in the racket during these months. "As quick as Mark or Sammy would hit a home run, the balls would be produced. Home run sixty-eight—thousands of them with a little sixty-eight on them. Sixty-nine—thousands. Seventy—thousands."

On August 4, McGwire stood at a major league high of forty-five home runs, leading Sammy Sosa by three and Ken Griffey Jr. by four. By the end of the month the great Mariners star had fallen off the pace, putting the spotlight on the other two who were tied at fifty-five apiece. McGwire hit two home runs on September 1 and another two on September 2 to push his total to fifty-nine. With nearly a month left in the regular season, it seemed a near certainty that he would reach the hallowed plateau of sixty and tie Babe Ruth's old record, and he did just that three days later with a shot into the left field seats at Busch Stadium in St. Louis. On the same day the unyielding Sosa recorded his fifty-eighth, keeping the pressure on the front-runner.

Although charges of steroid use by the two sluggers have in recent years rubbed some of the shine off the home run chase, at the time people across America got very, very excited about it. With Sammy hot on Mark's heels and both of them bearing down on the ghosts of baseball's past, the chase stirred people not only because of what the two were doing, but because of who they were: the ebullient Cubs right fielder, blowing kisses and tapping his heart after each of his home runs; and the super-sized first baseman (sportswriters liked to refer to him as "Bunyanesque") joyously lifting his ten-year-old son into his arms at home plate after rounding the bases at Busch following his stirring, nationally televised, Roger Maris-tying sixty-first. Sosa's Cubs were playing the Cards that day, and Sammy joined in the stadium-rocking ovation by applauding from his position in right field. The next day, when McGwire hit his record-breaking sixty-second, his rival jogged in from the outfield to congratulate him during the on-field celebration. The muscled Californian, who stands a head taller than his Dominican-born counterpart, picked him up and hugged him enthusiastically.

This was another thing that made the chase so memorable: the clear affection each man had for the other. During this series the two posed for pictures together: McGwire, his red goatee speckled with gray, in his red Cardinals jersey and cap, his thick right arm around his comrade's shoulders; Sosa in his blue Cubs uniform and cap with the red "C" outlined in white, both players grinning widely. One such photograph, with the word "AWESOME!" splashed across the front of their jerseys in large red letters, appeared on the cover of the September 14 *Newsweek*, turning the magazine into an instant collectible for fans and forgers around the U.S..

Unlike ordinary fans, though, the forgers and their pals did not hang onto their issues for long, signing and selling them as fast as they could get their hands on them. "We started seeing dual sigs on this cover right away," said Fitzsimmons. "Photos of McGwire and Sosa together, with dual sigs, were very popular too."

Working through their undercover agent, Fitzsimmons and McKinney would request signed photos of McGwire and Sosa hitting home runs sixty through sixty-six, and in McGwire's case, on up through seventy. "We're pushing, asking for signed photos, and they have no problems supplying them," Fitzsimmons said. As for the bogus McGwire autographs that had triggered the Missouri investigation, "many of these were emanating from California," said the agent, though surprisingly perhaps, they did not come from the pen of Greg Marino.

"We shied away from him," Marino explained. "McGwire was one of the activists who was complaining about forgeries. We were making so much on everybody else. Why do somebody who's gonna be a problem?"

With the fastest pen in the West out of the McGwire business, that left the field open for another prolific California forger, Mike Moses, who may have been responsible for the forgery that embarrassed *Tuff Stuff*. "The sig came from a company that did business with Moses," said Fitzsimmons, "so it could have been a Moses."

An inch over six feet with blue eyes and short blond hair, the thirty-year-old Moses was a well-known member of the small, interconnected band of forgers and distributors that lived along the southern coast of California and wreaked such autograph havoc on the country. He lived in a lovely custom tract home in a gated community on a hill in Newport Coast. His sexy brown-haired wife Robyn was a full partner in her husband's business, Universal Authentic Memorabilia, which sold universally inauthentic memorabilia. The couple, who had one small child and would soon have another, drove a new Chevy Suburban paid for out of the proceeds of the family business.

A big sports fan, often dressing in warmup suits and team jerseys, Moses ran a sports card shop in Laguna Niguel before starting Universal Authentic Memorabilia. Sports Alley sold legitimate autographs as well as the other kind, and inevitably Moses came under the watchful eye of Anthony West. But instead of trying to avoid West, Moses called him one day to tell him about Shelly Jaffe, who, said Moses, was dealing frauds and needed to be stopped.

"This was what they all did," said West with a sigh. "They'd tell on each other. It was a jealousy thing. One of them would see another one making all this money that they wanted to make, so he'd call me to try to get the other guy busted."

In this case the guy Moses was trying to get busted was his friend. "I like Mike," said Jaffe, who went out socially on at least one occasion with Moses and his wife. "He was a businessman doing his business."

During the home run chase and before, Mike would call Shelly at home and they'd share a laugh about the outrageous fakes being sold on the cable shopping channels. Moses penned some of these fakes, and Jaffe sold some of them. "It was a joke," said Shelly, who estimated he unloaded "hundreds of thousands of dollars" in forgeries over cable TV. Also calling Shelly to yuk it up was Nate Harrison, who was placing Greg Marino forgeries on the channels and watching from his home at the same time Shelly and Mike were watching from theirs. Moses had a wide-screen TV set up in his garage along with a Lifecycle machine and treadmill, so he could exercise while talking on his cell and watching his creations being hawked over the air.

Moses was also a friend of Dave Tabb's. Mike had served as a groomsman at Dave's wedding, and the czar of Hollywood Dreams had employed him as a forger though he didn't much like his overly aggressive criminal style. "He was careless," said Tabb. "He'd throw empty baseball boxes of balls he had forged into his trash that people could see. He had a hard time keeping secrets. He would invite people over to his house and people would see something and ask, 'Is it fake?' And he'd say yes. He never quite got it that when you are dealing in something illegal, you should keep it on the down-low."

In early October, a few days after McGwire's historic seventieth, John Ferreira was lounging at his desk at the Nihon Trading Company flipping through the pages of the November issue of *Tuff Stuff*, the same magazine Moses may have burned with his Big Mac forgery. The flipping stopped when he landed on a series of ads in the front of the magazine. Sitting up in his chair, Ferreira was astounded by what he saw: pages and pages of blatant forgeries for sale. Forged Muhammad Ali boxing gloves, forged Barry Bonds bats, forged Alex Rodriguez sports cards, forged Jerry Rice-Joe Montana helmets, forged Wayne Gretzky hockey pucks, forged Allen Iverson sports cards, forged Lakers team jerseys, forged Jack Nicholson basketballs, forged photos of Drew Barrymore, Leonardo DiCaprio, Salma Hayek, Jennifer Lopez, Adam Sandler, Billy Bob Thornton and Bruce Willis, forged photos of Affleck-Damon, Lawless-Sorbo and Redford-Newman, forged movie posters of "The Godfather" (nine sigs), "Titanic" (seven sigs) and "Pulp Fiction" (11 sigs). Scattered across these gaudy, out-there, catch-me-if-you-can pages were photos of Magic Johnson, Willie Mays, Steve Young, Samuel L. Jackson, Linda Hamilton, Lucy Lawless and Kevin Sorbo all with pens in their hands—the classic dodge of showing pictures of celebrities autographing things as if they were autographing the things in the ad.

Ferreira knew, with certainty, these were all fakes because of the colossal number of items listed and the low, low prices being asked for them: a measly twenty-four bucks, for instance, for a McGwire-signed photo when an authentic one, if authentic ones even existed, went for two hundred-fifty, easy. But the agent had to hand it to the guy behind the ads. In a box on the last page, Universal Authentic Memorabilia issued this pronouncement: "We have worked with the local authorities to help put people who are selling fake autographs in jail." While blatantly selling forgeries he was bragging about throwing forgers in jail. What balls!

Ferreira put down the magazine and called the number listed in the ad. Moses answered, identifying himself only by his first name. Emboldened by the boldness of the ad, Ferreira placed a five thousand dollar order on the spot. Much to the agent's delight Mike did not say he could not possibly fill such a large order so quickly. Did not say it was impossible to find genuine examples of such rare and valuable celebrity signatures. Did not say anything of the sort.

What he said was: See ya in a couple days.

And true to his promise, Moses, looking tall and lean and blond in a jersey and warmup suit, showed up at Suite 100 of the Nihon Trading Company two or three days later. He had entirely filled the agent's order, which consisted of the following forged items: six Michael Jordan basketballs, nineteen Jordan photos, six Jordan-Pippen-Rodman photos, fifty-one McGwire photos, thirty-one McGwire baseballs, twenty-one McGwire-Sosa photos, seventeen McGwire-Sosa baseballs, twenty-four Sosa photos, eighteen Sosa baseballs, two Griffey-Sosa-McGwire bats, nine Griffey-Sosa-McGwire bats, twenty-four Tony Gwynn baseballs and seven Gwynn photos.

To show his pleasure with the transaction Moses marked down some of the historic dual-signed McGwire and Sosa photos, selling them for ten bucks apiece. He also threw in, for free, two McGwire trading cards, a Kobe Bryant-Tim Duncan-Juwan Howard-Grant Hill basketball, Mike Tyson and George Foreman boxing cards, and four Foreman-Joe Frazier-Muhammad Ali boxing gloves. It was Moses's custom to throw in free items on a large order, calling it "a package deal." Over the next year he and Ferreira would do many such package deals.

"At first he was like all the others, feeling things out," said the agent. "It was a game we were playing. Then after he sold me some things and he wasn't arrested, his attitude was, 'Let's get more money from this guy.'" The more money Moses got, the more comfortable he felt. "Moses gave up Tabb in a second," said Ferreira, who happily played the sometimes antagonistic friends against each other. "I was acting very personable but it was a front. I'd talk good about Tabb in front of Tabb but when I was talking to Moses about him, Tabb was a scumbag—you know, that sort of thing."

Once Ferreira got onto Moses, FBI surveillance did the same. On November 5, the agent placed another giant order and the next day surveillance followed Mike's Suburban from Newport Coast to a mall and professional building on Camino de los Mares in the sleepy, well-to-do beach community of San Clemente. He swung into a parking lot in the rear of the building and disappeared inside the center where he had an office, reemerging with a box of memorabilia in his arms. Helping him carry things were a man and woman in their sixties, and they made several trips back and forth from the office to the SUV. Loaded up and ready to roll, Moses said goodbye to the pair and sped off.

The Suburban returned to the freeway and headed down the coast to—no surprise here—the Nihon Trading Company, where surveillance faded away. Inside, Ferreira paid $6,000 in cash to Mike and wrote a smaller check to his wife. As much as the crooks would let him Ferreira always tried to pay by checks. Even if, as in this instance, Moses insisted on cash, Ferreira would make up some story about how he only had so much cash on hand and could he pay some of the tab by check? When Moses said yes, it gave the feds a way into his wife's bank account where they could track who else she was doing business with.

Also at this buy, Moses made what proved to be a revealing admission—that the Babe Ruth cuts that were part of this order came to him via Rino Ruberti, Moses's partner in Universal Authentic Memorabilia. These cuts all had certs from J. DiMaggio Company, establishing a clear link between Moses's group and Bray-Marino.

While the FBI learned much about Universal's operation from surveillance, most of its best information came from Moses, who trusted Ferreira and provided damaging admissions about himself and his business. "Moses used John sort of like a priest, as his confessional," said Fitzsimmons. "He talked, and John listened."

"I was his best buddy," agreed Ferreira, who had lunch and dinner with Moses several times and visited his home once. "He confessed things to me, told me about his problems. Personal things, everything. He had complete confidence in me."

One time, while handing over a pile of fake merchandise, he included a signed Ken Griffey Jr. photograph, telling the agent to sell everything else in the order but not the photo. It was real, and he was giving it to him free of charge.

"You're not like everyone else in this industry," he told Ferreira. "You're an honest criminal."

The Universal Authentic Memorabilia operation consisted of three families: Mike and Robyn Moses, Rino and Karen Ruberti, and Karen's parents, Scott and Mary Louise Harris, the elderly couple spotted by the FBI loading stuff into the back of Mike's Suburban. The Harrises helped out as needed, using their bank account to launder money and allowing their son-in-law and his partner to set up a credit card account and business account through their bank. When Mike delivered that first big order to Ferreira in October, the agent wrote a check for part of the bill to Scott Harris.

Rino and Karen Ruberti were peers and friends of Mike and Robyn, and like them, they were a good-natured, attractive, sun-kissed California couple who were paying for their gleaming beach lifestyle, in part, by hustling counterfeits. A tall, green-eyed blonde, Karen Ruberti worked the phones, filled orders and made pickups and deliveries similar to what Robyn Moses did. A more central figure in the company—and a pivotal one in the conspiracy as a whole—was her husband Rino, who may have been the prettiest of them all.

"Mr. Cool. Mr. GQ," was how Dave Tabb described him. "He was a laid-back surfer-type."

A blue-eyed, blond-haired handsome man, Rino put the flip in the flip-flop mafia. As cool as they come, he had an easy-does-it, hang-loose attitude. Most everyone in the racket who dealt with him said they never saw him without a smile on his face. He lived near the ocean; had a blonde stunner for a wife; did judo to keep fit; and his wallet bulged with crisp new bills. What was not to smile about?

People who did not know him tended to pronounce his name "rhino," which he disliked. So to avoid that he usually spelled his name "Reno," which was the way he said it and the way he wanted others to say it.

Before hooking up with Moses, Rino operated as the Sports Card Kid; that was his DBA for the legit business he had selling baseball and Pokemon cards out of his van. He sold to people like Jon Hall, and at some point the owner of Del Mar Sports Cards introduced him to John Marino. After that the Sports Card Kid had a brand new thing to peddle out of his van: fake autographs. Normally suspicious of outsiders, the Marinos liked Rino, granting him the high honor of letting him enter their house, though he never saw Greg forge in person (this was reserved only for a precious few). But Gloria loved his GQ looks and style, and he always went along with her system, putting the money in her hands while flashing that golden smile.

"My mom and John dealt with him all the time," said Greg. "He was a stand-up guy, an honest guy. He never tried to pull any tricks like some of the other guys. He always paid the prices we asked."

Among his duties, Rino acted as a runner between Moses and the Marinos. As bold (or reckless) a forger as he was, Moses never did dead people, conceding that aspect of the business to Greg, who forged vintage cuts as well as living stars for Universal. This kept Rino busy shuttling up and down the coast in his new white Chevy Astro van. FBI surveillance first picked him up on a run to W.W. Sports Cards when he was dropping off a bunch of fakes for authentication. A few days later he returned to pick up these goods—now with J. DiMaggio Company certs—and breezed off again looking for all the world like he was about to go catch a set at Trestle's and then finish up the day with some fish tacos and Coronas. But instead he motored across town to a Petco parking lot where he met Gloria and John Marino. They quickly unloaded some stuff into Rino's van alongside the material he had gotten from Bray, and then he headed back up the coast towards home.

It was a good run, a fun run, flying alongside the white sand beaches and the blue water with the blue sky overhead and the sun shining and a hundred grand in fake merchandise in back. Slip in a CD, crank up the volume, roll down the windows and breathe in that good salt air. Rino made the two-hour round trip between San Clemente and San Marcos-Escondido once or twice a week, often tailed, discretely of course, by puzzled FBI surveillance agents who could not understand why their subject never got permanent plates for his van, driving around with a temporary paper license taped to the rear window. The agents wondered aloud about this to Fitzsimmons and McKinney, who were puzzled by it too.

Ferreira didn't know the answer either, but he was finding out many useful things about Rino from Moses and Jon Hall, who was also selling him some of the wildest fakes the FBI had ever seen. Whatever crazy-ass, off-the-wall autographs Ferreira asked for, the quiet, outwardly law-abiding shopkeeper produced them for him. Once Ferreira placed an order for cuts of George Washington, Thomas Jefferson, Abraham Lincoln, Theodore Roosevelt, Woodrow Wilson and Harry Truman, and Hall came up with them—all Greg Marino forgeries—in three days. As with all his dealings with the agent, he insisted on cash payment only, refusing to take a check.

Another dealer who had grown more relaxed was Chip Lombardo, who had stopped using the code word of "secondary" and was now openly saying the f-word to Ferreira. At a meeting at Nihon he delivered eight one-dollar bills signed by Ruth and Gehrig for $2,960, explaining how forgers made the sigs on the bills look old. At another buy he told how John Marino bought photos from supply houses and turned them over to his brother to sign. Chip cracked up Ferreira (and McKinney in the monitoring room) with a line about how "Mickey Mantle still has one arm out of the grave doing autographs." This was not the same conversation, however, when he joked that he had obtained some memorabilia "just signed" by a basketball superstar who had been dead for years.

During this time Tim Fitzsimmons began running pen registers on some of the subjects, notably the Marinos and Bray. But the registers, also known as trap and trace, only provided the phone numbers of incoming and outgoing calls; investigators could not hear what was being said over the line. For this they needed to tap the phones, and to do that they needed the permission of a judge.

Fitzsimmons and Halpern had worked for weeks on the proposal to obtain the taps, first passing it by FBI Headquarters and the Department of Justice in Washington for their approval. Once this occurred, in December 1998, they submitted the sixty-page proposal to United States District Court in San Diego seeking permission to install wire taps at W.W. Sports Cards, Greg's and Kathy's apartment, and the forgery factory on Smokewood Place. Based on the evidence from surveillance, the trap and trace, and not least, the information and admissions obtained by Ferreira, the government sought to establish a number of crucial points: that the subjects being pursued were a single disjointed but unified criminal conspiracy; that they were using their phones to commit these crimes; and that by tapping the phones, investigators would find evidence of this criminal activity.

The memorabilia boys were potentially on the hook for mail fraud, wire fraud, racketeering, money laundering, trafficking in counterfeit goods, tax evasion and conspiracy. There was still much the FBI and Justice Department did not know about their activities, but Judge Marilyn Huff felt there was enough. She signed off on the proposal, and the FBI had what it wanted.

The frustration felt by investigators for so long turned to exhilaration. At long last, they were in. And the person who had largely gotten them there was Ferreira. "John helped establish that there was in fact a conspiracy," said McKinney. "Also contributing were the surveillance teams that tracked the Marinos and others." Fitzsimmons agreed: "John's investigation kick-started everything and led to the wiretaps."

Even Phil Halpern offered grudging praise. "Hats off to John," he said. "He worked at his job and he definitely got better at it. He was a friendly guy and some of the subjects opened up to him. Even when he didn't draw them out to say [incriminating] things about themselves, they'd say things about other people that were useful. Without him we wouldn't have gotten the wiretaps."

He added, "Sometimes it's better to be lucky than good."

17

Come the start of the new year the FBI placed taps on the phones of Wayne Bray and the Marinos. These were remote taps, meaning that the connection was made not to a surveillance van camped out in the neighborhood as is so often depicted in the movies, but rather to the FBI's Aero Drive office in San Diego. One of the agents working the wire was twenty-seven-year-old Adam Lee. Lee wore a goatee and had a hipster's flair for cool lingo as well as a real passion for the ops side of his job—"the cloak and dagger stuff," as he put it. After earning his law degree and serving as a political aide for a California state senator, he decided that a career in law or politics held nothing close to the appeal of being a cloak and dagger man, and so he joined the FBI. San Diego was his first field office, and he'd been in the white collar unit for a little over a year when Fitzsimmons tapped him for the Bullpen wire.

This was no honor. Working a wire was typically assigned to a young agent like Lee who was still wet behind the ears. He had no strategic role in the case, at least in the beginning. Sitting with the taping system at his desk, wearing headphones, he listened to the intercepted conversations and typed up summaries of what he heard into his word processor. "It was grunt work," he said. Still it was his first time on a wire and despite the routine nature of the assignment he got into it, largely because they were investigating a group. For him, group cases were far more compelling than ones that targeted individuals because they involved lots of different people and personalities. And Bullpen, he was finding, had lots of personalities, notably Gloria Marino.

Lee knew immediately when Gloria came on the wire; her New York accent and "cigarette-ravaged" voice were unmistakable. "She was definitely in control," he said. "That was clear. If you assessed the family like a corporation, Angelo was a silent partner, a member of the board. John was in marketing, and Greg headed up research and design. Gloria was the CEO."

She told people what to do, handled the money, adopted a more efficient accounting system, kept track of incoming and outgoing orders, helped with setups and went on pickups and drop-offs, all the while keeping close tabs on the progress of her dream castle rising in the hills. Because she was such a large presence despite her small size, and because she always seemed to be around the house and knew what was going on with everybody, her sons came to her whenever the business hit a snag.

"Ma," Greg said anxiously to her one day. "You know where the black book is, right?"

Greg was at his Beaumont Glen apartment, Gloria at Smokewood Place. "I don't see it anywhere," she said, glancing around the living room and kitchen, the two places her son forged when he was at the house. "I don't think you brought it over yesterday."

"Huh?"

"I don't think you brought it over."

When Greg insisted that he did, she said, "I don't think so."

"Yes," said Greg firmly.

"No," said his mother more firmly.

Losing the black book (actually, there were several of them) represented a potentially grave matter, for it contained the genuine exemplars Greg referred to when he forged. Without the books, work—and making money—stopped. "It might be on the side of the couch there," Greg suggested in a hopeful tone.

"I looked," said Gloria, sounding annoyed. "You just brought in the jerseys, Greg."

"Oh, last night?" Greg was trying to recall. "No, I didn't bring it then but in the afternoon, I thought."

"You weren't here in the afternoon," said Gloria, who had no trouble remembering. "You did the order at your house."

The two of them went back and forth some more—Greg vaguely thinking he brought it over to the house, his mother telling him decisively no, he did not—until Gloria came up with another place he might have left it. "Must be in the car," she said.

"It's not. I already checked a million times."

"Then maybe you left it at Wayne's."

"No, it ain't there," said Greg, frustrated. "He said it ain't there."

After a flurry of panicky calls John Marino solved the crisis by finding the book amidst the clutter of unsigned memorabilia in the Smokewood Place garage. Greg had accidentally left it there. When John called his brother to tell him the good news he mentioned that on one of Greg's forgeries the *b* looked like an *s*. Even so the forgery "passes," he said.

It was a busy wire, with lots of calls coming in and going out. One of the voices belonged to that of Phil Scheinman of Smokey's. He talked about an order with Kathy, who told him to send his $4,000 check to Smokewood Place and to make it out to Gloria. They also spoke briefly about a pending order of Phil's regarding Michael Jordan memorabilia. The contents of this conversation were relayed to Fitzsimmons. He clicked onto eBay and noted with interest that Smokey's was auctioning off a number of pieces supposedly signed by Jordan.

John fielded a call from another big client of the Marinos, Barry Delit. The owner of the Rookie King, a card shop in Pottstown, Pennsylvania, Delit had been referred to the brothers by a family friend. This friend bought his pot from a Philadelphia source who knew Delit. The source told the friend about Delit, and the friend told the Marinos, and before long Delit and the family were doing business together. In gratitude for hooking them up with such a good customer, the Marinos kicked back a grand a month to their friend.

On this call Delit ordered ten Beatles 8x10s, two DiMaggio balls, two Ted Williams balls and a bunch of cuts, adding that he wasn't happy about a previous order of Albert Einstein cuts. Some of the Einsteins were bad, Barry complained, and he asked if he could return them and get a credit on a future order. John threw cold water on this idea, bluntly telling him they weren't taking back any merchandise and there'd be no credit. The disgruntled Delit placed his new order anyhow.

Listening in on how John handled people over the phone, Adam Lee said, "I got the feeling he fancied himself a tough guy. Blustery and sometimes bullyish. He and Greg talked about going to the gym and working out, but they were hardly what you'd call physical specimens."

John complained in a call to Greg about how he was having trouble with dipping—how he had done five balls but none of them looked any good. Then he whined about it to his mom, saying how Sissy, the family cat, had gotten into the shellac and was messing everything up. "She's touching the balls and knocking them over, and they're bad enough already," he moaned.

Gloria consoled him by telling him to choose the two best balls of the lot. They'd pick one of those, and sell that one.

First shift on the Bullpen wire began at six a.m. and lasted until two or three in the afternoon. The second shift went until midnight when the FBI signed off for the day. Lee worked two shifts a week, listening in when the conversation dealt with counterfeit memorabilia and clicking off when it turned to drugs and sex. The law required Lee and his fellow agents to "minimize"—turn off the receiver and stop listening within thirty seconds—if they overheard conversations that were not pertinent to the criminal activity under investigation. After minimizing he could tune back in for a spot check that again had to conform to the thirty-second rule. If no criminal activities were being discussed, he had to tune out again. But if there was chatter about the racket he could remain dialed in.

After each recorded conversation, he typed up a line sheet that included the date, time of day, the subjects who were talking and a summary of their dialog. Drugs and prostitution are illegal activities but this was a counterfeit memorabilia case, so his write-ups focused on that. He understood that Fitzsimmons, who read the line sheets every day, did not want to waste time wading through gossip that was irrelevant to the crimes at hand.*

Over the course of the investigation Fitzsimmons prepared one-sheets on the subjects, which included their photos and pertinent information on them. But most of what Lee knew about the gang came from the impressions he gleaned over the wire. Angelo, he thought, "was not much of a presence. Along for the ride." In one conversation Gloria criticized her distracted, artistic-minded husband for putting a Jerry Rice forgery on the wrong place on a football. Like many star athletes the former 49ers receiver had pet signing habits, autographing footballs in the same spot most of the time. But Angelo had not signed the ball in the Jerry Rice way, and in a morning pickup and delivery at an abandoned Vista gas station, Gloria learned about the mistake from Rino Ruberti, who returned the ball to her as unacceptable. Irritated, she sharply expressed her displeasure to her husband.

Gloria's strong presence in the racket aggravated another strong presence, Wayne Bray, who never clashed directly with her but who frequently bumped up against the rules she had imposed. Not one to accept being placed under someone else's rules to begin with, Bray, of all the guys in the business, felt the sting of these changes most keenly because he did not regard himself as just another one of the guys. Who started this thing after all? Whose idea was cuts? Who came up with the authentication scam? The answers were Wayne, Wayne, Wayne, and after all he had done for the family, after all the money he had sent their way, he felt he deserved better treatment from them. But instead of loyalty, what was he getting from them? He was getting screwed, that's what. He used to get a break on prices. Not anymore—not with Boss Gloria in charge. He used to get his orders

---

* One subject not directly related to the investigation that was of interest to the FBI was the ring's gambling activities. After the bust the FBI questioned the boys closely about Marty the Money Man and his offshore bookmaking operation, which investigators learned about through the wiretaps.

handled first—not anymore. He felt sure Gloria was giving better prices to other guys and pushing his orders back in line, playing favorites with a bunch of Johnny-come-latelys who were trying to horn in on what he and Greg had built.

Predictably, Nate Harrison sided with his bud in this power struggle. "Wayne wanted to run it like a business, but they [the Marinos] were giving other guys better deals, better prices, better treatment," said Nate. "They put limits on how much Wayne could spend, for instance. He was angry."

Nate had also encountered backups in the Marino supply line, but there was far less friction between him and the family, owing to his far less intense personality and his more dialed-down approach to the racket. While selling millions of dollars in counterfeits, he still worked at his own Nate-the-Skate pace, playing video games and hanging out and having a good time. Wayne, in contrast, never skated, and the same could be said for Stan the Man, too. Stan applied pressure to fill his near-constant stream of big orders and Wayne, feeling the heat, disliked being jerked around by the family with so many dollars at stake.

The Marinos, for their part, had their own issues with Bray. They felt strongly he had taken advantage of Greg—being one of the guys, the chief offender in fact, who had short-counted him at times and not paid the full amount as he should have. Greg had recruited his mother to protect him from being ripped off, so she wasn't about to back down from Wayne or anybody else who tried to put the squeeze on her son.

The tension between the two camps sometimes broke out into the open in arguments overheard by Lee and the other wire agents. But the anger flamed out quickly, as Bray and the Marinos weren't about to throw this thing away on petty turf battles and personality clashes. In one kiss-and-make-up phone call, Wayne told John not to worry about his family selling to other people because he, Wayne didn't want to interfere with the Marinos' ability to make a living. John responded with the ultimate compliment, saying, "Everyone knows you're the godfather of the memorabilia business." Greg then came on the line and in a further gesture of reconciliation, told Wayne that his latest order was just about done and he could pick it up that evening. It was all good, bro.

The W.W. Sports Cards wire was as active as the ones into the Marinos, with Wayne fielding calls from the likes of Dick Laughlin, who was looking to buy an old Lou Gehrig comic so he could get a Gehrig forgery on it, and Lowell Katz asking about Gehrig and Ty Cobb cuts and some blank certs he could fill in as he saw fit. Katz owned a Long Beach shop, The Beautiful and Unusual, whose most beautiful and unusual pieces were often frauds. Another of the voices heard on the wire belonged to Big Ricky Weimer, who was in the market for a Ruth ball and wondered if Bray had any for sale.

"Got a beautiful one here," said Wayne. "Sell it to you for $1,300. It's probably worth six thousand."

Big Ricky explained he had a customer who wanted to buy a Ruth-Gehrig combo-signed ball, and he asked if Bray had any of those around. "Yeah," said Wayne without enthusiasm. "I got a shitty one I'll give you for six hundred bucks."

Big Ricky then asked if they could take the beautiful Ruth ball and "add"—that was the word he used—Gehrig's signature to it.

If Wayne could have reached his hand through the phone and throttled Big Ricky's throat, he would have done it. It was a given that you could take a Ruth ball and increase its already substantial value by adding the sig of a star player associated with him in baseball history, someone such as Gehrig or Roger Maris or Mark McGwire. It was also a given that you never said anything like that over the phone, and as soon as the words came spilling out of Big Ricky's mouth Bray heard a click on the line.

A click. Like the phone was being tapped.

"You hear that?" he said. "It was like a clicking sound."

You had to be careful over the phone. Bray knew that, and as a member of the inner circle Big Ricky should have known it too. One reason they used nicknames was to confuse anyone in law enforcement who might be listening over the line. Last names were seldom mentioned. Often they referred to people only by initials—"W" for Wayne or "G" for Greg. Sometimes they combined an initial with a nickname: Little M, for instance. Little M could have been anyone with a first or last name beginning with M—Mike Lopez, Mike Moses, Jack Morgenstern, Rick Mitchell, perhaps even a Marino. Only those within the group would have known that Little M was Mike Bowler. Even better was not to use any name or initial at all. Just refer to the thing that needed to be done and leave it at that, assuming, of course, that when you referred to that thing you spoke in code as well, never saying the f-word or implying it. What you said was "take care of" or "authenticate" when referring to a blank piece of merchandise, and the guy on the other end got it because he was speaking with the same forked tongue. And you never, ever told someone to blatantly "add" Gehrig's signature to a Ruth ball because Gehrig had been a stiff for decades and anyone who did such a thing would obviously be committing a crime.

But Wayne could not say any of this to Big Ricky because that click might have meant that the authorities were listening in, and if that was the case, his words were being recorded too. So what he said, in a loud, exaggerated tone was: "Oh yeah, I'm on the PHONE with you," and this woke Big

Ricky up so they could get through the rest of the call without any more damaging comments.

This conversation turned out to be a pivotal one for the FBI. The judge's wiretap order was not open-ended; Halpern and Fitzsimmons had to report back to her every week or so to show that investigators were in fact finding evidence of criminal activity as they claimed they would. Unimpressed by what the FBI had discovered, Judge Huff shut down the wire for two days in January. Then the FBI produced the Bray-Weimer dialog about the Ruth ball. Big Ricky's loose talk changed her mind. The wire could go back on. Adam Lee and his colleagues could keep listening.

The wire turned FBI surveillance from cold to hot. Gone were the days when special agents sat around doing nothing special in the Smokewood Place neighborhood while Greg and John held a pizza party for their friends. The wire guys passed information to Fitzsimmons and McKinney, who passed it on to those in the field. Investigators now knew what the memorabilia boys were going to do before they did it. The wire also provided leads on some new and intriguing characters in the racket, guys they did not know about before, newcomers such as Mikey the Runner.

Mikey the Runner's real name was Michael Tapales. Also known as Little Mikey due to his small size, he was an LA guy who ran errands for Mike Moses. In the memorabilia trade, runners were people who hung around places where celebrities might be spotted—trendy restaurants, hotels, nightclubs, movie premieres—and collected their autographs. Runners do exist, but their main purpose in the industry may be to provide a convenient cover story for dealers when they are questioned about how they came to possess a bad autograph.

Where'd I get it? Oh, I got it from a runner.

Of course, if the person asking the questions doesn't buy that, dealers just invent another stretcher. Got it in trade. Got it in a private signing. Got it from the star's agent. Most fraudulent dealers have a scoundrel's love for a good story, saying whatever it takes to get the customer to go away and leave them alone.

Mikey the Runner may have collected genuine autographs but it was not how he made most of his money in the trade. That came from selling and distributing fakes, and FBI surveillance picked up his trail during a meet with John Marino outside an AM-PM mini-mart in Escondido. At this meet John was selling five 500 Home Run baseballs packaged in shrink wrap, an All-Star bat, a Yankee team bat, a Yankee legends bat and other signed merchandise. The agents watched as Mikey popped the trunk of his shiny new gold Taurus and stowed the stuff inside. Then he handed over the cash and as John was counting it out he walked across to a pay phone in the lot where he punched up W.W. Sports Cards. The FBI knew he was calling there because the wire guys heard Mikey come on the line asking how to buy certs for the material he was getting from John. Wayne wasn't there, so Mikey left a message that Bray picked up later. The next day, when Mikey flashed over to W.W. Sports Cards to pick up the certs, surveillance tagged along for that transaction too.

On this particular deal Mikey was representing Moses, whose partnership with Rino Ruberti had recently collapsed. The Sports Card Kid had split from Universal Authentic Memorabilia and gone off on his own, leaving Moses without someone to make the run between San Clemente and North County. So, for a time, Mikey the Runner took over the job, sporting up and down the sunswept coast with dollars in the form of autographs in the trunk of his Taurus. Unlike the handsome, smooth-gliding Rino, Mikey the Runner never got in good with the Marinos; he was strictly an outsider, meeting them at neutral locations well away from their house.

After getting the goods from John and the certs from Wayne, Mikey the Runner drove the order to the Camino de los Mares office of Universal Authentic Memorabilia. The FBI shadowed this deal too, picking up Moses as he loaded everything into his Suburban and took it over to Carrow's on Avenue Pico in San Clemente where he was seeing a client. The parking lot of Carrow's sits across a small ravine from San Clemente High, the home of the Tritons. Along the edge of the ravine is a row of Italian cypresses, and on the far side of the cypresses lies the vibrantly green baseball field where the Tritons play their home games. Here, within view of this youthful field of dreams, Moses delivered the shrink-wrapped balls and the other corrupted pieces to John Ferreira. The agent paid him with a $1,150 check and six grand in cash.

Another example of how the wire was suddenly making everything go smoother occurred a few days after Valentine's Day when the FBI heard Jack Morgenstern tell Bray about five "bad" Jackie Robinson and Roberto Clemente balls he had sold. These balls were truly bad because they had been manufactured after Robinson and Clemente had died—a fact Morgenstern learned the hard way: from the customer who had bought them from him. Unable to come up with a convincing explanation as to how the autographs of dead men could appear on balls made years after they stopped breathing, Jack had no choice but to refund every stinking penny of the guy's money.

It was embarrassing to be caught in a lie like that. Embarrassing, and potentially dangerous. Adding to the sting was being forced to cough up with a full refund, so the unhappy Morgenstern took his grievance to the Godfather of Memorabilia to see if he could get some justice.

Wayne was actually the original source for the balls. Unaware of the date of their manufacture, he had brought them unsigned to Greg. But Greg was blameless in the matter; his job was to sign, sign, sign, and leave authentication issues to the others. Wayne sold the balls to Mike Bowler, who assumed they were good when he sold them to Morgenstern, who assumed the same until his disgruntled customer pointed out otherwise. Having paid five hundred bucks apiece for what were now worthless forgeries, Jack was out $2,500 of his own money, not to mention all that potential profit that had slipped through his fingers.

Not only that, Jack's customer was so ticked off he had called Jim DiMaggio to hassle him about authenticating balls that were such obvious fakes. First DiMaggio denied issuing the certs, claiming with self-righteous indignation that he would have never bestowed his seal of approval on improperly autographed merchandise. When this story didn't quite take flight, he invented another one about how a batch of his company's blank certs had been stolen from his car. These certs, he speculated, must have been improperly filled out without his knowledge and passed on to the customer.

The Godfather of Memorabilia agreed that he and Little M should make good on Morgenstern's loss, which made Jack feel better. As for what to do about DiMaggio, well, that was another story.

Bray had recruited the personable ex-restaurateur to be part of the scam because of his famous last name, and DiMaggio had earnestly done his job, issuing certs for tens of thousands, if not hundreds of thousands, of Greg Marino products. But there was a difference between a good fake and a bad fake, or even a bad fake and a godawful fake, and DiMaggio either could not tell the difference anymore or no longer cared because he was certifying everything he saw, good, bad and godawful.

Wayne's unhappiness with DiMaggio's work, as well as DiMaggio's desire to run his own thing, caused another of the schisms that occurred so frequently in the racket. Splitting apart from the sham authentication company he had founded, Bray started another sham authentication company, Sports and Celebrity Authentic Autographs. Meanwhile his former partner stayed in business, retaining his company name and much of his old client list and regularly advertising in the trade journals to bring in more clients and maintain his cover as a legitimate business. "J. DiMaggio Company is an impartial and non-biased authenticating service, interested only in verifying that your signatures/autographs are genuine," reads one of his advertisements. As if to symbolize his company's impartial judgments, each ad carried a clip art image of the blindfolded figure of Justice, holding scales in one hand and a sword in the other.

DiMaggio was now competing against his former mentor in the authentication racket, but it wasn't much of a contest. Because of his headstart in the business, the clients he had developed and most importantly, that powerhouse name, the J. DiMaggio Company issued much more phony paper than Bray's rival start-up.

His refund in hand, Jack Morgenstern returned the bad Robinson and Clemente balls to Bowler, who quickly found a buyer for them: none other than John Ferreira, who was showing up in all the right places. Morgenstern had called Ferreira the day after Jack had spoken to Bray, pouring out his tale of woe not bothering to disguise the fact that the sigs on the balls were forgeries and their author was Greg Marino. Fascinated to learn that Morgenstern planned to give the balls back to Bowler, the agent called Bowler and negotiated a deal with him, saying that his Japanese clients would never notice the incorrect manufacture date. Ferreira paid $1,750 for the five balls, which ended their odyssey on a shelf in the Aero Drive warehouse.

This purchase completed a near-perfect circle of evidence for the FBI that included, significantly, recorded admissions by the crooks that they knew they were trafficking in fakes. Another aspect of the case that began to show results during this time was the financial investigation. Although a few insisted on cash only, Ferreira gave checks to most of his subjects. Even Dave Tabb, who regarded the agent's insistence on paying by check irritating and suspicious, accepted them from him. The agent's ability to pass on checks to the subjects allowed Maura Fahy, a special agent with the Criminal Investigation Division of the IRS, to track what was going on in their bank accounts.

Along with Fitzsimmons, McKinney, Halpern and Ferreira, Fahy was a core member of Bullpen's investigative team—the one female, the one non-jock. In her early thirties with long brown hair and a roundish face, Fahy, who carries a sidearm when on the job, worked in the same downtown San Diego building that houses the United States Attorney's Office. She frequently caught the elevator up to Phil Halpern's office because the IRS needed subpoenas to gain access to these normally confidential bank accounts, and Halpern was the one preparing the requests for the judge. Her primary FBI contact was Fitzsimmons. He took her on surveillance runs so she could get a sense of the people she was investigating—"so they weren't just names and numbers to me." She also listened to selected recordings and watched videotape to round out her understanding of the subjects.

Fahy described Fitzsimmons as "even keel. You have to push him pretty hard to get him mad. He doesn't get excited much." One area that did excite him—and Halpern and McKinney too—was all the big sports names involved in the case. "They were like little boys enjoying all the sports stuff. I didn't know sports or care," said Fahy, who once overheard the men discussing Ty Cobb.

"Who's Ty Cobb?" she asked.

"You don't know who Ty Cobb is?" came the astonished reply.

A movie buff, Fahy's interest landed on the celebrity side of things. Before joining Bullpen she was visiting her sister in Phoenix and they went to a movie together, stopping at a Hollywood Dreams display in the lobby. Her sister bought an autographed 8x10 of Tom Cruise. After becoming part of the investigation Maura had to tell her that her favorite star's signature was almost certainly bogus.

Fahy formally entered Operation Bullpen in the spring of 1998, just before the home run chase sent the memorabilia trade spinning crazily into overdrive. Designated by the IRS as a "primary investigation," meaning it was in a preliminary stage, she first had to answer a fundamental question: Did the IRS have a case against these people? Scouring property records and other publicly available information, she ran criminal background checks on the subjects and using their social security numbers, studied their returns on the not-publicly-available IRS computer system, comparing their declared income against what was known about the most lavish aspects of their lifestyle. She concluded without doubt that the free-spending memorabilia boys were hiding illegal income and not declaring it on their returns.

By November of that year Fahy felt confident about her case, and it moved into a full-blown subject criminal investigation. The preliminaries over, "I started building what I needed to build"—aided, two months later, by the onset of the wire taps. One of the things she started building was a spreadsheet that covered the known subjects and their web of financial activity. "Ferreira would write a check to a dealer, and we'd follow this check as it made its way through the banking system," she explained. " The bank marks routing numbers on the back of each check it processes. We could see the local bank branch where the check was drawn from, and we'd subpoena the records of this account. Gag orders were placed on the subpoenas because we didn't want to tip off anybody. Once we started looking at these accounts we could see what other activity was going on, and we found out who the Marinos and Bray were doing business with. Some of these people the FBI didn't know about. We told Tim about them, and they came under investigation too."

Federal law requires banks and savings institutions to report every cash transaction of $10,000 or more through a Currency Transaction Report, or CTR. People try to avoid having a CTR issued on them through a technique known as "structuring." They make cash deposits under the $10,000 limit but usually in a structured way—$5,000 this week, $8,000 the next, $6,000 three weeks after that. Fahy was hip to structuring, and watched for it in the accounts she was following.

The Marinos had four bank accounts, at least two of which were used to hide their illegal earnings. These accounts were in the name of Gloria and her daughter Andrea, who was married and living in New Hampshire. Chatting frequently with her mother from back East, Andrea knew how the rest of the family was making money out in sunny California. The wire tap recorded her giving advice to her mother on how to hide money, and she let Gloria use her name and social security number when Gloria set up these accounts.

The Marinos were "savvy enough to know they had to be careful," in Fahy's words, and they generally limited their cash deposits to one or two thousand dollars at a time. The most glaring exception to this exercise in caution occurred when Gloria made her $50,000 cash drop at the Palomar Savings and Loan to buy the land for the dream house. While Gloria served as bag lady for this transaction, the joint owners of the property were listed as Andrea and Greg Marino. The savings and loan issued a CTR for this deposit, and Fahy tracked it down and used it to build her case against the family.

Because the Marinos were so absorbed with the house—the topic came up frequently over the wire—it became a focus of the investigative team too. Surveillance agents snapped pictures and watched, with fascination, as the five-acre parcel was staked off for construction. Architects, engineers and the general contractor carrying rolled-up drawings under their arms walked the land, gesturing and talking amongst themselves. Heavy machinery rolled in to clear and grub the site. Boulders were moved and rises in the land leveled to create a pad for the two-story, 6,500-square foot mansion. The area chalked for the driveway was graded. A spot for a gardening cottage was cleared away. The isolated getaway in the hills became increasingly busy and noisy with the sounds of construction. Trucks carrying sheet rock and building materials negotiated the narrow mountain roads. Carpenters, laborers and other workmen moved about the land as the foundation was poured, the framing went up, and the roof was hammered into place.

The main architectural feature of the house was a grand central living room with high vaulted ceilings. Attached to this great room on either side were the two wings of the house with three bedrooms and four bathrooms downstairs. Two of these bedrooms were spacious master suites (one for Gloria and Angelo, one for Greg and Kathy), each of which opened onto the backyard patio and featured a private garden area and views of the hills. Upstairs was a three-bedroom, two-bath arrangement for John and his children. Two of the bedrooms led onto balconies with equally expansive views.

The grounds were to be bounded with high wrought-iron gates. A wide driveway would bring visitors up to an elegantly designed covered entry area, whereupon they would disembark from their vehicle, walk down a short path lined by flowers, and enter the front door into the great room with its majestic ceilings. The west wing of the house had a two-car garage; the east wing, two one-car garages and the detached garden cottage. The plans called for extensive landscaping of the grounds, a sculpture fountain in back and perhaps a vineyard in the outer areas. But the landscaping would be done last. The first order of business was the house. The family wanted it finished as fast as possible, and this meant paying cash, cash, cash to the men doing the job.

On February 23, Angelo Marino wrote an $8,000 check to the general contractor, a man named Victor Miller. On that same day Angelo made an $8,000 cash deposit to his bank account to supply the funds for the check. Two days later Angelo and Victor Miller held a phone conversation in which Angelo shared the good news that a county building official had been up to the house and it had passed an early inspection.

"Did it?" said Miller.

"Yeah," said Angelo.

"Right on."

Angelo then moved to another topic, one that he urgently needed to speak to Miller about: how he was going to pay him in the future. To pay the contractor, Angelo had been forced to put a chunk of cash in the bank, never a good idea if it could be avoided. But it turned out that Miller would have taken cash, which would have been much safer.

"Uh, you know I didn't know you wanted that," said Angelo, broaching the difficult subject. "Uh, you know, cash. So you coulda told me. I had to run to the bank. Put the cash in."

"Oh," said Miller. "Steve [Miller's associate] was just wondering where the coin was and I said I got a check. So he says, 'I thought this was a cash job,' and I said, 'Well, uh, I don't know…'"

"Nah," interjected Angelo, "I'll give you the [cash], if you want it that way. I'll give it to you. I had cash. I ran to the bank."

Miller understood. "Yeah. Then you're gonna go to the bank anyway. Just for the cash."

"Yeah, right."

"From now on…" Miller began, but Angelo anticipated what he was going to say and jumped ahead to the next question: "So, so, I'll give it to you?"

"Yeah," said Miller.

So their pact, in halting phrases, was struck; from then on cash was king. The foundation cost $45,000. The Marinos paid cash. The roof: $20,000. Cash. The windows: $39,000. Cash.

All this cash going out made Gloria shake her head. "Thirty-nine thousand for windows," she sighed. "I didn't pay that much for my first house."

Despite her amazement at the cost of things, she understood the benefits of dealing in cash. "Give them a little cash," she said. "That makes them very happy, you know what I mean?"

The Marinos paid the plumber with checks but also with cash, the cash being the thing that got them a lower price for the work being done. They felt that the construction price tag of $650,000 would have been much higher if they had paid for it by conventional means.

Angelo's chat with Victor Miller was picked up on the wire and relayed to Maura Fahy, who uncovered evidence of Angelo's cash deposit and the check written by Miller. Then, on the first of March, something came over the wire that startled everyone on the team.

It was a conversation between Wayne and Greg, and Wayne's voice crackled with nervous intensity. Gone was his customary bravado. In its place was genuine alarm and what sounded like fear. He had just found out about a federal investigation into the sale and distribution of counterfeit memorabilia, and it was real. No bullshit this time, he told Greg. They were in trouble.

18

"We need to talk," said Wayne.

The urgency in his voice made Greg pause. "Is this about bad things?" he asked.

"Potentially. It's some serious shit. But maybe we can come up with something."

It was close to noon. Wayne was at his shop and wanted to talk in person. Greg said he could meet him at two that afternoon. But not five minutes after they hung up Wayne's phone was ringing. It was Greg. He couldn't wait that long to find out what was going on. "You know you got me jumpy now," he said.

"You should be," said Wayne emphatically.

"This about Little M?" Greg asked, using the code name for Mike Bowler.

"Not particularly. But I'm not gonna be doing anything for him in the future." Wayne added, "We just need to sit down and talk."

Greg said he heard that all right. "We have to be smart and close. I'll shut everybody off for months if we need to."

The tip-off about an investigation had come in that morning's *Wall Street Journal*. "Pressure on eBay to police its service is likely to grow after the company's disclosure of a federal probe into transactions on its site," read the front page teaser in the What's New column. The article inside revealed that the federal government had asked eBay to "produce certain records… relating to an investigation of possible illegal transactions in connection with the company's website." The reporter didn't know what those illegal transactions were, and the government and eBay weren't saying, but you didn't have to be a rocket scientist to figure it out. Ebay had already thrown Lowell Katz and Barry Delit off the site because of complaints about what they were selling, and Mike Bowler and a bunch of others were using it to move tons of product. This was why Wayne no longer felt safe dealing with Bowler, and Greg said from now on the family wasn't messing with him either.

After hanging up with Wayne, Greg called his brother to tell him what was happening. Shocked and pissed, John expressed disgust for all the "Internet shit" that was mucking up the marketplace for them. But Greg pointed the finger at somebody else who was to blame for their problems. "DiMaggio will authenticate anything when he needs money. We should have never let him in. That was a big, stupid thing by Wayne."

Greg thought the J. DiMaggio Company was approving so many forgeries with so little regard for their quality that it couldn't help but draw the attention of the law. One thing he was sure about, though, was that DiMaggio was more at risk than they were. "They're not gonna look at the guy who's sellin' 'em or doin' 'em," he told his brother. "It's the guy authenticatin' 'em."

"I know," said John. "It's the guy authenticatin' 'em."

"Exactly. They're the crooked ones doing it."

"That's easy to figure out."

"Yeah it is," said Greg. "That's probably why it's so open though, 'cause everybody authenticates shit."

Authenticators included their names and phone numbers on their certification documents, making it easier for law enforcement to track forgeries back to them. Greg, on the other hand, just signed things, and it was harder to connect him to bad stuff, he felt, unless somebody was blabbing or being stupid. And could that somebody be DiMaggio? Or what about Little M and his pal Chip Lombardo? Or ornery old Shelly Jaffe? He sold on eBay too and he had a personal thing against Wayne to boot. Any one of a half-dozen or a dozen guys could have tipped off the feds and hell, might already be secretly working with them.

That's why they needed to "go out Appalachia," in Greg's words.* Get everyone together and hold a meeting and talk it out. Greg felt strongly all the core guys should be there, plus Rino Ruberti. "He's our only connection to LA. We gotta know what the hell's going on." He also felt that Rino needed to know how to handle Little M when they cut him off.

Greg and John decided to make a list of all the people they'd been dealing with, especially the heavy Internet players, and see what everybody thought—who they could trust and who they couldn't.

---

*The term is actually "Apalachin," referring to a 1950s meeting of Mafia bosses in which they came together to discuss business in the upstate New York town of Apalachin. Greg said he first heard the expression while watching the Billy Crystal mob comedy "Analyze This."

"We need to tighten up," Greg said. "Like when we do business over the phone. We need to automatically hang up when someone screws up."

The Apalachin meeting—or Appalachian, if you prefer—took place four days later at Coco's Café and Bakery at the Plaza Camino Real shopping center in Carlsbad. It was a warm overcast Friday morning, and Greg and John drove in together, standing outside by their car until the other guys showed up. Greg was bearded and rumpled in a T-shirt and sweats, and his big, mustachioed brother could have been his bodyguard. Typically somber and intense, Wayne pulled up in his Land Cruiser about the same time as the Marinos. He was in his work vehicle: no Mustang or Harley today. No flashy rings or gaudy baubles either. Today was all business.

Rino arrived in his familiar white Astro van with the temporary plates in the rear window, stepping out and greeting the others with a smile and thumb shakes all around. Nate the Skate hadn't come yet, which wasn't a problem. He was just running a little late. He'd be there.

One guy was missing, though. A guy who said he was going to be there. Someone remarked he may have been trying to skip out of it altogether. This didn't sit well with any of them, but especially Wayne. He had called this meeting, he and Greg, and they expected everyone to show. So where the hell was Little Ricky?

He was at home. His wife was at school and his new son, less than a year old, was at his grandparents. He wasn't in hiding, though in some ways it felt like it to him. Earlier that morning he had called Greg to confirm the time and place of the Apalachin but the truth was, he didn't want to go. "I thought it was stupid to have a meeting," said Mitchell. "I had my own thing and I wasn't stepping on anybody's toes. Why did I need to be there?"

He had even shared his concerns the night before with his wife. "There's something kinda weird going on," he told her, without being too specific about what the weirdness exactly was. "A bunch of the memorabilia guys are having this meeting and they want me to go, and I don't want to go."

His wife supported him fully. If you feel strongly about it, she told him, don't go.

His unease about the meeting mirrored his feelings about the racket in general. He had been in it for close to two years, sold hundreds of thousands of dollars in fakes, and he still couldn't get something that Jim DiMaggio had told him out of his head. He and DiMaggio had gotten to know each other through the racket, and Mitchell called him "a good guy" and "a smart man." DiMaggio evidently felt the same about Rick because one day he took him aside at the Vista office of J. DiMaggio Company. It was early evening and Mitchell, still in his insurance suit and tie, had stopped by on his way home from work to get some Marino fakes certified. After they finished their business the older man sat the younger man down and looked him straight in the eye.

"Rick," he said, "you're not like the other guys. You have the potential to make money in legitimate ways. I guarantee you this won't last. You have the chance to walk away from this. Do it. Get out of the business. Walk away."

This abrupt talk startled Little Ricky and on the drive home that evening, and for weeks and months afterwards, he thought long and hard about what DiMaggio said, though he ultimately chose to ignore it. How could he not? It is one thing, and quite a predictable thing at that, to repent from your criminal ways once you've been pinched. It is quite another thing to stop breaking the law if you've never been caught, even if you know what you're doing is wrong. While breaking the law DiMaggio was telling Little Ricky not to do what he himself was doing and apparently intended to keep right on doing because the money was so damn good.

And that was Little Ricky's dilemma, shared by all. How do you walk away from all that cash on the table when it's yours for the taking and nobody is stopping you? DiMaggio couldn't do it and neither could he. So he kept making money in his profitably quiet way, going up to Vegas on the weekends and gambling and partying away those long, hot desert nights.

On one of his trips to Vegas, Little Ricky brought up a big order of counterfeit stuff that his client-turned-friend was supposed to buy but couldn't—not enough coin. The client already owed him $15,000 from previous deals they'd done. Pile another ten onto that if he accepted this order, and he'd be into Rick for twenty-five grand and that was more than he could handle.

But the baseball card trader remembered that his friend had something of value in his garage. "What about the Ferrari?" Rick asked.

This was the candy-apple red two-seater that his client owned and the two of them had cruised the clubs with. "What about it?" said the client, not seeing where Rick was headed.

"It's worth about twenty-five, twenty-six, right?"

"Yeah, I suppose."

Rick made him a proposal: his Ferrari in exchange for the ten grand in new goods plus the fifteen they'd wipe off the back books. His friend chewed on it a while and finally said yeah, okay, count him in. They drew up an agreement and each of them signed it and it was done. Little Ricky claimed possession of his very own Magnum P.I. car, shipping it back home to San Diego where it mostly sat in the garage, a captive of his growing unhappiness with his secret life.

It—the unhappiness, the guilt, the sense that he was badly messing up his life—had been present from the beginning, but in his mind he had compartmentalized it to some degree. There was Little Ricky, the peddler of counterfeits, the gambler, the party boy; and there was Rick Mitchell, college graduate, respectable businessman, husband and father. This last development, the birth of his son, was what changed everything, broke down all the compartments he had carefully created to separate the Rick Mitchell side of his life from the Little Ricky side.

What a father he was! What a role model! He felt like such a louse when he thought about the damage he was doing to his wife, the mother of his child, and their relationship. But at least that part of his plan he could feel good about: After all this time she still didn't suspect a thing about the Little Ricky side of him.

But after the birth of his son he had steadily become a little more like the man his wife believed he was. His Vegas trips became less frequent, in part because she needed him around the house more but also because he wanted to be there, changing diapers, feeding his kid, helping out at night, doing whatever, just to be around his son and wife and spending time with them. While he still liked going to Vegas, still got a charge out of gambling, it wasn't quite the same. Something had turned inside him.

The Ferrari represented this change. Cruising down the Strip in it seemed natural and right; back home with his wife and kid, it seemed out of place and wrong. He took a few spins around town in it but most of the time it remained shuttered from view with the garage door down. He preferred for others not to see it because he preferred they not see that side of him. Similarly, he was sick of the racket, sick of the lying and the secrecy and the gnawing fear in the pit of your stomach that any minute the cops were going to find you out and toss your sorry ass in jail. It had been a helluva ride, no question, but more and more he was beginning to think the ride was just about over. And deserved to be. He wanted to come clean with his wife and go back to being Rick Mitchell, full-time. But how? How could he do that?

His phone rang. He picked it up. It was Wayne, breathing fire.

"Get over here," he told him. "Now. If you don't get your ass over here, you will never see me and Greg again. We will cut you off."

After Rick's first memorabilia trip to Vegas, the first time he had sold forgeries, Wayne had threatened him if he tried to get between him and Greg. This message was similarly harsh. This wasn't kid stuff. This was real, man. Get your ass over here.

Reluctantly, Little Ricky got in his car and drove over to the meeting. His house wasn't far from Coco's, and he showed up in only a few minutes. The guys were still standing by their cars waiting for him. Greg, his best friend in the group, greeted him warmly. Wayne barely acknowledged him. Nate had still not appeared but they decided to get a table and he could meet them inside.

Entering Coco's, there was a cash register in front. A sign said, Please wait to be seated, and a stand against a wall held a stack of newspapers for sale. No one took one. The cash register sat on top of a glass cabinet with bakery goods displayed on shelves inside it. One of Coco's selling points is its pies, and a selection—apple, boysenberry, cherry, Dutch apple, banana cream, chocolate cream, lemon meringue—was arrayed on the shelves. This morning the cabinet also featured crumble-topped coffee cake, scones and muffins.

A hostess greeted them. To the left of the register was a window section with four small booths that looked out on the parking lot. There was also countertop seating here. With five in their party and one more on the way, neither of these areas was appropriate, so the hostess asked them to follow her. Along the front of the restaurant was a long rectangular section that consisted of four tables and booths—again, too small and crowded an area for their party, an assessment the hostess made in an instant as she led them into the main dining room.

This room featured two smaller booths on the wall to the left, tables in the center and four large window booths along the far wall. One of these booths was clearly the best place for a party of six to sit, but as the group stood awkwardly in the center of the room waiting for the hostess to direct them, they could see as well as she that there were no seats for them. All the booths were occupied.

What they did not realize was that the booths were occupied by FBI.

In one booth, a man and a woman posed as a married couple. FBI. In the booth next to them, another man and woman. FBI. In the other booths in the room, more FBI. And in the tables in the center, still more FBI. In all, fourteen undercover agents—seven women, seven men—sat in this section of Coco's.

One of them was Jeff McKinney, wearing sunglasses and a baseball cap pulled down on his forehead. Since he had done surveillance on Bray and the Marinos, he figured it was possible they might recognize his face. But neither Bray nor the Marinos were paying any attention to him; they just wanted to sit down.

McKinney had coordinated the surveillance for the meet, which the FBI knew about in advance, of course, because of the wire taps. The plan, as he said, was "to pack the restaurant with agents," a plan it carried out successfully—too successfully, as it turned out. With the main dining room jammed with diners ("It was their best morning in years," joked McKinney), the staff at Coco's, which had no inkling of the drama being played out in its restaurant that morning, opened the rear dining room. And so the hostess led the group into this separate section, leaving behind McKinney in his cap and shades and thirteen other chagrined federal agents.

Between the main dining room where the agents sat and the rear dining room where their subjects were being seated, two large wait stations stood against either wall. Containing silverware, racks of dishes, a coffeemaker and beer and wine taps, these stations had wooden partitions around them that were so massive that, except for a small aisle in the middle where people could pass, they formed an almost solid wall. The result was that the agents could not see or hear what was going on in the rear dining room, rendering them useless. All they could do was sit there and have breakfast like the regular couples they supposedly were.

Fortunately for the FBI, McKinney, whose undercover philosophy was to expect the unexpected, adapt to the changes and roll on, had a backup plan. Waiting until the gang was comfortably settled, he casually slid his long legs out from under his table, walked back across the restaurant past the cash register and down the aisle of the small window section that looked out onto the parking lot. Just beyond this section was an alcove with restrooms and a pay phone on the wall. McKinney did not use his cell because he wanted everything to look normal in case one of the subjects happened to go to the bathroom and see him. He slipped two quarters into the slot and dialed the cell phone of Jake Gregory, a tall, slender, brown-haired FBI agent with horn-rim glasses. McKinney told him what had happened and what needed to be done.

"Come in," he said. "Be close."

FBI surveillance had watched as the gang pulled into the Coco's lot. Once they went inside eight to ten more agents staked out the shopping center in case they were needed. Gregory was one of those agents. So was Tim Fitzsimmons. Both were paired with female agents on the thinking that it was less suspicious for a couple to be out for breakfast on a Friday morning, rather than a man by himself.

Gregory's partner was Caroline Hoag who, like the other agents, worked in the white collar crime squad of the San Diego FBI. But until this moment she had not taken part in Operation Bullpen and knew little about it. "My knowledge of the case was not extensive," she said. "I didn't know the names of the subjects. But I was on the same squad as Tim and Jeff, and agents often help out other agents at big moments in a case. And I knew this was a big moment. These were the kingpins of the fraud racket in southern California, and they were going to have a sit-down."

Dressed casually ("like what you would expect if you were eating at Coco's."), with blondish hair and soft features, Hoag has the pleasant, almost bland appearance of a white middle class suburban homemaker—certainly not someone one would suspect of being FBI. She and the professorial-looking Gregory were the first of the outside couples to enter, following the same route traveled by the memorabilia boys past the fourteen agents having pancakes and eggs in the main dining room. But when they reached the rear room and the hostess tried to seat them at a booth too far away from the subjects, Gregory, thinking fast, complained that the bench seats aggravated his bad lower back and could they please sit at a table? The hostess obligingly put them at a table right next to the group, in a perfect position to hear what they were saying. As the hostess gave them their menus and explained that their waitress would be along in a minute, Gregory and Hoag said nothing, each of them unfolding a copy of that morning's *Union-Tribune* and turning to the section with the crossword puzzle in it.

In a moment or two Fitzsimmons and his partner came in and sat down near Gregory and Hoag, followed by another pair of agents who did the same. The FBI had the gang nearly surrounded, and the gang didn't suspect a thing.

For Fitzsimmons, this was a moment of some emotion, though you couldn't tell it by his face or anything he did or said. He and his partner inspected the breakfast menu, their waitress brought them coffee, and he ordered a short stack of pancakes. After the waitress left, taking their menus with her, they, too, became absorbed in their newspapers as Fitzsimmons sneaked glances at the men he had been chasing for more than two years.

Even with the wire providing access into the gang's private conversations, there was still some confusion within the FBI about who was who. Not Bray and the Marinos but other guys such as the two Rickys: Who was Little and who was Big? At times the wire agents were not clear which one was being referred to over the phone. But now, sitting only a few paces away from them, Fitzsimmons knew exactly who he was dealing with: bearded Greg and brother John, blond-haired Rino, clean-cut Rick, and finally joining the table and taking an empty chair that had been saved for him, Nate Harrison. Dressed in a T-shirt and jeans, with long brown hair and a baby face, he was the youngest in the group.

At the head of the table, running the meeting, was Wayne. Broomstick-skinny, he was not an imposing figure except, somehow, he was. The way he spoke and carried himself suggested authority and power. Among these guys, within this group, he was clearly strong, an intimidator. The other commanding presence at the table belonged to Greg, whose manner was more easy-going than that of his tightly-wound partner but equally strong in his way. He was loud and gruff at times and because of who he was and what he did, they all deferred to him, including Wayne.

Since the onset of the wire taps Fitzsimmons had listened to some of the tapes, particularly if Adam Lee or someone else had told him about a good conversation he needed to hear. But in the days leading up to the Apalachin all the tapes were good, and he listened constantly. "They were nervous," said the case agent. "They were getting panicky."

Leaning slightly over from his table to try to hear what they were saying, he picked up snippets of dialog about the *Journal* article and eBay. Fitzsimmons himself had been in touch with eBay in recent months, as well as the New York Department of Consumer Affairs which was conducting a separate fraud investigation into certain eBay sellers. Some of these sellers were familiar names to Fitzsimmons, who had begun trading information with eBay attorney Rob Chestnut and a company investigator, Kevin Kamimoto. While counterfeit dealers relished the anonymity they had online, they could not escape one routine aspect of modern commerce: the credit card. Ebay required that every dealer provide a valid credit card number (as well as the name of his Internet service provider). The company's listing fee and sales commission were charged against the card. In an attempt to conceal their real name and address, dealers often used aliases and P.O. boxes, but they could not easily get around the credit card requirement. Once eBay captured this information, together with the subpoena powers of the government, investigators could trace the sales activity of the most suspicious dealers. Since these transactions were computerized, the details of every deal done on the site—date of the auction, names of the seller and buyer, what was sold and for how much, the credit card info—flowed into the company database. In the early days of the scam a match or paper shredder could make past business disappear. But in eBay's chunk of cyberspace there was no destroying of records; everything you did there was more or less permanent. This data, summarized "down to the penny" in Fitzsimmons's admiring words, was transferred to a disk and shipped to his office on Aero Drive in San Diego.

The waitress returned with their order, and Fitzsimmons put down his paper and started in on his pancakes. But it was frustrating for him. Now that Nate had arrived and the talk had begun in earnest, he was too far away to hear the details of what they were saying. The agent in the best position was Caroline Hoag, who could hear them clearly except for the elderly couple talking in her ear.

"That was the one annoying thing," she said. "A couple of senior citizens were sitting near me and talking really loud. It made it hard for me to hear. I wanted to get them out of there."

But the seniors were actual Coco's diners, not FBI agents, and Hoag could not shut them up without drawing attention to herself. So she concentrated harder without making it appear she was concentrating at all, pretending to do a crossword puzzle. The crossword gave her a plausible reason to be holding a pencil and writing things down. What she was actually doing was writing down what the fellows were saying.

So were Gregory, Fitzsimmons, his partner and the other FBI couple when they were not eating. Solving the crossword puzzle was a popular activity that morning in the rear room of Coco's.

Coco's Friday special consisted of two eggs cooked to order, a choice of bacon, sausage or turkey patties, buttermilk pancakes, hash brown potatoes, toast, muffin or biscuit and crumble-topped coffee cake. Hoag ordered breakfast because not to do so would have looked wrong, but she passed on the special and had something light. When her food came she only nibbled at it, absorbed as she was in her crossword puzzle charade and straining to hear what was being said at the next table over the noise of waitresses coming and going, the loud older couple, innocuous pop songs playing over the Coco's sound system, and dishes occasionally clattering at the wait stations. For her, this was "the gotcha moment" of the case. Several times while she was writing things down in the margins of her paper she thought, "Oh, this is good. This is really good," because the men were openly discussing their criminal activities.

This was most satisfying for her—the fact they did all this loose talk in front of her. "The meeting was held to discuss strategy so they could be united against law enforcement," she said. "The idea that they would think so little of a female that they would be boisterous and talk about what they were doing in front of me, and then to have no clue that this female was listening to them and taking notes on what they said. That was fun."

All of the subjects were having breakfast except for the clean-cut one, who was nervously drinking coffee. Since she did not know their names she assigned each of them a number based on their seating position at the table. When that person said something, she scribbled his number down next to his quote. It was impossible to write down everything they said, so she made sure to get the most damning statements. She heard Nate Harrison say, "There are too many things going on. It's not normal." He was referring to the unusually high number of complaints he was receiving for the merchandise he'd been selling. Everybody got complaints now and then but a whole bunch of his clients had been ragging on him lately. It wasn't right, and it bugged him.

She heard Wayne describe Shelly Jaffe as "scary," which made Greg ask, "Scary how? Scary FBI?"

Wayne's contempt—and distrust—for Shelly was plain. Originally able to buy directly from Greg, Shelly had lost this privilege after Wayne had assumed control of much of Greg's business affairs early in the enterprise. But their dislike for each other started to get in the way of making money, an unacceptable development, and Wayne turned Shelly's account over to Nate. This was fine with Shelly, and Nate liked it too because with Jaffe's orders now coming through him, it put more money in his pocket. Gradually the grizzled veteran took a liking to the kid, and he and Nate often talked business and called each other to yuck it up when they saw their bogus products being hawked on TV.

Being friends, Nate stuck up for Shelly and vouched for him. You didn't have to worry about him going over to the FBI.

Greg admitted to feeling paranoid. He told a story about how he was sure he was being followed the other day in his car. The guy behind him was right on his tail, slowing when he slowed, turning when he turned. Finally at a stop light Greg started yelling at him like in a road rage incident. But the guy wasn't the law; he just happened to fall in behind Greg in traffic.

One person's name who did not come up in the discussion was John Ferreira. A major source of suspicion early on, he was no longer seen as a threat to them. Besides, no one at the table did business with him. They were more worried about their own clients, agreeing as a group to cut loose anyone who seemed suspicious and not bring in any new people until things cooled down.

Wayne recommended taking it one step further: shut things down for a while. "Let's not call it off but take some time off," he said.

Greg thought this was a good idea and so the others went along with it, although his brother wasn't keen on it. "It's a pain in the ass," said John. "But I'll do whatever it takes to keep Greg happy."

Worried about being caught with a bunch of fakes if the law came calling, Little Ricky asked what he should do with the stuff he was storing in his house.

"Get it out of your house," Wayne told him.

"Should I bury it?"

"Yeah. Bury it and put it somewhere for twenty years. You and your kid can dig it up."

This drew some laughs that quickly died away. They had been living a kind of bubble life, working their scam for years without being caught. In certain moments some of them felt they'd never be caught. Now, the threat of an investigation—no, it was not a threat, it was happening—had jolted them all. The bubble appeared ready to burst.

But it hadn't—not yet. And maybe it never would if they stayed tight and smart and let things chill for a while. Wayne proposed taking a month off. After that, they'd see how they felt, see how things looked. They all agreed to that. In the meantime they'd look into hiring an attorney to represent them as a group if the law made a move against any one of them.

"Okay, this is it," Wayne said. "Everything at this table stays here. And if we're approached by law enforcement, we have two words for them: 'Fuck you.'" As if to underline the point, speaking loud enough so that every diner in the room could hear him, he added:

"Fuck the FBI!"

Breakfast over, their meeting done, the guys stood up, tossed some bills on the table for a tip and left. When they passed through the main dining room an undercover couple stood up with them and nonchalantly followed them to the cash register as they paid their bill. Then when the gang stepped outside to their vehicles, surveillance agents took their photographs.

Back inside the restaurant, Hoag went straight to Fitzsimmons, who drew a diagram of who was sitting where and supplied the names of each. She then matched the number she had given each subject with his name, furiously writing down everything she remembered them saying before she forgot it. Gregory and the other agents in the room did the same, cleaning up their scribbled notes and writing down everything they had heard.

The subjects having departed, the agents in the main dining room started filing out too, stopping to pay their bills at the register before heading out to the parking lot. But the kingpins of the southern California fraud racket did not immediately drive away once they left the restaurant. Wayne, Greg, John, Nate, Rick and Rino were still standing by their vehicles, shooting the breeze with one another, when all these men and women started pouring out of Coco's at the same time. They walked out to their cars, got in and drove off almost as a group. All the guys noticed this and thought it was kinda weird. But there were so many weird things going on lately no one gave it another thought.

19

Afterwards Greg drove home and called his dad. Everything went well, he told him, except he was sure someone tailed him from Coco's.

The wire guys listened in on this call, and it produced still more satisfaction for the FBI. Surveillance units did in fact follow a few of the Apalachin's participants, but not Greg. Coupled with his admission about road rage, the master forger with the confident pen strokes was clearly feeling shaky. And based on what they had said at their breakfast sit-down, his pals were feeling a little jumpy too.

"They had the feeling they were being watched," said McKinney. "And they were."

The pressure on Greg came not only from the FBI, whose presence he could vaguely sense but not confirm, but also from the people seated around him at the table that morning. These and so many other guys in the racket depended on him; if he didn't work, nobody made money. Some of them had families and small children, mortgages and bills. Lots of them came to him in a panic because they'd gotten into a jam with their bookie or whatever and needed money in a hurry. All were running businesses, in some cases million dollar businesses, built on him and his productivity. Their demands were simple but extreme. Sign, sign, sign.

Greg's family had also come to rely heavily on him. His gifted right arm had brought them money and things, with the promise of more money and things to come. The *Bada Bing* floated on a sea of falsity; so, too, did the cruiser they were planning to replace it with: The *Casa La Mare* or Castle on the Sea, named after the area in Sicily where Greg's grandparents had lived. This custom-built, forty-two-foot Maxum was to contain a satellite dish, bait tanks and other special features for fishing and partying. Its cost: $350,000. The Marino brothers planned to trade in the *Bada Bing*, put down a hundred grand in cash and take out a loan for the rest, paying it off as fast as Greg's pen would let them.

Putting more heat on him was the house, always the house. Indeed everyone in the family was sacrificing for this Castle on the Land, working harder and longer hours and taking less money to make it happen. Ordinarily Gloria split the take three ways between the three branches of the family, but the high cost of construction forced her to cut back on each person's income and pour the savings into the house. "We were paying off the house as it was being built," said Greg. "I never saw a lot of cash during that time. I had spending money but most everything I was making was going into the house to get it done."

Greg, the first-born son, was providing everything for everybody, and he felt the burden of their expectations. If they were going to finish the house and buy the new boat and do all the other things they dreamed of, it was up to him. If his parents were going to truly retire and live free of worry in the comfort and ease they deserved, it was up to him. And if none of these things happened, whose fault would it be?

Some days Greg signed from the moment he got up in the morning until he fell into bed dead-tired at night. The intensity of his workload matched the intensity of the demands on him, and he started getting into crystal. "When I had to go fifteen hours straight and all this stuff had to be done in a day," he said, "I didn't have a problem with doing a line of crystal to get through it all." Pot was still a constant, used mainly to help him relax. The crystal was to keep him going and going and going, and it did. In the process it destroyed what remained of the craftsman's pride and pleasure he had once taken in his work. All he cared about was moving the crap through. Garbage in, garbage out.

On March 8, three days after the Apalachin, Greg had one of those days when he went fifteen hours straight and needed crystal to get through it all. That was the day Joe DiMaggio died, and the gang, despite its agreement to suspend operations for a month, sprang back into action. That morning Stan the Man ordered a thousand DiMaggio baseballs from Wayne, who turned around and called his local equipment supplier for the blanks. But the supplier, thinking along the same lines as everybody else, first wanted to know if Wayne wanted to buy some signed DiMaggio baseballs.

"Are they certified?" Wayne asked.

"Sure," said the supplier. "Every one of them comes with a cert from Stan's Sports Memorabilia."

Greg had almost certainly signed these balls and Wayne had sold them to Stan. He certified them and sold them to another party who sold them to Wayne's supplier. The supplier was now trying to sell them back to Wayne, complete with Stan's certs. Wayne declined the offer but did take every blank ball the guy had in stock.

Starting with Mickey Mantle, the guys had made a killing with the death of every prominent celebrity. Another example of this occurred in May 1998 when Frank Sinatra sang his last song. That day or soon thereafter Bray rolled up to Beaumont Glen with a thousand or so Sinatra 8x10s in the back of his Land Cruiser. Greg, who had already heard the sad, uplifting news, was ready for him, blasting "New York, New York" out of the open windows of his apartment. With Frank providing the background tunes, they polished off those thousand photos and plenty more after that.

Like Sinatra, DiMaggio suffered through a long and well-publicized illness, and autograph racketeers across the country, hoping for the worst, had stocked up on Joe D. merchandise. After it was announced that the Greatest Living Yankee was no more, they pounced, and Joe D. photos and balls flooded a market already brimming with Joe D. fakes.

The Land Cruiser arrived at Greg's with six hundred blank baseballs, four hundred DiMaggio 8x10s, four dozen blank helmets and six dozen blank bats. Remembering how he had motivated Greg after Mantle, Wayne said that if Greg filled Stan's order he could do better than an Explorer and buy a new Expedition.

"I tagged Stan's card for $20,000 after that one," said Wayne. Suddenly back in overdrive, he and the guys loaded up Greg's apartment and Smokewood Place with gaggles of Joe D. merchandise. Rocking and rolling on crystal, Greg pumped it out. Over the wire the FBI got a sense of how busy things were when Gloria remarked to Andrea that their garage was crammed full with merchandise because "J.D." had died.

"Who's J.D.?" asked Andrea.

When Gloria told her it drew a sarcastic laugh. "Yeah," said Andrea. "Everyone will believe he signed all those things before he died."

"Shut up!" said Gloria, knowing how dangerous it was to talk like that over the phone.

But Andrea didn't like being told to shut up and said so. "I'm getting nauseous about everyone talking in code all the time," she told her mother.

The women switched to more pleasant topics and talked about the dream house. Gloria said she had hidden $100,000 in cash to help pay for its construction. When dealing with contractors, she explained, there were "certain things I can pay by check and certain things I've been paying by ca—" She stopped suddenly, hearing her sons come in the front door. Not wanting them to hear her talking about such things over the phone, she said, "Oh, let me go. They're back," and hung up.

This was the last significant conversation recorded by the FBI in March and well into April. After the DiMaggio death boom, the memorabilia boys made good on their vow and ceased operations. Since there was no reason to keep listening if there was nothing to listen to, the FBI shut down its taps on Bray and the Marinos. Suddenly, everything went silent.

With the wire turned off and no one in the FBI certain when it would be turned back on, if ever, the investigation shifted its focus back to John Ferreira and his ongoing campaign against the outer ring of subjects. One of these subjects was Jim Bellino, whose name had surfaced earlier in the investigation during the California attorney general's raid of Hollywood Dreams. The state had used Bellino to determine if some of the things being sold by Dave Tabb were bogus, not knowing that Bellino himself was authenticating and selling fakes. Chip Lombardo and Mike Bowler had introduced Bellino to Ferreira, and among the items the agent had bought from him were two forged Babe Ruth balls for $6,700. Each of these balls carried a COA from Forensic Document Services, Bellino's company.

Ferreira had visited Bellino's office in Orange but come away without any admissions. "I tried the nice guy approach but it didn't work," said the agent. "He was close-mouthed, a tough cookie to crack."

So Ferreira and his colleagues in the FBI decided to see if there was another way to get the cookie to crumble. At the time Mark McGwire was at the height of his fame, having just set the single season home run record. In January 1999, his seventieth home run ball had sold at a New York auction for more than $3 million, still the most ever paid for a single piece of sports memorabilia. Conveniently for investigators, McGwire lived in the off-season in Newport Beach, about a twenty-five minute hop down the freeway from Orange.

Fitzsimmons contacted the player's representatives, who relayed the information that the FBI wanted to speak to him. When the FBI calls people usually listen, and McGwire invited Fitzsimmons over to his home in Newport Beach. On this occasion, and two other times during the off-season, the agent arrived with some of the McGwire-signed merchandise acquired during the investigation. "He looked at tons of Riddell mini-helmets and Cardinal batting helmets, all signed on the bill of the helmets," said Fitzsimmons. "There were baseballs, jerseys, photos. One time I spread out a bunch of bats for him to see at his agent's office. He said, 'I haven't signed that many bats in years.' He appeared to be staggered by how much bad stuff there was."

Every single thing McGwire inspected—every bat, every helmet, every jersey, every photo—was fake, and many of them had been certified by Forensic Document Services. Angry, he said, about all the kids who were being ripped off in the scam, the slugger agreed to cooperate in a plan to catch the authenticator.

The scheme had a few steps to it. First Ferreira wrote and signed a $20,000 check made out to McGwire's charitable foundation for children. He never made this contribution; it was a sham. On the memo line of the check, it read, "Charity." The FBI made a poster-sized copy of the check so it was big enough for two people to hold and the names and the amount could be seen clearly. Ferreira and Fitzsimmons then drove up to the Long Beach office of Jim Milner, McGwire's business agent who managed the foundation and was also in on the scheme. Milner and Ferreira held the check between them and smiled as Fitzsimmons took a picture of them. Additionally, Milner composed a letter on foundation stationery, later signed by McGwire, thanking Ferreira for his generous gift.

The next step was to take some pictures of McGwire and Ferreira together. The 1999 baseball season was now under way and the Cardinals were in Los Angeles for a weekend series against the Dodgers. So Ferreira and Fitzsimmons, joined by McKinney and Halpern, journeyed up to Dodger Stadium to see McGwire before the Friday night game. They all dressed casually and badged their way into the visitors' locker room. But when they appeared, McGwire, his shirt off and his game face on, didn't recognize them. He had never seen Fitzsimmons out of a suit and he thought they were sportswriters. "What do you want?" he barked.

Fitzsimmons identified himself and McGwire remembered, and things went more smoothly from there.

After McGwire threw on a black sleeveless T-shirt, the five of them retreated into a training room and closed the door. First Ferreira and McGwire posed for their fake buddy picture. Then McGwire signed two baseballs—one with his name, the other with the inscription: "To John Thanks for everything Mark McGwire." Their business done, the prosecutor and the agents got to be fans for a moment. Ferreira, Fitzsimmons and McKinney posed for a picture with McGwire who, in a gesture of camaraderie, threw his arms around Ferreira's and McKinney's shoulders. Halpern did the picture-taking, then received his own keepsake. Having brought along a photo of McGwire hitting his record-breaking seventieth, McGwire signed it for him. Ferreira had also brought a *Sports Illustrated* with McGwire on the cover, and the slugger inscribed it to Ferreira's daughter. Bidding their new friend goodbye, the investigators stayed around for the game and saw one of McGwire's teammates, Fernando Tatis, achieve a first in baseball history by hitting two grand slams in the same inning. St. Louis won in a romp, 12 to 5.

The feds next moved to their target. Since Ferreira's usual demeanor had been a bust with Bellino, his colleagues argued for a change in approach—harder, tougher, more like a criminal. The ever-agreeable UCA said he'd give it a whirl, and on his next visit to Forensic Document Services he came on like a major asshole. Swearing and bragging and dropping the f-word all over the place and parading around with the two signed McGwire balls and the pictures of him and McGwire and him and Milner with the $20,000 check, Ferreira said he knew that all the garbage he was buying was bad and that all his customers knew it too. So to cover his ass he had dumped a load of money into Big Mac's foundation. You know, to help the kids. All that crap.

Trying to close the deal, Ferreira told Bellino he should do the same—make a donation—because he was dealing lots of forgeries too, right?

If he was, he wouldn't say. The cookie still would not crumble. All this tough talk made Bellino nervous or, as the agent put it, "hinked up." Failing once more to crack his subject, Ferreira took his balls and photos and left, and the hinked-up owner of Forensic Document Services was undoubtedly happy to see him go.

Later Ferreira framed the McGwire foundation letter and the photo of him and Milner, and posted them on the wall of the Nihon Trading Company. In a visit to Nihon one day, Dave Tabb noticed the picture and asked the agent about it. With his mind on something else, or just not thinking like a UCA in that moment, Ferreira dismissed the check merely as a tax write-off and said nothing more about it. If there had been a chance to snare Tabb in the net originally set for Bellino, the agent had blown it. Afterwards he apologized to Fitzsimmons for his lapse.

The Bellino episode was a reminder of the undercover problems encountered by the FBI before the wire taps. But by mid-April the flip-flop mafia had resumed business as usual, and the wire clicked back on.

Once again the wire guys started hearing incriminating chatter: Gloria telling Greg that John had "prepped" a shipment of blanks and they were ready for him to sign; Greg telling John to bring the black books over to his place, adding that he had worked five hours the day before and made three thousand bucks and that John's cut was ten percent; and Gloria and her daughter chattering about money, Andrea estimating that her mother was making $10,000 a week.

"Yeah," said Gloria, and Andrea put a point on it: "You're making money hand over fist."

On April 21, Bray's voice came on the line in a conversation with Gloria. She told him they were raising their prices on team-signed material because it represented a lot of extra work for Greg—multiple sigs on a single piece of merchandise, compared to one sig on one piece. Further, they were raising the prices for vintage cuts as well, saying that all cuts would cost the same regardless of when a player had died.

Startled by these new prices, Wayne argued that a player who had died recently should cost less than a player who had been dead a long time.

"Yeah," said Gloria, "but they're dead." Dead was dead, in her view. Whether a person died last week or last century made no difference to her. Besides, she said, Rino had been paying these higher prices all along and the family wanted to bring everyone else in line.

The price increase came up again with Gloria and Big Ricky Weimer, who wasn't happy about it either. But, he said, at least he wasn't crying about it like Wayne. "Why would I cry? I don't need a hundred, two hundred jerseys done. He [Bray] made a million dollars. I didn't make no million dollars."

Never one to shy away from good gossip about money, Gloria speculated that Stan the Man had made $10 million in the racket. Big Ricky agreed this was possible, saying that Stan had made gargantuan money selling gargantuan amounts of crap on cable TV. He added that he had sold lots of crap on cable, too.

Another member of the inner circle, Dick Laughlin, could be heard whining about the new prices, but by this time Gloria had run out of patience. She told Greg that for all she cared, Laughlin could take his business to Mike Lopez.

The FBI could only speculate why Gloria, who had always been tough in dealing with the boys in the racket, appeared to be in such an uncompromising mood. If they wanted to play, she seemed to be saying, they had to pay. Raising prices reflected the need for more money because of the dream house, but it also suggested that after the Apalachin she had developed a case of the nerves too. This was a dangerous game they were playing, and in the past two months it had gotten more dangerous. But even she did not anticipate how dangerous it was about to become.

20

The phone rang in Phil Halpern's office in the Federal Building. Calling him was an attorney named Ray Gomez, with an office in North County. It was a busy day and the AUSA had a million things on his mind, and in a distracted tone he asked what he could do for him.

Gomez replied that he was representing a major figure in what he believed was a federal investigation into counterfeit sports memorabilia.

This got Halpern's attention fast, though he stayed cool. "How'd you get my name?" he said, sounding disinterested.

Gomez said he got it from a friend who knew the AUSA from his past steroid prosecutions. Halpern, the friend said, was the man who handled the big sports cases at DOJ. If there was a federal investigation being conducted into counterfeit sports memorabilia, Halpern figured to be at the center of it.

"I don't comment on investigations," said Halpern. "Now tell me why you called and I'll see if I can help you."

Gomez explained that his client was a member of the inner circle. He had intimate, firsthand knowledge of the activities of the conspiracy. He was a husband and father who felt that his actions were hurting his family and wrecking their lives. He had grown tired of the lying and deceit and the feeling of always being watched and never being able to trust anyone, and he had experienced a real change of heart. For these reasons, and more, he was ready to cooperate with the government in its investigation.

Halpern thought, "There must be a leak. Somehow, someone has found out about the investigation and it is no longer a secret." But he said none of this to Gomez. Instead he took down his number and still playing it cool, said he'd get back to him after he discussed the matter with his colleagues.

As soon as Halpern got off the phone he punched in the number for Tim Fitzsimmons. "Tim," he said. "We got a problem."

He recounted his conversation with the attorney, saying a major figure in Bullpen had decided to come forward. The agent got it instantly. He hung up with Halpern and called McKinney, and the three of them dropped everything else in their schedules to meet in Halpern's office that afternoon. The first crucial issue they had to resolve was whether or not to reveal the fact of the investigation to Gomez and his client.

"This was a huge decision," said Halpern. "You don't say, 'Oh, this is a unique and wonderful opportunity.' You must address this problem immediately. Something like this could blow the whole case. Years of work and more time and surveillance than you can imagine could go up in smoke. Once we confirmed there was an investigation, there was a potential for disaster. If the subject decided not to cooperate he could tell everybody. He could make one phone call and coast to coast people would stop doing business in a minute. End of story. End of investigation."

Even if the investigators agreed to meet with the subject, and a meeting occurred, that did not necessarily guarantee his cooperation. He might not like what the government had to say and decide not to accept its offer. Having had the existence of an investigation confirmed to him, he could walk out and make that call to his associates. They could then destroy evidence, get out of the racket, go underground. Similar things had happened in other cases Halpern had worked on. "You gotta understand," he said. "You're dealing with a criminal. You have no idea whether or not you can trust him."

McKinney felt similarly apprehensive, saying, "If we tipped our hand to him, tried to come on strong and blow him out of the water and tell him his only chance was to cooperate with us—if we did that, and then he said no, we'd be done. We were all concerned this might be the end of it."

Another thing to be considered was the progress they'd been making because of the wire. It was delivering real admissions, real evidence of illegal behavior, and they were building cases against the subjects they had not been able to before. If they tried to turn this guy and it blew up in their faces, it would destroy the wire too. The gang would know about it and its usefulness would come to an end.

The other unknown was the subject himself. Gomez did not give up his name in that first conversation with Halpern. Nor did he divulge it when Halpern called him back after Halpern's meeting with the agents. But the attorney did provide enough supporting information that investigators were able to piece the clues together and figure out the mystery man's identity. The knowledge of who this man was convinced them that the potential benefits of a meeting far outweighed the risks.

Things moved fast. The day after Gomez made his call, Halpern, Fitzsimmons and McKinney appeared at the attorney's office in Vista. Ushered into a conference room, they sat down at a rectangular table and waited. It was no surprise to them when a moment later the door opened and Gomez entered with his client. It was Wayne Bray.

The driving force behind the Bullpen enterprise had been unhappy with his creation for some time. Some of his unhappiness arose from those voices in his head that never seemed to shut up, telling him that what he was doing was wrong. Some of his unhappiness had less to do with morality and more to do with business. Gloria's price increases had pissed him off anew and he saw it as one more example of shoddy treatment by the Marinos. He felt they were jerking him around and whenever he tried to get Greg to hear his point of view, his partner basically blew him off. Wayne did not appreciate being treated like that and other voices in his head, the meaner ones, called for revenge.

Then there were all the other people he had to do business with besides the Marinos. Liars and thieves abounded, and screwing the other guy before he screwed you was part of the game he'd been playing, just like constantly looking over your shoulder and watching what you said and who you said it to. There was this irritating, paranoid sensation that had drilled its way into the back of his skull and taken up permanent residence there that the law had its eyes on him and that if he screwed up or someone close to them screwed up, they were all dead. All of this was kicking his ass physically and emotionally. The handfuls of pills he swallowed like candy every day never seemed to take his headaches away, not entirely anyhow. He needed pills to knock down the pain in his head and pills to sleep, and his stomach churned day and night worrying about how exposed he was, how vulnerable.

This feeling that he was only as strong as the weakest guy in the racket nagged at him relentlessly, and he hated it. Any number of lame-ass, broke-dick guys could put him in prison for years with one little call. Being suspicious by nature, nothing Wayne had experienced in his life had taught him to disobey those instincts. The TRUST NO ONE sign he gave to Greg was no joke. He had meant it; it was the code he lived by. Trust no one except your closest friends, and keep an eye on them too.

In early April, during the pause in the ring's activities, he had taken his wife and kids to Honolulu. They stayed on the beach at the Outrigger Hotel, taking breakfast in bed every morning and gazing out the window of their suite at Diamond Head and the turquoise waters of Honolulu Bay. He slipped hundred dollar bills into the palms of the guys carrying their bags and bought a gold Presidential Rolex watch for fourteen grand and whatever silly extravagances his wife and kids wanted. Then, after two weeks of living life large, he had come home to hear how Boss Gloria was raising prices whether he liked it or not. Talk about a come-down. If he needed any more convincing it was over between him and Greg's family, this was it. He was as sick of them as they were of him.

But he went along with Gloria's dictates and did his usual drill—ordering blanks from his supplier, driving them over to Smokewood Place, picking them up after Greg signed them, driving them back to his shop, certifying them and shipping them off to Stan the Man. He had done this countless times but for some reason, something didn't feel right to him. He placed another order and went through the same routine, only to have the feeling come back to him, even stronger this time. "I believe in intuition," he said. "It just felt weird to me."

It was weird all right; it felt like ghosts were shadowing him. With an uneasy feeling that things weren't right, and trusting the rightness of that feeling, he made some discrete calls and found out the name of an ex-Department of Justice investigator who had gone into private practice. Explaining what he wanted, but not saying why, he hired the dick to follow him around town on his errands to the Marinos and elsewhere. "Basically he performed counter surveillance," he said. "He was watching to see if anyone was watching me."

Sure enough, someone was. After a day on the job the investigator confirmed Wayne's hunch. Those weren't ghosts; that was the FBI. "They have you," the investigator told him. "They have you locked down."

So that was it. Now he knew. But, having gained this knowledge, what should he do with it? At Coco's he and the others had agreed to hire an attorney if the law ever confronted any of them. That resolution, if it meant anything at the time, meant nothing now. Wayne didn't tell any of the others what he had just learned. From now on he'd take care of his own skin and let everyone else's skin take care of itself.

The number of people with whom he could speak in confidence, never many to begin with, had narrowed to one: his wife. At this late stage of the game there was no reason not to confide in her. His desire to protect her was falling apart like everything else. So, the evening after he saw the investigator, he came to her and spoke to her in the living room of their San Marcos home. It was late at night and their two young sons were in bed. Careful not to wake them, he talked in urgent, hushed tones, telling her everything, letting it all come tumbling out, the pain of this moment revealing itself in his face. As he talked he looked pale and ravaged like he had lost weight, if that was possible.

His wife listened intently, trying hard to calm her emotions and hear what her husband was telling her. If she had suspected nothing about his illegal activities, or if she had known some things and suspected the rest, or if she had known everything all along and had chosen to look the other way for her own reasons (trips to Hawaii and expensive jewelry are nice after all)—whatever her actual state of awareness of the scam, it all changed for her that evening with her husband speaking softly to her in that super-serious way of his while their boys slept like angels in the next room. She cried. He cried. He said he was sorry for hurting her. Naturally, with so much coming at her all at once, some of it confused her. It was hard to absorb it all, hard to understand it—the FBI was following him, and he had hired someone to follow the FBI?—until her husband, with his flair for the dramatic, showed her the cash.

This cash he had stashed away in secret places in the house and elsewhere. Now he was bringing it out to prove that his wildly improbable claims were not exaggerations, that he had gotten them into a screwed-up awful mess and here was the proof. There was maybe $350,000 in all, in twenties, fifties and one hundreds, and he piled them onto the table in the living room and when some bills fell on the floor he picked them up and piled them onto the couch and chair, while his wife looked on in admiration and horror. There wasn't anything happy or fun about this money; it was terrifying. It no longer represented freedom, but the freedom they were in danger of losing.

"What do I do with it?" he asked her. "Sneak out in the middle of the night and bury it somewhere?"

Nobody knew about this secret stash except for Wayne—and now, his wife. Once she saw it she understood the full dimensions of the trouble he was in, and how he was not going to be able to get out of it.

"Turn yourself in," was her answer.

He had no other choice, she told him. What if he tried to hide the money and the FBI was watching and they caught him? How would you explain having all this cash and really, there is no explanation except you've been seriously breaking the law. But even if you hid it and got away with it, that money would still be there, buried in the ground or whatever. It'd always be there, calling out to you, and because of that you'd never be done with this thing. And you had to be done with it. It had to end. Now. For you, for us, for the two dirty-faced angels sleeping in the next room. They had to put it behind them, once and for all, and the only way they could do that, truly, was for him to give up the money and go to the authorities.

Unhappy with what his wife was saying, but willing to trust her instincts, the next morning he went to see Gomez and hired him to represent him.

Gomez put in his call to Halpern, and the "big throw-down," as Wayne sarcastically referred to it, was arranged. When Bray walked into the conference room it was the first time, to his knowledge, he had ever laid eyes on the three men in suits seated at the table. McKinney and Fitzsimmons recognized him, though. "It was a pretty dramatic moment," McKinney said with understatement. "We knew he was the central player in the ring and he was the one leading the charge for the united defense of the gang." He, Fitzsimmons and all the agents at Coco's that morning also knew who had told the FBI to get fucked. Now this same big talker had come to them with his hand out looking for a deal. For them it was dramatic, and oh so sweet.

Next to McKinney was Fitzsimmons, the classic G-Man who would seem to have little in common with the tattooed, chain-smoking ex-meth head across the table from him. But their bios did have at least one shared interest. Fitzsimmons had lettered in tennis in his senior year at Auburn, and tennis was Bray's favorite sport before he got kicked out of high school for drugs and partying and teen rebellion. In many ways the struggle between the two resembled a kind of tennis match with each man trying to anticipate, and react to, the other's moves. Although Bray, of course, could never be sure he was actually matched up against the FBI, he played the game very well, repeatedly frustrating the investigators. But his opponent across the net was nothing if not determined. Miscues here and there, while irritating, were not going to distract him from doing what needed to be done. Fitzsimmons kept applying the pressure, persistently hitting the ball back until the man on the other side caved. Game, set, match, FBI.

Taking the lead in the discussion, Halpern revealed to Bray that yes, there was a federal probe into his activities. "But if you say one word about it to anyone," Halpern told him, "we'll charge you and nail you."

The prosecutor made sure sure Bray understood it was in his self-interest to cooperate. Without collecting another piece of evidence the government could bring a case against him right now—and a powerful one at that. He listed the crimes Bray could be charged with and the prison time he was potentially looking at.

Wayne betrayed no emotion as he listened to the sharply-worded message being delivered from across the table. What finally got to him was when Halpern brought his wife and father into the negotiations. The AUSA cited the fact that Bray had used his father's mailing address for his illegal activities. Bray said he had done so only once, and that his father knew nothing about what he was doing. Nevertheless, said Halpern, his father could be subject to criminal prosecution. His wife could possibly be charged as well.

Bray felt like throwing up. "I'll do anything," he said.

After Bray rolled, Halpern and the agents had achieved one of their aims in coming into the meeting. "We had three main goals for the meeting," McKinney said. "One, we had to convince Wayne that he was ours, that he was not in a position of power. You could tell by looking at his face that he was convinced. Two, once we had him, we wanted him to tell us enough things to lock him in. And three, we had to convince him that he could trust us."

Pursuant to goal number two, the three men asked Bray a series of questions—"Twenty questions," Bray derisively called it—to see if he was going to be a legitimate source of information or if he was going to lie to protect himself or other people. After hearing his answers Halpern and the agents left the room to talk in private. They evidently liked what they heard because in a few minutes they returned to say they'd accept Bray's offer, presenting him with a typewritten statement outlining the terms of his cooperation.

Bray and his attorney reviewed the statement. If he agreed, he was pledging his full and total cooperation. In exchange the government gave him no guarantees or promises although Wayne realized, as did everyone else in the room, that becoming a cooperating witness would only help his case—that he could receive a lighter sentence from a judge than he ordinarily would have based on his crimes.

Wayne signed the document and slid it back across the table to Halpern, and the deal was done.

Neutral in their manner and words, Halpern and the agents were pumped. They had successfully turned a subject who could blow the case open for them. Their questions and Bray's answers persuaded them that he did not know about the investigation before the meeting and that the FBI had done nothing to tip him off. They also felt that the information he had provided had locked him in even more and strengthened their already strong case against him.*

Things speeded up still more. After the meeting McKinney and Fitzsimmons followed Bray to his house and thoroughly went through it. Then they accompanied him to W.W. Sports Cards and searched it too. While there, they conducted another interview, this one on tape, in which Wayne further locked himself in. They also discussed how to proceed with the next phase of their fast-developing plan: having him go undercover.

When Bray went to see other gang members at their houses and places of business, it was decided, he'd wear a wire. But when the guys visited him

---

Bray said nothing at the time about his counter-surveillance of the agents. To this day Fitzsimmons remains skeptical it ever occurred; McKinney is willing to concede that Bray is smart enough to have pulled something like that off.

at his shop, the FBI wanted to get pictures of them as well as sound. The camera needed to be concealed and yet provide wide coverage of the front room of the office where Bray did most of his business. Looking around, the agents observed the framed movie posters and pictures of Hollywood stars on the walls. Also around the office were a variety of novelty items such as the menacing white Storm Trooper's mask from "Star Wars," one of Bray's favorite collectibles.

Bingo. They had it. The perfect place for the camera.

The next day FBI technicians installed the camera inside the Storm Trooper's mask and mounted the mask like a stereo speaker on an upper corner wall. Surrounded by other pieces on the wall and perched above a glass display cabinet that contained baseball cards and other memorabilia, it was perfectly in keeping with everything else in the shop. The lens of the camera was in the eyes of the mask. The techs ran wires from the back of the mask into the wall to a recording unit hidden in another room of the shop. One microphone was installed near the mask, and another was placed in a broken-down box on the far side of the office in case one of Bray's customers wandered over there while they were talking.

It was a slick setup. Time was wasting. They fell to it in a flash.

21

Bray made his first recorded call for the FBI in mid-May, placing an order with the Marinos. Two days later he dropped off the blanks as he had so many times in the past, only this time he was wearing two microphones attached to his chest under his loosely-fitting Hawaiian shirt. Hair-thin wires ran from the mics to a recording device hidden in the crotch of his pants. From the outside everything appeared normal.

His order included two Hank Aaron jerseys, three George Brett jerseys, four Yankee batting helmets, eight Robin Yount jerseys, ten Ted Williams jerseys, twenty-three Mantle jerseys, and sixty-six DiMaggio jerseys and helmets. Fitzsimmons and McKinney knew exactly how many pieces there were because they had counted every one. On every piece they had also put a marking from a black light pen invisible to the naked eye.

The Aaron jerseys were 500 Home Run Club items and needed multiple sigs, as did the Yankee batting helmets that were to feature the autograph of every player on New York's 1998 world championship team. John prepped the pieces and Greg speedily signed them, Wayne chatting the brothers up as they worked. In payment he counted out $2,270 in cash for Gloria—money that had also been counted previously by the FBI.

Afterwards Wayne bundled up his things in large black plastic bags and drove them back to his shop where he met McKinney. The agent had tailed Bray from W.W. Sports Cards to Smokewood Place, and back again. While Wayne was inside with the Marinos, McKinney had parked on a nearby street listening to their conversation via a transmitter in Bray's recording unit. The reason for the close watch on Bray was not because the FBI didn't trust him, although this was certainly part of it in the beginning. Rather, McKinney was backing him up just as he had backed up Ferreira on his undercover meets. If something went wrong and his man needed help, the agent was ready to provide it.

McKinney was Bray's primary FBI contact, and the agent and his former adversary worked together every day over the spring and summer starting with this, his first undercover assignment. When Bray talked on the phone to guys in the racket, McKinney was in the room with him. McKinney wired him up on many occasions and covered all his meets, listening in through Bray's transmitter. When Bray returned to the shop after a meet McKinney was there to retrieve the tape from him. Along with Fitzsimmons, he counted and marked every piece of merchandise before it left Bray's shop and inventoried it when it came back in. The same with the money. Bray used his own cash, the cash he generated from buying and selling fakes, but the FBI now kept his books for him and counted every bill that passed in and out of his hands.

McKinney, Fitzsimmons and Halpern all coached their new operative on his undercover techniques, but he was a quick study and didn't need much coaching. "It took a guy with big balls, a bright guy and a smooth talking guy to do what he did," said McKinney. "I knew Wayne could walk in and talk circles around those guys. He had undercover experience without ever being one."

"We talked to him and rehearsed scenarios with him," said Halpern. "We got him on the phone with Tim in his office and they'd do role playing games. A guy says this, you say that. We'd offer some ways to talk about things in a natural way. He had to make it clear that what he was selling was a forgery, but he couldn't say it was forged. If he did the guy would hang up on him. But Bray was quick. He could turn the conversation so that the guy's intent was clear—that he was doing and selling forgeries. He understood in many respects what he needed to know and do better than Ferreira. He knew what it takes to get admissions."

Bray, said Fitzsimmons, was "cool as a cucumber." Before a meet Wayne would joke about how nervous and amped up he was, but he never showed it on the job. Even Bullpen's UCA was impressed by how quickly he took to the job. "He listened, he was sharp, and he got us more players," said Ferreira.

One of the biggest players was Stan Fitzgerald, and Bray, now in secret alliance with the FBI, methodically set about to bring him down. It was Bray's idea to have people around the country place orders with Stan for specific items such as the two Aaron 500 Home Run Club jerseys. The FBI marked the blanks before sending them over to the Marinos. After they were signed the jerseys were sent to Stan. He in turn shipped them onto the customers who had ordered them, not knowing that they were undercover

FBI. The agents returned the jerseys to San Diego, where McKinney and Fitzsimons placed them under a black light to see if their original markings were there. And they were.

"I spent a lot of my time placing orders," said Wayne, "basically tricking people to buy stuff."

Opening up his American Express records to the FBI, he revealed that Stan the Man had paid him more than $3 million for counterfeit memorabilia. In the past year Stan had sent him more than one hundred shipments of blanks, and later in May another big shipment came in from New Jersey, this one consisting of eight 500 Home Run Club bats, a couple dozen George Brett jerseys and stacks of 8x10s of Tupac Shakur, Sam Kinnison and other dead celebs. When the UPS truck dropped off the goods at 133 North Pacific, McKinney was there to receive them with Bray. The agent counted, recorded and marked the order before Bray turned it over to the Marinos.

The FBI ended the wire taps but continued to record all the calls going in and out of W.W. Sports Cards. So McKinney listened as Bray took a call some days later from Stan, who was ticked. He said he had 20,000 customers and was getting three hundred calls a day for merchandise and where the hell was his stuff? He had been waiting and waiting for Wayne to get it to him and every day there was nothing. Wayne came up with some excuse to calm Stan down and later that day, followed secretly by his FBI escort, he drove over to the Marinos to pick up the order, paying Gloria $4,500 in cash. Along with the vintage photos there were pics of living celebrities, and one of them was of Timothy Dalton that Greg had mistakenly signed as Pierce Brosnan. [Both Dalton and Brosnan played James Bond in the movies.] When Bray finally sent this shipment off to Stan, he included the Dalton photo and attached this note to it:

> Stan, this is the kind of shit I have to deal with using Greg. I ate twelve Dalton photos plus the autographs 'cause the asshole signed Pierce Brosnan's name on them. I continually get no refunds from them—they're assholes—I already talked to you a little on the phone but I have a guy that's better than Greg at the Hollywood sigs. I start using him next week tell me what you think. I'll continue using them to get you your vintage as well as Mantle-Joe-Ted and other guys that only Greg does. [Signed] WB.

This note, written with McKinney looking over his shoulder, reflected Bray's frustration about doing business with the Marinos, which Stan was aware of. Its real purpose though was to get Stan off his back. Wayne, once the most reliable of suppliers, had suddenly gone flaky on him, not supplying all of Stan's orders or supplying them late. Stan's customers were getting on his ass and Stan was getting on Wayne because of it—an unacceptable development for McKinney and Fitzsimmons. They needed to keep Bray in business and his activities running normally, but they also wanted to keep counterfeits out of the marketplace as much as they could. So they had him continue to fill Stan's orders, just not everything he asked for. And to explain these repeated failures Wayne shoveled blame onto Greg and his family. Since the Marinos and Stan never talked with one another, neither could check the truthfulness of this story, or the lack thereof. Wayne had always been so careful, so sharp, that lapses of this kind were out of character for him. And while Stan was pissed at him, he was not suspicious because Wayne had always been the best of crooks, the least likely member of the gang to be a rat.

After sending off the package, Wayne called Stan to see if he had seen the note inside.

"Yeah," grunted Stan. "I read that note in there."

"You did read the note?" said Bray, repeating the question to make sure they got it on tape.

"Uh-huh." That the former deputy sheriff had read the note and was now acknowledging its contents was evidence that he knew he was dealing in fakes. And Wayne got him to admit this without either of them saying the f-word.

Wayne went on to talk about the forger who was supposedly better at the Hollywood stuff than Greg. This person was a fictional creation, invented by Bray as a means of talking about forgery in a different way and possibly gaining more admissions from Stan. But what if Stan made a request to use him in the future? That wouldn't be good. Wayne solved this potential problem by bad-mouthing this nonexistent forger too, explaining how he had mixed up the James Bonds just like Greg, only he had signed Pierce Brosnan's name on Timothy Dalton's photo. If the asshole was no more reliable than Greg, why deal with him? Presto! A person who had never existed vanished from discussion.

In a canny piece of foresight Gloria Marino had once bestowed the nickname of the Fox onto Wayne, who turned out to be cleverer than she ever expected. Greg's nickname was the Gingerbread Man. The inspiration for these names was the well-known children's story in which a gingerbread man escapes from the oven of an old woman and races through the forest eluding a number of hungry animals until a tricky fox finally catches and eats him. The parallels between this story and what Wayne was doing extend only so far, however. For in the children's story the Fox does not also eat the Gingerbread Man's mother, father, wife and brother. The close-knit Marino family had always feared doing business with strangers but it was a person on the inside, one of their most trusted associates, who sealed their fate.

On June 2, a few days after the exchange with Stan, Wayne drove over to the Marinos to pick up another order. On the drive over, indeed before all of his undercover meets, he talked into the mics taped to his chest, introducing the recording by stating the date, time and who he planned to talk to. Following these preliminaries he slipped a disk into the CD player of the Land Cruiser and recorded some music onto the tape. He did this as a way to relax but also to entertain the female clerks at the FBI who transcribed the tapes he gave to McKinney. Although he had never met them, Bray felt that these women liked him and were rooting for him to do well. Their only request, relayed to him through McKinney, was that he quit cursing so much. This he could not do, but he did enjoy giving them a musical treat at the start of each tape.

Two of his favorite musical preludes were Johnny Cash's "I Walk the Line" and "Ring of Fire." Just for laughs he sometimes slipped in "In-A-Gadda-Da-Vida." But as he rolled up to the Marinos on this particular day, his choice may have been another of his favorites, Alice Cooper's "No More Mister Nice Guy."

He turned off the music as he parked on the street in front of the house. He grabbed his keys and the briefcase sitting on the seat beside him, and got out. He shut his door and beeped the doors locked. Somebody was washing a car in the driveway out front, and Bray nodded and said hello as he walked past. The Marinos' front door faced away from the street onto a side patio. He knocked on the door, and it swung quickly open. Wayne had called ahead and they were expecting him.

Greg and John were there. So were Nate and Big Ricky. When he came in they were in the living room watching a Padres-Cubs game on TV. John had some money on it and everyone was into it, laughing and talking loud and being rowdy. Both Greg and John greeted him with friendly, booming voices, telling him to come in, sit down, watch the game. Wayne said he'd be right there, setting his briefcase on top of the kitchen table. He popped the case open and left it on the table as he joined the guys in the living room.

There was nothing unusual about any of this; Bray always brought his briefcase on business calls to the Marinos and everywhere else. This was how he carried his papers, his pills, his pens, his cash. And it was like him to leave it in the kitchen when he was jawing with Greg and the others. The difference was, this wasn't his briefcase; this one came compliments of the FBI.

It was a heavy, black briefcase identical to his normal one except for the hidden video and recording equipment installed inside. The camera lens looked out through a pinhole in the side of the case. Bray clicked the camera on before he stepped out of his vehicle, and it had recorded a shot of the guy washing his car in the driveway. When Wayne set the case down and popped it open on the kitchen table it was already on and filming. He had placed it at one end of the table so it would have a clear view of the kitchen and anyone who happened to sit at one of the four chairs there, namely Greg. Bray's job was to get Greg out of the living room and into the kitchen where the briefcase camera could catch him in the act.

The FBI badly wanted this. McKinney and Fitzsimmons had seen thousands of examples of Greg's work; surveillance agents had watched it pass between hands outside mini-marts and pet stores; Ferreira and so many others had paid huge sums for it; and the wire guys had listened to people chatter on and on about it. But after all this time they still had not seen Greg forging, a potentially devastating piece of evidence if the case ever went to trial. Having jurors actually see Greg spinning autographs with his own hand would make the case against him a slam-dunk, they felt sure.

Wayne didn't stay in the living room long, returning in a moment to the kitchen where he set a box and a few baseballs out on the table. He was smoking a cigarette. So was Gloria, who was around the house but not watching the game. When she passed through the kitchen she glanced at the balls Wayne was laying out and said nothing before leaving again. Really, what was there to say? Greg was about to forge some balls, so what? Creating fakes was a daily part of the household routine. The banality of this moment—at least for the Marinos—was seen most vividly, and poignantly, when John's nine-year-old son came into camera range. He noticed the ball on the table, looked at it and walked away without a second thought.

After setting the balls out, with seeming nonchalance but utmost care, Wayne took one into the living room. Greg didn't want to leave the game so he signed on the couch without bothering to look at an exemplar of the autograph he was forging. He had done it so many times before, produced so many single-signed balls of this guy, he didn't need to. The signature was Babe Ruth's.

Wayne returned to the kitchen with the ball, talking loudly so Greg and the guys could hear him from the living room but playing to a different audience they knew nothing about. "This is a $6,000 baseball now," he said admiringly. "Greg, you ever done one this good? It's perfect."

As he spoke he blew on the ball to dry it. "You've got to blow on it," he said out loud, though he was alone in the room. Once the autograph was dry he placed the ball in the box.

The Ruth ball was only one of many pieces in Wayne's order, which included nearly two hundred photos of athletes and celebrities: Johnny Bench, Yogi Berra, George Burns, Jack Dempsey, Derek Jeter, Mel Gibson, Rocky Marciano, Nolan Ryan, Frank Sinatra, the Beatles, the casts of "Friends" and "Seinfeld." There were also thirty-two jerseys, five baseball gloves and vintage Jimmie Foxx, Lou Gehrig and Ty Cobb balls besides the one now bearing the Babe's signature. Wayne also needed a Gary Cooper cut and a sig added to a cast shot of "M*A*S*H."

The excited voices in the living room carried into the kitchen as Bray stood calmly holding a bankroll of one hundred dollar bills in his hand. When you are on a surveillance camera it is important to count the money out loud so that a jury or anyone else who views the tape later will know exactly what is going on. The agents asked Bray to do this and he did, counting the bills out one by one and saying aloud, "One hundred, two hundred, three hundred, four hundred, five hundred..."

In the meantime Gloria reappeared in the kitchen, hovering around him. He handed the five bills to her, and she slid them into a pocket of her pants. Meanwhile John's son passed within view of the camera again, drinking a can of soda.

"Why are you drinking soda?" she snapped, a cigarette perched in her lips. Drinking soda apparently struck her as an unhealthy habit.

Saying nothing, the boy fled the room.

About this time Greg, bearded with black bushy hair, got bored with the game and joined Wayne and Gloria in the kitchen. He slid a chair out, sat down at the table. Vintage pen in hand, he glanced at a black book that had been brought in and set on the table, leafing through it to find the page with the Gary Cooper exemplars. In front of him was a piece of paper ripped from an antique book. Without hesitation he dashed off the sig—and the FBI had what it wanted. Wayne peeled off a fifty for Gloria, and she slid the bill into her pocket with the others.

Then a huge roar erupted from the living room, John's booming voice rising over all: "Goodbye! Bye-bye!" Sammy Sosa had smacked a three-run, ninth-inning home run to win the game for the Cubs, 9 to 8, as well as a tidy pile of dough for John. Greg dropped his pen and rushed back into the living room to see the replay as John provided the color commentary. "Watch this shot! That's gone, baby!" he said happily, singing a mock funeral dirge for the Padres as he came back into the kitchen, followed by his older brother. They were both buzzing with excitement.

Returning to business, Greg sat down at the table as Wayne handed him the "M★A★S★H" photo, which had the phony sigs of the entire cast except for one of its minor stars, Larry Linville. Greg said he'd never heard of the guy. "He's dead, he's dead," Bray muttered, and with a bored expression Greg found Linville in the book and polished off his sig. Gloria moved back into camera range, grasping for another bill.

Bray took the "M★A★S★H" photo, the Cooper cut and the Ruth ball when he left the house that day, turning them over to McKinney at W.W. Sports Cards. The agent confiscated the special FBI briefcase as well, so that when Wayne returned to the Marinos the next afternoon he was carrying his regular black briefcase. On this visit he paid Gloria close to six grand in bills and she gave him two paper receipts—more evidence for the FBI. She and her family noticed nothing unusual about Wayne's behavior or his briefcases. They were the perfect pigeons. And they made the mistake all pigeons make. They trusted.

22

At the same time Wayne was jamming up Stan and the Marinos he was setting his sights on Shelly Jaffe. He and Shelly had never gotten along, but they still did business from time to time so it was no big deal—nothing out of the ordinary—for Wayne to give him a call to see if he was interested in buying some stuff from him. Shelly said okay, bring it over, he'd take a look at it.

McKinney saw Bray at his shop before the meet, which was the usual routine. Sometimes they met at Wayne's house first thing in the morning and drove separate vehicles over to W.W. Sports Cards. But mostly they met at the shop, the agent always careful to vary his route and park on a side street, never on the asphalt strip in front of 133 North Pacific. The two always talked before the agent showed his face. If Wayne expected a visitor he gave a heads-up and McKinney stayed clear. And since it was protocol for guys in the racket to call ahead before coming over, the agent could be at W.W. Sports Cards without much worry of someone dropping in on them unannounced. Still, he remained alert.

McKinney and Fitzsimmons felt strongly that even before Wayne's flip, they could have dished up enough red meat to a judge to send him and the Marino brothers to prison. Ferreira's work, they also felt certain, would deliver some of the outer ring guys. But that was it. That was all they had to show for all their time and effort, and that was definitely not what they had in mind when the case started. They wanted more than that, much more. They wanted everybody: Kathy and Angelo and—conclusively, no wiggle room—Gloria. They wanted all the inner circle players. They wanted Stan the Man and Stan the Man's wife and Stan the Man's mother. They wanted out-of-staters like the Scheinmans and Barry Delit. They wanted big-time players like Dave Tabb and the small-time guys who had just come along for the ride. And with Bray on their team, they knew they had the one guy who could deliver all that for them, who could make Operation Bullpen the big, headline-grabbing, lead-the-network news, crime-fighting and public relations success story they had always envisioned it to be.

What made Bray so special, besides the skills and aptitude he showed for undercover work, was his knowledge of everything and everybody. Now he was putting all that hard-earned knowledge on display, naming the names of people the FBI knew about and others it knew nothing about. With this windfall of information McKinney and Fitzsimmons had developed a list of subjects—more gingerbread men, as it were—for the Fox to go after, one by one. And Shelly's name was at the top of the list.

Wayne made the hour and a half drive up the coast to Tustin in the afternoon, McKinney tailing behind and peeling off when Bray turned onto Yaqi Court with the basketball hoop on the street and a house flying the Stars and Stripes out front. With "Walk the Line" playing on the CD player, he pulled up outside Shelly's place and shut off the car. When he rang the bell Shelly called out from upstairs and told him to come up to the office where, years before, Greg Marino had gotten his start as a professional forger. The mustachioed, balding Shelly, clad in shorts and sports shoes with his big glasses on a string holder around his neck, did not get out of his chair when Wayne appeared, and nobody shook hands.

Almost immediately, Shelly sensed something was wrong. "He started acting funny. He's trying to sell me some stuff, and he starts making all these calls and telling me, 'I'll get you certs for these,' and he's saying how he's going to call Donald Frangipani and these other authenticators. The way he was acting, all these calls he was making to people, I knew. My gut instinct told me. I thought to myself, 'This is no good.'"

So Shelly asked him straight out, "Are you wearing a wire?"

Wayne didn't blink. "No," he shot back. "Are you?"

But Shelly didn't believe him. "He was wired and I knew it," he said. "I tried to catch him and I reached out for him to feel his chest."

As he did so Wayne pulled away, though not fast enough because Jaffe got his hands on him. "He patted me on the chest and missed feeling the wire by a quarter of an inch," said Wayne.

Though he missed the wire, Shelly was so convinced Wayne was wearing one that he began speaking past him and directly to the FBI as if there were federal agents listening on the other end. "Come talk to me," he said. "You got me. Now let's get some of the big guys…"

Listening from his car parked in the neighborhood, McKinney tensed, wondering how to react if Shelly stayed aggressive and kept pushing Wayne. As it happened Shelly backed off and made no more lunges at his visitor. Wayne regained his usual command, and they started talking business normally. Wayne even sold some things to Shelly, who paid him cash. When Wayne left the house less than a half hour later, his secret was still intact. Returning to his vehicle, he made his way out of the subdivision and back onto I-5 with McKinney close behind.

Alone again in his office, surrounded by the heroic portraits on the walls of the great DiMaggio, the man who had spent a lifetime brokering deals in the steel industry felt strongly that he was screwed. He punched in the number for Nate Harrison, who, over the past year, had become much more than a business associate to him. They had gotten to know each other so well that Shelly regarded him with real affection, almost like a son.

Nate was at home—one of two houses he had bought largely by selling fakes—when Shelly called him.

"We're finished," Shelly told him bluntly. "Wayne is working for the FBI."

"What?"

"Wayne is working for the FBI," he repeated.

Nate thought Shelly was talking crazy. Wayne? The FBI? No way.

So Shelly told him the story of what had just happened—how Wayne had come in talking wild and how Shelly had grabbed for the wires that he knew Wayne was wearing. He didn't find them but that didn't change his mind. "We're dead. They know who we are and what we're doing and everything else, and Wayne's working with them."

Nate still didn't believe what he was saying. "You're wrong," he said.

"No," Shelly insisted. "I'm right."

"No," Nate said forcefully. "He's my friend. He wouldn't do that."

"He's not your friend," said Shelly.

Recalling the incident years later, Bray admitted that he had blundered with Shelly—that he had come on too strong, too fast, and that it had raised the suspicions of an already suspicious man. "I didn't like Shelly, so I didn't want to spend a lot of time with him. I was aggressive in my questioning, more aggressive than I should have been."

After his early successes with the Marinos and Stan the Man, he may have also been overconfident. Or he may have simply run up against someone who was as street-smart as he was, and as skeptical of the inherent goodness in people. But nothing more came out of the incident. Since Shelly did not talk to the Marinos, he did not share his suspicions with them. And even if he had, they would have ignored him. Trust cantankerous Shelly, an outsider, over their main man Bray? Gimme a break. The only inner circle guy who was close to Shelly was Nate, and Nate was devoted to Wayne. And despite his suspicions, Shelly had not found a wire on Wayne—indeed, after all that he had bought some things from him and even suggested as Wayne was leaving the house that they do some more deals over the summer. So Bray and the FBI kept on with their plan of luring more gingerbread men over to W.W. Sports Cards.

One of those was Big Ricky. Once Wayne had to shut Big Ricky up for talking stupidly and blatantly about Ruth and Gehrig forgeries over the phone, but those days were done. Now, asking innocent but probing questions, controlling the conversation while letting it meander, Wayne let him go on and on about how to disguise a baseball by sanding off the Rawlings label on it. With the label removed you could dip it in shellac, bag it in dog food and sell it for thousands.

Big Ricky bought dozens of blank certs from Wayne on this visit, and dozens more on another. Why does a person need so many blank certs? Because you can fill them out yourself to give cover for the frauds you're selling, and you don't have to dick around with Jim DiMaggio or some other authenticator who wanted a cut of the take.

After putting away Big Ricky, Wayne moved on to Dick Laughlin, who asked him in a confidential manner if it was safe to talk in the shop.

"No problem," Wayne reassured him.

Laughlin bought a baker's dozen worth of fake photographs from him. In a later visit he confided that he felt the Marinos no longer respected him because they were treating him so poorly. Wayne offered his heartfelt sympathy, and when Dick walked out of Suite D that day he felt as if he had found a soulmate with whom he could confide.

He was wrong. He was toast, too.

Like Jaffe, Mike Lopez was one of the pioneers of the racket in southern California, a short, stocky LA forger who had done work for Bray back when Bray was cutting his teeth in the trade. Also like Jaffe, the FBI had known about him a long time but didn't have much on him, owing to the fact that Mysterious Mike was such a cool and crafty operator. "He was tough to crack, very cautious and careful," McKinney said. "We discussed him a lot, how to approach him. We did role playing games and went through this whole spiel on how to approach him, none of which Wayne followed."

Reaching Lopez on the phone, Wayne came up with a novel technique for getting a criminal to let down his guard. "Mr. Lopez," he said in a mock serious voice, "this is Special Agent Wayne Bray of the Federal Bureau of

Investigation. I was wondering if I could speak to you about an investigation we're conducting into memorabilia fraud."

Standing next to Bray when he made this pitch, McKinney was "floored. There is no way I would have approved of him using this technique if he had told it to me ahead of time." But the agent could only listen and wait to hear how Lopez would respond.

"Okay, Special Agent Bray," Mike said with a laugh, "I'd love to help you out."

"It worked," said McKinney admiringly. "Lopez played along, and that's how we got him."

Special Agent Bray began milking information from Lopez, who bragged that he was going to give Greg Marino "a run for his money" by venturing into Greg's specialty of dead people. Lopez said he had Ruth and DiMaggio down cold but he was still perfecting the half moons in Greg's masterpiece, Mickey Mantle. Wayne invited Lopez down to San Marcos to do some work for him, and Mike, in an unusually outgoing mood because of Bray's joke (what he thought was a joke), said yeah, no sweat, he'd come down.

Mike made at least two appearances in the shop on North Pacific that was no longer safe. Located in an upper corner of one wall, the camera inside the Storm Trooper's mask had a clear view across the office to a desk set against the far wall. The placement of the desk was no accident. That was where Lopez sat when he forged a Joe DiMaggio photograph, some Joe Montana and Dan Marino lithos, and a Dan Marino on a Dolphins team jacket. Happy in his work, Mike bragged about how he had been into counterfeits "way before a lot of other people." He talked openly about how he had scammed a cable shopping network for three quarters of a million bucks. After that things had gotten a little dicey for him but, he assured Bray, he was "ready to play again."

A couple of weeks later Lopez came back to W.W. Sports Cards to play some more, showing up in droopy black shorts and a white T-shirt. He signed the autographs of the entire Lakers squad on three basketballs, Michael Jordan and Larry Bird on some other basketballs, a bunch of quarterback sigs and a pile of Joe Montana lithos. Then, as if that wasn't enough for one day, he helped package everything up and ship it to Wayne's supposed client in Hawaii—actually an agent in the FBI's Honolulu office.

Lopez asked Bray if he thought Stan Fitzgerald would be interested in buying some of his fake-signed NFL jerseys, which he was offering at a discount price of under two hundred bucks apiece. Wayne said he'd talk to Stan about it, and never did.

At another point Lopez was signing some sports autographs when he came to a hockey star whose name he didn't recognize. "Who's Rocket Richard?"

"He's an old Hall of Fame hockey name," answered Bray.

But a more telling conversation occurred a little earlier, when Lopez first sat down at the desk against the far wall and noticed a Michael Jordan poster with a fake Jordan signature on it. "Hey," said Mike, "who does those Jordans over there?"

Wayne didn't need to look to know who did those Jordans. The guy who did them was the best damn forger in the business, his former close friend and partner, a man who was an artist compared to the guy he was dealing with today. If Wayne felt any emotion at this moment, he did not show it.

"Greg," he said.

"He does it pretty good, then. He does it better than I do."

"Yes, he's really good," said Wayne.

"He makes that slant," said Lopez, continuing in his admiration for the forgery.

"Yeah," said Wayne blandly, "he's got that slant."

Lopez insisted on being paid in cash, which was no problem. Wayne counted the cash out loud while standing in front of the camera, and the no longer mysterious Lopez took the money within camera range too. He didn't know it yet but like everybody else now doing business with Wayne, he was screwed, totally screwed.

Little Ricky Mitchell's name was the next to be crossed off the hit list. Wayne called on him at his house in Rancho Bernardo and found the new father in a talkative mood, anxious to buy and sell. Little Ricky asked Wayne to get him some counterfeit vintage balls for his Vegas clients, requested hundreds of blank contemporary balls that he could take to Greg, ordered some of those wonderfully useful blank certs, and said he had a fake Babe Ruth-signed bat he was willing to part with for six grand.

The genuine Ruth signature, not Greg's version, was a subject of discussion when Little Ricky visited Wayne's shop soon after that. The two were talking about aspects of Ruth's signature—how the *e* on Babe ends sort of high, details of that nature. Wayne maintained that Ruth's sig had a certain slant to it, and Rick said no, it had a different sort of slant. So Wayne asked him to give him a demonstration.

"Come on," he said. "Show me. Show me what you mean."

This was unusual for Wayne to ask something like this, but Little Ricky didn't think anything about it. Retreating into the back of the shop, he traced over an exemplar of Ruth's and brought it out to show Wayne. "This is how it's done," Rick said. "This is the way Ruth did it."

All of this was being recorded, on FBI audio and videotape, and this evidence helped finger Little Ricky not just as a counterfeit distributor and wholesaler but as a forger too—a charge he adamantly denies. "I never forged and Tim [Fitzsimmons] will back me up on that," he said.

Whether he forged or not, for some time it had been Little Ricky's deepest desire to quit the business and end his double life. Unbeknownst to him, Bray had granted his wish for him.

For three days in late July the investigation shifted to the Georgia World Congress Center in downtown Atlanta, site of the annual National Sports Collectors Convention. The National—"the Disneyland of card shows," as one observer called it—attracted thousands of dealers from around the country, and many more thousands of collectors interested in buying what they had to sell. Also in attendance were John Ferreira and Upper Deck investigators Anthony West and Kathy Wichmann.

Both Ferreira and the West-Wichmann team were hunting the same prey: the sellers and distributors of forgeries. And with more than 1,200 tables on the crowded convention floor, there were lots of potential targets for them. The show's main attraction was the special section reserved for celebrity signings. Among the stars present were Reggie Jackson, Ryne Sandberg, Joe Montana, Magic Johnson, Bill Russell, Joe Frazier, Pamela Anderson and buxom pro wrestler Sable. They sat at tables and signed rapidly and profitably as long lines of people waited patiently for their autographs and to get their picture taken with them.

Amidst this noisy, crowded jumble, Ferreira and West-Wichmann found an abundance of fakes being sold alongside legitimate merchandise. Each of the investigators noted the booths with the highest concentration of counterfeits, reporting back to Fitzsimmons and McKinney who were also on scene.

But the normally placid and soft-spoken West was furious when he and Wichmann saw who else was at the show. "It got our blood boiling," he said. To their disgust, one of the biggest crooks of all was making the rounds of the convention floor and chatting up dealers like he was their best friend.

Wayne Bray.

Neither Fitzsimmons or McKinney had told West that Bray had come over to their side. But Ferreira knew, just as Bray now conclusively knew that Ferreira was FBI. In their first meeting since their brief, hostile encounter at W.W. Sports Cards early in the case, the two men spoke a few words to each other in the hotel where they were staying. Then they split apart. Though both were undercover, the two had different assignments, different circles they were moving in. Bray was in his own orbit, and it wasn't a good one.

"It was horrible," he said.

His job in Atlanta, as in California, was to trick guys, but increasingly the job was getting to him. When he had started, fearing for what could happen to his family if he did not cooperate fully, he had poured himself into it. The anger and energy and calculated intensity he brought to all things he brought to undercover work too, and to be sure, a part of him relished its cloak-and-dagger nature. He knew why he was good at it: He looked and talked and acted like a criminal, and so the other criminals trusted him. Still he felt a deep sense of loss about what he was doing. Here he was, destroying what he had helped to create and bringing down his friends in the process. Yeah, he was doing the right thing blah blah blah, but he never realized how doing the right thing could make him feel so bad. His one big shot in life, his one big chance at being rich folks, was over. Something of this scale and scope and crazy-ass ambition wasn't coming around for him again. He'd never be this lucky, or unlucky, again. It was his thing, and he'd blown it.

The FBI had rigged him up with another secret agent gizmo for the convention, building the recording unit inside a cigarette pack he carried in the front pocket of his shirt. The microphones were taped to his belly. Since he was a smoker it was a totally natural setup, and none of the guys he was tricking suspected a thing. Though he gave nothing away on the outside, on the inside he was a mess. That bored, I-don't-give-a-crap look he had, those droopy, heavy-lidded eyes, the vibe he gave off to strangers that he was somehow walled off from what was going on around him—if that was ever true, it wasn't true anymore. He was completely tuned into what he was doing, and it was making him sick.

One of the guys he jammed up at the National was a small-time Orange County card dealer named Forest Golembeske. He'd known Frosty, as people called him, for years. With Wayne leading him on and every word being recorded by the bogus cigarette pack, the good-natured Frosty chatted openly about buying some fake Ruth balls. After talking to Frosty and some other people Wayne started to feel dizzy and a little light-headed, and he found his way through the jumble of tables to a men's room in a corner of the hall. There, he retreated into an empty stall, closed the door behind him, got down on one knee, and heaved into the toilet again and again until there was nothing left. In a while he started to feel better. He stood up, walked over to a sink, threw some water on his face, stuffed a gob of pills down his throat, and headed back out into the maze of tables.

23

As productive as the investigation had been, some nagging problems had developed with it, problems that needed attention. One of them had to do with Stan the Man, whose business was booming like never before, surpassing even the golden days of the home run chase. In August, in only one sign of how rosy things were, his wife had ordered nearly 8,000 certs from Wayne, each flimsy piece of paper representing an item that had been sold, or was about to be sold, by Stan's Sports Memorabilia.

The only thing stopping Stan from selling more was Wayne's repeated inability to deliver the goods he wanted, on time and in full. Stan didn't like problems of this kind; they irritated him. And when Stan the Man was unhappy, so were McKinney and Fitzsimmons, who wanted Wayne's operation to appear as normally corrupt as it had always been. Their plan to reel in more subjects was falling into place, but they weren't done yet. More fish were still out there, and some big ones too. They needed to keep up appearances a while longer and preserve Wayne's cover.

One of Stan's shipments consisted of both blanks and signed material, including sixty balls with fake DiMaggio sigs. Enclosed was a note from Stan telling Wayne to "upgrade the J.D. balls to J.D. + Mantle combo's." He also said not to throw away the certs Bray had made for the DiMaggio balls, implying that they'd be changed once the balls were upgraded with Mantle sigs. After receiving this shipment Wayne called Stan to explain, once again, why he'd only been able to come through with a portion of his most recent orders, blaming the Marinos as usual but also committing the unpardonable sin of mentioning them by name.

"I'm trying to punish the Marinos for, uh, dickin' with me," he said.

Stan quickly cut in, telling him not to say their names over the phone. "I know who everyone is," he said curtly. He added that he had just sent off three dozen 500 Home Run Club jerseys, instantly giving rise to the issue anew. If Wayne didn't fill this jersey order promptly, as well as the one that had just come in, this was going to make Stan even grumpier than he already was. And at some point, if that point hadn't already arrived, he would begin to wonder why the mastermind of the enterprise had turned into such a lousy crook.

To solve this problem, Wayne and the FBI decided to shift Stan the Man's account over to Rino Ruberti, who had become a rising star in the racket after splitting off from Universal Authentic Memorabilia. In an appearance before the glowing eyes of the Storm Trooper, Rino had admitted that he owned more than $100,000 in stolen Upper Deck cards. He sold some of these cards to Wayne and bought certs from him for Ruth, Einstein and Reagan baseballs. Despite his beach boy style Rino had a man's ambition to make money, which made him a natural fit with the relentlessly enterprising Fitzgerald.

As Wayne and the FBI saw it, with Rino taking over Stan's account, Stan would no longer have the supply problems he had encountered with Bray. This would keep Stan happy and take the pressure off McKinney and Fitzsimmons to release counterfeit material into the marketplace. Meanwhile, Wayne could keep tabs on both Stan and Rino by supplying them with certs from SCAA, his bogus authentication company. Telling Stan why he was making the change, Wayne said he was so sick of the Marinos he just couldn't deal with them anymore. Because Rino was tight with them, he was in a better position to deliver the goods to Stan. Wayne spun similar lies to Rino, who was thrilled to have such a hugely profitable account land in his lap. He'd be happy to work with Stan, no problem. And he liked the Marinos and they liked him, so that side of it seemed good too.

The Marinos, however, were not as pleased by the switch. It made them suspicious. "We wondered about Bray when he gave up Stan's account," said Greg. "I mean, this was Stan the Man, Bray's big account, and he's handing it over? That was weird."

Another request by Wayne earlier in the summer had struck Greg as weird, too. During one frenetic week Wayne had brought in an order for 1,000 photos—one hundred Mantle/Maris combos, one hundred John Lennons, fifty Jerry Garcias, fifty John Waynes and more. This was followed shortly by another order for more than 3,500 baseballs signed by the likes of Satchel Paige, Cool Papa Bell, Roy Campanella, Lefty Gomez, Thurman Munson, Roger Maris and other dead guys. Greg didn't think twice about any of this until Wayne asked him for some cuts of Abraham Lincoln.

Sitting at the kitchen table at Smokewood Place, with Wayne standing by, Greg put down his antique pen and picked up the paper he was supposed to use. "I don't think this is old enough," he said.

"Don't worry about it," Wayne assured him. "No one will notice."

Greg shrugged. It ultimately made no difference to him whether he signed Abe Lincoln or Abe Vigoda. "I wasn't the one selling it, so I didn't care." He put down the paper and picked up his pen. "Here, you want the signature. Take it."

But it wasn't so easy to brush off the switch of Stan's account. It worried the Marinos until Wayne explained that he was going to get a piece of Rino's business with Stan. Now that was the guy they knew, keeping a finger in every profit-making pie. "If he had given up everything without wanting a percentage, that would've been different," Greg said. "But Bray was still getting a percentage of everything Rino did with Stan. So we didn't think anything more about it."

To help Rino with the transition to Stan's account, Wayne visited him at his place in San Clemente, delivering three hundred blank SCAA certs, an SCAA authentication stamp, and a note from Stan saying how the cuts and photos should be sent directly to Stan's framer. A few days later Rino showed Wayne the nine pages of fakes that he had authenticated using the SCAA certs, including numerous individual photos of Richard Nixon, Gerald Ford, Jimmy Carter, Ronald Reagan and George H.W. Bush, and some other ones of all of them together. That same day a big cuts order came in from Stan: three Bruce Lees, three Spencer Tracys, four Ernest Hemingways, six George Gershwins, six Martin Luther Kings, ten Humphrey Bogarts, ten Janis Joplins, ten Groucho Marxes, ten Elvis Presleys, twelve James Deans, fifteen Marilyn Monroes and hundreds more. Not long after this came a quickie order for fifty signed 8x10s of Hillary Clinton and twenty-four of Jackie O.

High on meth and pot, burned out and distracted, working day and night to finance his and his family's dreams, earning piles and piles of cash of which there never seemed to be enough, Greg burned through all these autographs and more. So much business was coming in from Stan that Rino asked Wayne about hiring Mike Lopez as a backup, doing whatever Greg couldn't get to. Even as they pondered this, another mammoth order from New Jersey lit up Rino's smoking fax machine: six Gilda Radner photos, twenty-five "Seinfeld" cast photos, fifty John Wayne photos, two hundred Satchel Paige baseballs, two hundred Thurman Munson baseballs, three hundred Roger Maris baseballs. The next day Rino drove this order down to the Marinos and gave Gloria twenty-five thousand in cash for some of their recent work for him.

During these final, cash-crazy days of summer, the Marinos received their now-infamous order for the baseballs to be signed by Mother Teresa. This order came through Rino who was filling it for another party that has never been identified. And although it surprised Greg even more than the Lincoln cuts, he signed all five of the balls on the sweet spot. Each ball received a certificate of authenticity from the J. DiMaggio Company; the certification number for one was 33298J, written down by the conscientious DiMaggio in the notebooks he kept for his business. Additionally, Greg signed three Mother Teresa photographs. In these photographs she is in a habit and clasping her hands with a prayerful expression on her aging, lined face. To the right of her face is her forged signature, and at the end of her signature are two scrawled, lower case letters that only handwriting experts and professional forgers would have known about: "mc." These initials stand for Missionaries of Charity, her religious order, and she customarily signed her name with them. So even at this late stage in the game, with the nonstop pressures to turn over material fast so they could sell it and take more orders and turn over more material, the guys still cared enough to get the details right.

Despite their initial hesitation the Marinos quickly got over their worries about Wayne and adjusted to the new order of things. Helping to smooth the adjustment was all the money that Stan, through Rino, was laying on them. Stan did $200,000 in business with Rino in August alone. And in the first two weeks of September, he spent another $289,000.

With the Stan the Man problem handled, Bray and the FBI took aim on Doc and Phil Scheinman, the father-and-son team that ran Smokey's Sports Cards in Las Vegas. Wayne had first approached Phil at the Smokey's booth on the floor of the National, getting in good with him by talking bad about Greg. "I told him I knew that Greg was supplying them with stuff, but that you couldn't rely on Greg so they needed to deal with me." Though the Scheinmans had done business with Greg for years, loyalty only counts for so much in the counterfeit memorabilia business, and Phil said he'd be willing to talk more with Bray at a later date. With McKinney and Fitzsimmons pushing hard behind the scenes, that date came quick. When Wayne returned to California he called Phil and they came to terms on a deal, with Bray offering to drop off the merchandise on his next trip to Vegas in a few days.

Wayne did not happen to mention that he'd be accompanied on this trip by two federal agents, Fitzsimmons and Maura Fahy.

The FBI had waited to introduce Fahy to its cooperating witness because, as she said, "people get very nervous talking to the IRS," criminals included. One reason was that on top of the threat of federal prosecution, the IRS could strip them of some or even all of their assets. As cool as he was with his undercover subjects, Bray was as rattled as anyone else by the specter of the IRS. When the cheerful, unimposing agent finally came to see him at his house in San Marcos, he was "visibly shaking," she recalled. Bray's cooperation agreement included a commitment to fully disclose his financial activities, and the two of them sat down with his income tax returns. "I had all his returns," said Fahy, "and I had talked to his accountant ahead of time to see how they'd been prepared. I had studied his Schedule C, and one year it said that the cost of goods sold for his business was $100,000 or thereabouts. I wasn't sure how he'd arrived at that figure, so I asked him to explain it to me."

"Okay, you've got me," the jumpy Bray blurted out. "It's fraudulent."

Fahy thought, "Okay, cool," because until that moment she had no idea the number was a sham. Saying nothing about what this revelation meant to her, she later recalculated his return, and this and other admissions by him led to the seizure of his Harley, his jewelry and other assets after the takedown.

Aware of what Bray's cooperation meant to the investigation—"He opened it up," she said succinctly—Fahy kept probing gently to find out more about the gang's finances. Through him, she learned about all the cash the Marinos were pouring into their dream house and how they were planning to dump the *Bada Bing* and trade up for a new boat with the help of Big Ricky Weimer. Greg and John did not want to be seen handling lots of cash so they asked Big Ricky to act as middle man, giving him $42,000 in bills. With this money Big Ricky bought cashier's checks that the brothers used as a partial down payment for the *Casa La Mare*.

As Fahy dug deeper and deeper into the financial affairs of the operation, she gained a growing sense of how big it was. "It had a lot of tentacles," she said, and these tentacles reached into every state in the U.S. and involved many thousands of individuals and businesses, far more than the ones she was looking into, and consumer losses in the hundreds of millions of dollars since the mid-nineties. The conspiracy was large and headless. The Bray-Marino ring and the other forgery rings around the country did not function like traditional organizations. There was no centralized decision-making structure, no one at the top telling those lower down what to do. The corruption was more sophisticated than that. The seemingly honest businessmen and businesswomen selling and distributing these dirty goods knew what to do without anyone having to say a word. They were part of the rip-off though they'd never be implicated in it or charged with any crime. And they kept silent about it because they had a vested interest in its success, and their complicity allowed the thing to basically run itself.

Fahy went with Bray and Fitzsimmons to Vegas as part of her ongoing financial investigations in the case. For budgetary reasons she stayed at a family-style motel while the two men booked rooms at New York-New York, the self-proclaimed "Greatest City in Las Vegas," on the Strip not far from Smokey's. Wanting this trip to be exactly like all of Bray's other trips to Vegas, at least outwardly, Fitzsimmons had asked Wayne beforehand what hotel he stayed at when he came to town. The answer was New York-New York, so the case agent, also on a government budget, booked the two cheapest rooms available. The rooms were reserved under Bray's name, but when he and Fitzsimmons arrived in the lobby to check in, the room clerk greeted them with a frown.

Studying the hotel's computer system, she saw that something was amiss. "Oh, Mr. Bray," she said, her frown turning to a smile. "We can do much better than this for you." Adding, with a glance over at the uncomfortable looking FBI agent standing nearby, "And we can take care of your business associate as well, for no extra charge."

The rooms were considered beneath the stature of a high-roller such as Mr. Bray, so the hotel upgraded their accommodations. During the wiretap phase of the investigation Fitzsimmons had developed a sense of the lifestyle that the memorabilia boys were leading, but it was not until he and Wayne checked into their luxury suites at New York-New York that he truly understood how glorious it must have been for them in their inglorious prime. "It was a palatial style suite, easily 1,000 square feet," said the agent, clearly impressed. "Wet bar, elevated king size bed, big screen TV, kitchenette, dining room, living rooms with chandeliers, sitting rooms, bathrooms with marble floors, this huge jacuzzi set up so you could watch TV while soaking in the tub. To me, this was an indication of how Bray had lived when he was in Vegas. He was known to that computer."

The meets at Smokey's went smooth. Always a fast worker, Wayne brought in some fakes and negotiated with Phil, who gave him a couple grand in cash and ordered some more. Less than a week later Smokey's shipped three boxes of blanks to W.W. Sports Cards—one count, mail fraud. Then came two checks in the mail from Smokey's for services rendered—two more counts, mail fraud. To conduct these deals both Doc and Phil had talked to Bray on the phone—four more counts, wire fraud. The FBI was right to bet on Bray. Smokey's had just been smoked.

Other bogus dealers smoked by Bray were Steve Allen, Barry Albert, Tim DiPinto, Bruce Gaston, Barry Goldberg, Lowell Katz and Rocky Rabadia.

The last man to be crossed off the hit list, the last man standing as it were, was Nate Harrison. "I avoided doing Nate," said Wayne, who didn't want to do him and kept inventing excuses as to why he couldn't. "I was always conveniently busy. Know what I mean?"

Not pressing the matter, McKinney and Fitzsimmons went along with his excuses until there was nobody left but Nate. He couldn't be avoided any longer. So Wayne did as he was told. He got wired up and drove over to Nate's shop off Mission Avenue not far from W.W. Sports Cards. Nate's little brother was there when Wayne arrived, but Nate quickly told him to go down to the 7-Eleven and get a drink or something. After he left the two friends discussed a deal for Mantle caps.

When the meet was over Wayne handed the tape over at W.W. Sports Cards per usual. But when McKinney and Fitzsimmons listened to it later, they didn't like what they heard. At all.

"Bray got a little from Nate but it wasn't good enough," said McKinney. He and Fitzsimmons saw that the Fox was trying to pull one over on them too, deliberately doing a poor job on Nate in order to fulfill the terms of his bargain with the government while saving his friend from prison. But the ploy didn't work, and the next time McKinney saw Wayne he told him that the tape was no good and he was going to have to do Nate again.

They were driving at night on a road in North County, coming back from a meet. Wayne listened to what the agent had to say and was quiet a long time before replying. "I'm not doing Nate," he said at last.

Up to this point he had hidden his real feelings about Nate from the FBI, but now he had to come out with it. Nate wasn't just a business associate or even a friend, he told McKinney. He was like blood. Wayne had brought Nate into the racket because he wanted for Nate what Nate wanted for himself: to get over, to be an earner. And look what had happened—Nate was standing on his own like a man. Besides, Wayne continued, he had always been straight with Nate and Nate had always been straight with him. And now he was going to screw him over too, the only guy in the whole world besides his father who had truly trusted him? No, not Nate, anybody but Nate.

"I'm not doing him," he repeated, more strongly than before. "I'm not."

Saying nothing, McKinney pulled the car to the side of the road and turned off the engine. It was a warm, quiet desert night. Stars were out. A big man, he turned his body slightly in his seat so he could speak directly to Bray. "You're doing him," he said firmly. His normally easy-going attitude had disappeared and in its place there was an edge to his voice, a sharpness that suggested that this was not a matter open to debate. "Now let me tell you why."

He briefly reviewed the terms of the cooperation agreement Bray had signed. Full meant full—nothing less. This was not something he could sweet-talk his way out of, cherry-picking only the subjects he chose to do. Wayne was doing really well. But if he refused to do Nate or only did him in a half-ass way, things were going to turn instantly bad for him. All the good work he had done up to that point would mean nothing and prison would be a certainty. "You don't get to choose," he said. "Your cooperation is complete and total. That's just the way it is."

Searching Wayne's face for a reaction, the agent waited a moment for this to sink in. A pair of headlights came towards them on the road and passed them by. Then he softened the edge and made a different sort of pitch. Wayne, he said, had done such a good job of jamming up the other guys that when the takedown came they'd have no choice but to cooperate with the government. If they cooperated fully, told what they knew, did what Wayne was doing—actively assisting the FBI in bringing down more subjects—they'd have a better chance of reducing their sentences. Nate deserved the same chance, said McKinney.

"Help us, and we'll give Nate the same opportunity we gave you. Nate has to know he has no other choice but to cooperate, and in order for him to see this you need to do him good. So he will make the same decision you did. So he will help himself in the same way you did. Now," said the agent with finality, that edge returning, "you're going to do him again. And this time you're doing him right."

He turned back in his seat, started up the car, and the two drove through the night in silence.

The scam had always been about money. Getting it, getting more of it, getting more and more of it and buying things with it: houses and vehicles and jewelry and chicks and high times. But in the end it wasn't about money and things. It was about things that weren't things: loyalty, friendship, trust. Now, according to the FBI's line of reasoning, the best thing Wayne could do for his friend was betray him.

Betrayal as an act of loyalty? By jamming Nate up he was helping him? Interesting concepts, these. Interesting or not, Wayne saw no other way out. He called Nate and arranged another meeting.

This one took place at Nate's house, upstairs in the game room. It was in the evening, after dinner. When Wayne came in he found Nate sitting on the carpet in front of the TV, skillfully working the hand controls on an electronic fantasy where bad guys are truly bad and you get to blow lots of things up. Nate kept his eyes mainly on the game and muttered a soft hello.

When Shelly called Nate to tell him what had happened that night at Shelly's house—how he felt sure Wayne was wearing a wire—Nate wouldn't believe it. Later in the summer, after a second meeting with Wayne, Shelly became even more convinced about Bray, repeating his accusations to Nate who still remained loyal to his friend. But Nate could not dismiss Shelly's charges quite so readily after Wayne had approached him about the Mantle caps.

"I was always very careful not to say the f-word," said Nate. "I had always talked in code and I had corrected people if they went out of code. Only I was less careful with Wayne because I trusted him. But at the office he was talking too openly about everything, and my brother was there with us. I had to get him out of the shop because he didn't know what was going on and Wayne was talking too much."

Nate wasn't sure what to think anymore. Part of him believed that Wayne had gone over to the FBI, and part of him believed that Wayne would never do such a thing, at least not to him. Another part of him figured that since he had gone this far with Wayne, he might as well go all the way with him, even if meant going down with him. Wayne was his best friend in the world after all, and Nate was going to stay loyal to him no matter what. Still, while they talked, Nate remained absorbed in his game, unable to look Wayne in the eye because he knew in his heart what his friend was secretly up to.

"I did what they asked," Wayne said years later, still bitter at this memory. "I got Nate to say what I knew they wanted him to say. That he knew everything he was selling was fake."

Then he went home and busted up his kitchen in a rage.

24

Preparations for the takedown moved ahead even as the FBI learned of a large counterfeit card operation in the Los Angeles area. This information came through Bray, who was doing business with a dealer named Barry Goldberg. "Goldberg started bringing Bray these counterfeit rookie cards of McGwire, Sosa, Tony Gwynn, Dan Marino, John Elway," said McKinney. "He had thousands of them, boxes and boxes, and he was selling and trading them for signed memorabilia. They were all freshly cut so we knew there had to be a factory somewhere in LA that was printing these cards. But we didn't know who was doing it or where."

Warnings about the high quality of these counterfeits had appeared in the collector press. "McGwire counterfeit called the scariest yet," read a headline in *Sports Collectors Digest*. "Hobby experts say this fake looks almost better than the original." An analysis by the magazine revealed only minute differences between the originals and the fakes, which had crisper printing and sharper color registration. Another report described the fakes as "extremely good. It takes some work to identify these counterfeits, especially the Marino." To determine the authenticity of the Marino card, the writer recommended that collectors compare a genuine card against a fake one, and studying them both under a microscope. Under ten-point magnification one could see that "the dot structure" in the tiny white area on the Dolphins helmet worn by Marino was slightly fuzzier on the fake cards. For those without a microscope or who did not own authentic versions of the cards, the only advice was: Buyer beware.

The counterfeits were all rookie cards, rookie cards generally being the most valuable of all trading cards because they are rarer and harder to obtain. The fake five were McGwire on the 1984 United States Olympic baseball team, pictured in his red Team USA jersey and cap with a bat resting on his shoulder; Sosa, in an uncharacteristic bunting pose; Gwynn, who had recently passed the 3,000 career hit mark and whose value to collectors had correspondingly increased; and the two superstar quarterbacks, Elway and Marino. The McGwire card was the most valuable with a list price of two hundred dollars.

Officials from Topps, which manufactured all but the Sosa card, reported seeing McGwire rookie cards entering the market in huge, unprecedented lots of more than 1,000 apiece. One eBay merchant sold five hundred in a single Dutch auction. Topps estimated that at least 10,000 of the fake McGwires were circulating in the marketplace, although the company admitted the actual figure could be much higher. By every estimate the number was considerable, and McKinney and the FBI recognized this as "potentially a multimillion dollar problem."

Goldberg, described by McKinney as "a smart, likeable New York-style dealer with salt and pepper hair," was not buying directly from the printer. Rather he was working with a middle man who had a pipeline into the printing plant. In order to get to this middle man, and thereby to the source, the FBI needed to get Goldberg to incriminate himself on tape. For this it once again relied on the talents of its cooperating witness.

"Our goal was to get Goldberg jammed up," said McKinney. "Once we jammed him up we figured we could get him to talk about where he was getting the cards. So we used Bray to jam Goldberg, and Bray got him a million different ways." Bray placed an order with Goldberg for thousands of cards. When he showed up to deliver the cards at W.W. Sports Cards, the plan was for some FBI agents to introduce themselves to him, reveal the evidence they had on him, and make their pitch on why he should abandon his unlawful activities. This unhappy surprise party for Goldberg was scheduled for October 13, takedown day.

John Ferreira also placed big orders with his subjects a few days before the takedown because the FBI, for reasons of evidence and to make a big media splash, wanted plenty of loot on hand to seize. While chatting with his clients over the weekend the agent casually inquired where they'd be on Wednesday. Everyone said they'd be home except Chip Lombardo, who excitedly relayed the news he'd be with his wife celebrating their wedding anniversary at a luxury hotel downtown.

"Oh boy, are you in for a surprise," thought Ferreira.

On takedown day Ferreira would remain at the Carlsbad RA, which would serve as command post for the operation. He would not participate in any of the raids, and he stayed away from a meeting held at Camp Pendleton two days before takedown. The FBI chose the Marine Corps base north of Oceanside as its meeting place because it needed a secure site where lots of federal agents could gather without worry of being noticed by the public. About two hundred FBI and IRS agents from San Diego and LA—half the total that took part in the busts—packed an auditorium there for a show-and-tell conducted by Fitzsimmons and McKinney. The case agent and co-case agent gave an overview of the investigation to the audience, explaining what to look for when the search teams entered the residences and places of business and how to distinguish legitimate signed items that should be left alone from the fakes that were to be confiscated. The agents played what McKinney called "a greatest hits tape" of the most outrageous things said by the flip-flop mafia over the wire and in the undercover recordings. The clear audience favorite was the video of Greg autographing the Gary Cooper cut on the kitchen table of his parents' house.

Maura Fahy spoke about the IRS side of things. In late September she and McKinney had conducted surveillance on the Alps Way house, noting that construction was about ninety percent complete with the landscaping set to begin. McKinney remarked, to the delight of the audience, that the Marinos would never realize their dream of moving in.

With the United States Attorney's office, Fahy had prepared a forty-two-page complaint for forfeiture on the house. In this document she described how it had been paid for solely by the Marinos' illegal earnings and therefore could be rightly seized by the government. The complaint contained a detailed accounting of Gloria's financial activities, including her $50,000 cash drop at the Palomar Savings and Loan and a transcript of her comments ("Give them a little cash. That makes them very happy, you know what I mean?") on how the family was paying the builders. Fahy would sign the complaint the next day, and it was to be filed the morning of the takedown with the Clerk of the United States District Court, Southern District of California.

Phil Halpern was the other core member of the team to address the gathering. For the takedown, sixty search warrants would be served on an equal number of homes and businesses in California, Nevada, Pennsylvania and New Jersey. (Later Florida would be added to the list.) Each warrant contained the name of the subject, his or her address, a brief description of the property to be searched and a list of the items to be seized: sports and celebrity memorabilia, counterfeiting material, customer lists, financial records, cancelled checks, income tax returns, business ledgers, telephone statements, Rolodexes, diaries, correspondence, computers. The warrants stipulated that "any authorized officer of the United States" was permitted to enter the specified premises and confiscate "the fruits, evidence and instrumentalities of criminal offenses."

One major goal of the takedown was to get confessions from as many ring members as possible. Though he did not mention it at the meeting, Halpern had placed a bet with McKinney over how many confessions they'd bag. McKinney guessed ten; the more pessimistic Halpern said none. He didn't think any of the subjects would roll over. The loser would buy the other dinner.

The searches were to be conducted by both FBI and IRS agents. The agents received plastic evidence bags and boxes with identification labels to hold the material they confiscated. Eight to ten agents made up a search team, FBI and IRS divided equally, with the FBI agents serving as team leaders. Each team had enough people to easily overwhelm any resistance they might encounter. But with so many agents at every location, it was thought—rightly, as it turned out—that the subjects would see the foolishness of resisting and allow for a peaceful entry and search. Still, all the agents would wear bulletproof flak jackets and windbreakers identifying themselves as federal officers, and carry guns.

Within each team McKinney assigned certain agents to interview specific individuals and, it was hoped, win their cooperation. Greg, John and Gloria Marino were considered the plum assignments. The canny Jake Gregory, who had been undercover at Coco's, was assigned to Greg; Adam Lee drew John; and Linda Bateman, a twenty-five-year FBI agent known as a person who wouldn't take crap from anybody, got Gloria.

One of the biggest one-day takedowns in FBI history took place early Wednesday morning, October 13, 1999, with teams of FBI and IRS agents knocking on the doors of counterfeit memorabilia dealers and forgers around southern California. Fitzsimmons and McKinney decided to first cover the home turf before rolling out the searches in the other states, their thinking being that if the local guys decided to cooperate, the FBI could have them call their associates back East and get recorded admissions from them. Then federal agents in the other states could knock on some doors themselves.

Bray received a day-long FBI escort for security reasons. No one could anticipate how the other memorabilia boys would react upon learning that the man who had most zealously enforced the code of silence was the one who had smashed it to pieces. Bray made calls for the FBI as the raids were rolling out, phoning guys who were waffling about whether or not to believe what the agents were telling them. He said yeah, believe it, the party's over, and you better reduce yourself. Another thing he did was trap Goldberg.

As planned, the smart New York-style operator with the salt and pepper hair showed up that morning at W.W. Sports Cards with a vehicle full of counterfeit cards, thinking he was about to land a sweetheart of a deal. Instead all he got was heartache. He and Bray brought the boxes upstairs and they were talking in the shop when they heard some noise on the steps outside. A knock on the door followed, and Wayne answered it. Gathered on the walkway was a group of agents in windbreakers and flak jackets.

"These guys are the FBI," Bray told the stunned Goldberg. "You better listen to what they have to say because you're screwed."

Bray departed with his escort while FBI Special Agent Jerry Brown, a soft-spoken former East St. Louis homicide investigator who had obtained confessions in a number of murder cases, started his tough, tense negotiations with Goldberg.

A husky, black-haired ex-Navy lieutenant, IRS Special Agent Dave White had entered the case over the summer, assisting Fahy in her financial probe of the ring. On takedown morning he found himself at the beautiful, two-story Newport Coast custom home owned by Mike and Robyn Moses. The lead FBI agent did the knock, and in a minute or two they heard Mike's voice from behind the door.

"Who is it?"

"We're federal agents. We have a warrant to search your house. Now open up."

While Fahy had focused on the Marinos and Bray, White's investigation had largely centered on Moses and Universal Authentic Memorabilia. Secretly tracking his financial doings for months, White had only seen pictures of him—pictures that showed him to be a somewhat out of shape, heavyset guy. But when Moses, shirtless and in gym shorts, opened the door, White could see that he looked trim and in shape.

"Man," said White, stepping inside, "you look great."

Moses sleepily thanked him, excusing himself to go get dressed as the rest of the search team crossed into the house. Like the other agents White wore a flak jacket and blue windbreaker with the words FEDERAL AGENT in large letters on the back. He carried an agency-issue Sig Sauer 9mm pistol, which he never unholstered. (None of the agents in any of the searches unholstered their guns.) As soon as he walked in he saw they had come to the right place. "Memorabilia was all over," he said. "Lots of Sharpie pens and material in the garage. In one place there were unsigned mini-helmets and unsigned jerseys. In another place were signed mini-helmets and signed jerseys. It was all arranged in a logical order."

One item found by the agents was Moses's combination lock briefcase. When White asked for the key and combination, Moses freely gave it to him and recited the numbers, calmly standing by while the agent opened it to find more than $100,000 in cash. The FBI later uncovered another $100,000 stored in what Moses thought was the safety of his bank safe deposit box.

Robyn shortly appeared with their two young children in tow. She was visibly upset, complaining, asking sharp questions, giving curt answers and upsetting everyone else, including her husband.

"Calm down," he told her more than once. "Take the kids and go to your Mom's."

As intrusive as this search was—searches of homes always engender more emotion from subjects than business searches—it was still an exciting event, and Robyn, despite her unhappiness, did not want to miss a minute of it. But her attitude, said White, was "ticking everybody off," including the female FBI agent who had been assigned to do her subject interview.

"I don't know who's advising you," she told Robyn, "but they're giving you bad advice."

Down the coast in San Clemente, Caroline Hoag was sitting in the home of Scott and Mary Lou Harris, the parents of Karen Ruberti. A veteran of many takedowns and subject interviews, Hoag had been with the FBI long enough to know instinctively when someone was lying to her. "Sometimes people ask me what our jobs are like," she said with a sigh, "and I tell them that it feels like we're getting lied to every day."

Hoag just knew that Mary Lou, who in four days would celebrate her sixty-seventh birthday, was lying to her. Upon entering the house Hoag had noticed forged Beatles albums in plain sight. When she walked back through, the albums were gone—and you didn't have to be Sherlock Holmes to figure out who had hidden them. But Mary Lou had her story and she was sticking to it. "I just knew she wasn't telling me the truth," the agent concluded wearily.

And she never did tell Hoag the truth, though she did confess later. Feeling bad about how she had behaved with Hoag, the repentant Mary Lou sent a message to her through another investigator: "Tell that nice woman from the FBI that I'm sorry I lied to her." It was the first and only time in Hoag's career a subject had apologized to her for lying.

The lying came to an end for Rick Mitchell, too. The Mitchells were doing a remodeling project in their backyard, and Rick had stepped outside to take a look at it with his baby boy when a posse of agents appeared. In total shock, he gathered his son up in his arms and went inside with them. "I was stunned," he recalled. "I remember coming into the living room and stepping over this plastic fence on the carpet that was my son's and feeling like I was gonna pass out."

Presenting him with a search warrant, the FBI pressed its case. "The agents were all over me, saying I could be prosecuted under the RICO act if I didn't cooperate. That I'd lose everything and go to prison and when I got out I'd have to start over with nothing. I was guilty, I knew I was guilty. But I didn't feel like I had anything to hide. Then the agents told me that Wayne had been working undercover with them and I said, 'Okay, now I really have nothing to hide.'"

The realization came over him that there was no sense trying to bluff anyone anymore, and with a leaden feeling he sat down with his son and played with him on the carpet while the agents systematically went through every room of his house. In the garage was the spiffy red Ferrari he had acquired in a trade with a client. To seal the deal Mitchell had signed a paper stating the terms of their agreement. A search agent found this paper in his office and since fake memorabilia was involved in the transaction, it provided the basis for the government to tow the car away.

The FBI and IRS worked at Mitchell's house all morning and into the afternoon. "They took everything," he said disgustedly. "Anything that had to do with sports memorabilia, they took." Dozens of Hot Wheel cars he was collecting for his son, ten plastic bags full of Starting Lineup figurines, stacks of old sports magazines and every card in his entire baseball card collection—more than 250,000 cards that Mitchell had been collecting since childhood. Nearly all of this was legal, unsigned memorabilia that was later returned to him, but the agents had no way of knowing this at the time and so they took it all. Since there was so much stuff that had to be counted, packaged and labeled, they carried it out of the house and laid it out on his driveway, in full view of the neighbors. The subdivision had never seen anything like it before. Federal agents in guns and flak jackets bagging and tagging baseball cards as boys rode by on bicycles and moms passing in SUVs slowed down to take a look.

School let out in the afternoon, and Mitchell's wife came home. When she pulled up, the driveway was still covered with stuff and men and women in windbreakers were loading boxes into a van. She got out of her car and looked around. Her expression seemed a mixture of concern and puzzlement.

"Honey," she said. "What's going on?"

"It's not good," said Rick.

Chip Lombardo's wife was equally stunned when, on the morning of their wedding anniversary, federal agents knocked on the door of their San Diego hotel room to notify them that their Del Mar townhouse was being raided. Her husband was also shocked to find out that the man he knew as John Freitas was actually FBI Special Agent John Ferreira, and that in the past two years his favorite lunch buddy had collected irrefutable evidence of his guilt. An agent gave Chip the number of the Carlsbad RA and said he could speak to Ferreira if he wished.

Of all the subjects Ferreira had worked during the case, Chip was the only one to call him that day. "He started out by saying, 'I don't hate you.' I could hear the fear in his voice. But we talked, and he ended the call by saying, 'I love you.'" This comment surprised the agent—"My reaction was, 'What? I'm just doing my job'"—and he tried his best to make sense of it. What he came up with was that the two of them had formed a real friendship, at least in Chip's mind. He knew that Chip had long contemplated getting out of the racket. This was his way of saying thanks to the man who helped him do it.

Nobody was arrested during the takedown; all the subjects slept in the same bed that night that they were in that morning. Dave Tabb learned about the bust not from the FBI but from Mike Moses. Moses called to say that the feds were at his house and Tabb, who was still in bed, promptly called his secretary to see what was going on at his Santa Ana office. She informed him that yes, the FBI and IRS were there, and they had presented her with a search affidavit. Wondering to himself why she had not bothered to inform him of this fact, he rang off and phoned his attorney.

On Yaqi Court in Tustin, Shelly Jaffe expressed little surprise when he answered his door to find a bevy of agents waiting outside.

"Well, you were expecting us, weren't you?" said the lead agent, slyly referring to how, during a recorded conversation, Jaffe had talked as if he was speaking directly to the FBI, trying to work out a deal before the bust.

"Yeah," he said with a resigned look. "Come on in."

Nor was Nate Harrison all that shocked when he heard some pounding on the front door of his house. He was in bed too. Groggily throwing off his covers, he looked outside his bedroom window to see the agents on the porch below. He tossed on his clothes and went downstairs to let them in.

That was when Nate found out, definitively, what his best friend had done. As an agent played for him the undercover tape Wayne had made of them talking in the game room that night, "it was like a fist tightened around my stomach. It was a bad feeling."

More bad feelings followed. At his office warehouse he had stored hundreds of caps, jerseys, balls, photos, cuts and other signed items. Nate estimated their street value at $1 million, and the FBI and IRS cleaned him out.

The knock on the door that Kathy Marino had always feared took place precisely at eight a.m. "Eight a.m. was the exact time everywhere," she said. "That was when the FBI hit everybody."

She and Greg were asleep in their upstairs bedroom at Beaumont Glen when a loud noise at the front door woke her. "It was like boom! boom! boom! I thought it was maybe the kids who lived in the unit below us." Wearing only the long T-shirt she had slept in, she got up without disturbing her husband and scurried downstairs in her bare feet. Peering out the front door peephole, she saw "a whole crowd of people" standing outside.

"Who is it?" she asked uncertainly.

"Open up, Kathy," said a female agent in a friendly tone. "It's the FBI."

This was when she thought: Okay, so this is it. This is what God has decided. It's time.

She opened the door to receive God's blessing and the FBI poured through, with Jake Gregory in the lead moving briskly up the stairs. Waking up to find the FBI in his bedroom was not how Greg had planned to start the day, "but I knew right away what it was for," he said. "I had always thought it could happen, though I didn't know how it'd go down. Wayne and I had talked about it a lot. Then when the FBI told me that he was the one who had turned, I thought, 'Well, that's it. We're screwed.' I knew right away they had enough evidence once they said his name."

The FBI had brought a copy of the briefcase video Wayne had made at Smokewood Place, asking if Greg wanted to watch it. He declined. He had no desire to see his former partner's handiwork. Instead he asked if he could talk to his mother. The answer was yes, and when he got Gloria on the phone he told her that FBI agents were all over their apartment.

"They're here too," she said quietly, sounding overwhelmed.

The FBI and IRS made their biggest show of strength at Smokewood Place, and this shocked Gloria and Angelo especially. As for John, he was in the kitchen fixing breakfast for his kids when the agents arrived. He stopped what he was doing to answer the door. While being presented with a search warrant, his mother rushed up to see what was going on.

"Mom," he told her. "It's the FBI."

The children weren't sure what to make of all these strangers suddenly entering the house, and the FBI agreed to let John finish getting them dressed and ready for their day. So John drove them off to school as the agents began their searches.

The place, as expected, was lousy with forged merchandise. Agents found roughly $75,000 in cash hidden in Gloria's and Angelo's bed.

When John returned, he started "strutting around," said Adam Lee, still denying his guilt despite ample evidence to the contrary. Anticipating this, Lee produced a copy of the forging video and asked John if he'd like to see it. Unlike his brother, John said yeah, let's see what you got.

So Lee slipped the tape in the VCR, and John sat on the couch in the living room and watched. The tape had a gray surveillance quality to it with a time counter running at the bottom of the screen. It lasted only a few minutes but packed a wallop. "It nailed John between the eyes," said Lee. "He cracked. He was no longer such a tough guy, if he ever was one. He grabbed a pillow with his hands and started to tear up, asking for his mom."

Before Lee would agree to this, he asked John to make a recorded call to another subject in the investigation, which he did. Then Linda Bateman brought in Gloria, who joined him on the couch. All of John's bluster was gone; he was a puddle. The husky six-footer curled up like a small child in his mother's arms and began to whimper pitifully.

"Mom," he said. "They got us on tape."

Word of John's fetal-like collapse was relayed back to the command post and spread quickly among the hundreds of search agents conducting the takedown. "Sometimes," said McKinney with a smile, "it's good to be an agent."

PART THREE

Rings and More Rings

25

Around noon on the day of the bust Kathy Marino left her apartment to go to Calvary Church for a moment of prayer and reflection. From there she drove to her in-laws' house where her husband and the other members of his family were sitting around in a daze. "It was surreal," she said, remembering that day. "It was like it wasn't happening. It felt like we were in a dream."

The search teams were at the house when she arrived, and they were still there after eight that night. Meanwhile the family sat in their dream state talking amongst themselves in the backyard and wandering in and out of the house as the agents moved about collecting and boxing the evidence. In the afternoon John went to pick his kids up at school and brought them home. He parked on the street because the FBI van was in the driveway being loaded with stuff.

Earlier in the day, before collapsing in his mother's arms, John had agreed to make a recorded call to Barry Delit, the long-time Marino family associate who ran the Rookie King in Pottstown, Pennsylvania. After John got Barry on tape, the second phase of the takedown began to roll out, with Pennsylvania agents knocking on Delit's door at about the same time New Jersey agents were calling on Stan Fitzgerald. Fitzgerald, it was said, ripped his phone out of the wall when he heard about the takedown. Even as the FBI was moving in on his homes and business, Stan was moving deftly himself, taking a half-million in cash to buy cashier's checks that he deposited into a bank account. The next week he used this money to buy a house on Bradley Beach on the Jersey shore, a house that years later would be seized by the government.

Besides having their world famous sports card shop raided by federal agents, Doc and Phil Scheinman suffered the further indignity of having the search filmed by "20/20." Tipped off ahead of time by the government, ABC News positioned its cameras in a concealed second-story location on Las Vegas Boulevard across from Smokey's, shooting a parade of agents carrying framed photos, posters and other signed artifacts out of the shop into an FBI van. At one point a clearly agitated Doc Scheinman stepped outside and gestured angrily at the agents, and this footage appeared on the program the following week.

All day long, trucks full of seized memorabilia rolled into the Aero Drive warehouse of the San Diego FBI. Agents unloaded the trucks and stacked the evidence according to where it came from and the subject or subjects it was associated with. When one truck pulled out, another soon pulled in. The sheer quantity of goods—cards, photos, posters, albums, video covers, magazines, movie scripts, framed cuts, lithographs, trophies, hockey pucks, hockey sticks, tennis balls, golf shoes, golf balls, baseballs, bats, caps, footballs, helmets, mini-helmets, jerseys, cleats, basketballs, sneakers, toy cars, action figures, guitars, tambourines—was enormous, worth an estimated $10 million. Many of the items were too big and bulky to fit into evidence packets or even in boxes, and large, sprawling heaps of stuff took up virtually every inch of floor space in the 20,000-square foot federal facility.

The FBI also bagged and tagged $200,000 in cash from Mike Moses's briefcase and safe deposit box, $75,000 from Gloria and Angelo's private bedroom stash, and another $135,000 in walking-around money from various subjects.

Jeff McKinney won his dinner bet with Phil Halpern; the FBI got eleven confessions on takedown day, one more than the agent predicted. More confessions followed two days later when the Marinos and twenty other members of the ring appeared at the United States Courthouse on Front Street in San Diego. Kathy Marino's feelings of unreality intensified still more when she entered the courtroom and saw so many of their friends and former associates sitting there. "It was like a movie," she said. "The court was packed. There were all these people. Some of them I knew, like Ricky Weimer. Some of them I didn't know, like Mike Moses, but I had heard his name so often I felt like I knew him. Mike Lopez was there. So was Little Mikey, who'd been in on the scam for about a week. I saw Little Ricky. His eyes were red like he'd been crying, and he looked at us real sad."

Nate Harrison, Dick Laughlin, Shelly Jaffe, Robyn Moses, Reno and Karen Ruberti, Scott and Mary Lou Harris, Dave Tabb, Mike Bowler, Chip Lombardo, Jon Hall, Lowell Katz, Bruce Gaston and Frosty Golembeske were there too, all of them sitting nervously with their attorneys in the rows of seats in the rear of the courtroom, all of them turning to look when the doors swung open and the Marinos came through.

One person notable for his absence was Wayne Bray. Bray felt, and the FBI agreed, that his presence might be a volatile one, and arrangements were made for him to make his plea in court on a different day.

"That was good. Because it wouldn't have been pretty to have him there," said Mitchell, expressing the sentiments of the group. "Wayne always said that if anything ever happened, he'd take the fall. 'Use me to authenticate,' he said, 'and I'll take the fall. Keep me posted on everything you're doing, and I'll take the fall.' Everybody believed him."

"He's a piranha," said Jaffe, never a fan of Bray's. "Take it, dude. If you're gonna get caught, get caught. Don't bury everyone else with you."

"Wayne was two-faced to everybody," said Kathy. "He had all of us snowed." Her husband felt the same, though some of his anger had to do with the fact that Wayne took down not just him and his brother but his parents as well. "He always said, 'Only trust me. Trust no one else,'" Greg said disgustedly. "And this is the guy who comes in with the wires. But the worst for me was bringing in my parents. He could've gotten me and my brother, whatever. But he had to get them too."

Despite their hard feelings toward Bray in the immediate aftermath of the bust, most of those in the courtroom that day had already begun to resign themselves to their predicament. Many expressed relief that the thing that had consumed them for so long was, finally, over. Still a number of uncertainties loomed ahead for them all, including the outcast Bray—the biggest ones being how much of their property and assets would be seized, and how much prison time they'd get.

Beginning with the Marinos, who were sitting in the jury box on one side of the court, the subjects entered their pleas. Kathy was the first to be called. She rose with her attorney and went to stand behind a podium facing the judge on the bench. Phil Halpern sat at the prosecutor's table, rising to stand behind a podium of his own. The attorneys and the judge talked legalities for a few moments, then the judge asked Kathy for her plea. "Not guilty," she said, per the instructions of her attorney. After this she followed a bailiff through a door in the back of the court, down some steps and around some hallways past the courthouse jail. "There were all these people in cells," she said with horror. "They looked like they were in cages."

The bailiff brought her to a room where she was told to wait. Greg, Gloria, Angelo and John joined her in succession after entering their pleas and following the same route past the cages of people. She made a joke to lighten things up but it didn't work. "Everyone was miserable," she said glumly.

The scene no longer resembled a movie; it was just depressing and sad. In a few minutes Tim Fitzsimmons appeared in the room to get their fingerprints and mug shots. He got what he needed, and they went home.

Over the course of the morning the others entered their pleas, took the long walk past the cells, were printed and photographed, and left. All the subjects were what attorneys and judges refer to as "Category Ones"—people with no previous criminal records who, if they hadn't got caught up in this crazy forgery thing, surely would not have found themselves in federal court being charged with multiple-count felonies. One of those was the teary-eyed Rick Mitchell, who had cried a lot over the past two days. His wife had had a rough time of it herself, her puzzlement and concern at seeing the agents at her house turning to feelings of shock and betrayal as she learned the full story of her husband's deception. She felt angry and hurt and deeply sad, and she cried, too.

But she had resources, and she called on them. Her uncle was an attorney, and he came out of retirement to represent her husband. "We met the day after the takedown at his office," Mitchell remembered. "I told him everything, and he told me you're in a heap of trouble. Cooperate and disclose everything you know. Do anything they ask you to do."

When Mitchell thought about what had gone wrong, and why, so many things came to mind—Jim DiMaggio's advice to get out of the business and how he had stupidly ignored it, how naïve he was to think that while the other guys might go down, he would avoid being caught. He knew for certain now what a disaster Coco's had been. All those agents pouring out of the restaurant while they stood around watching them. In retrospect it's obvious they're FBI, but at that moment "you don't really believe it. It can't really be FBI, can it? Then they show up at your house and you know it is."

McKinney and Fitzsimmons conducted extensive post-takedown interviews of the gang. Their questioning of Rino Ruberti uncovered one of the smaller but persistent mysteries of the investigation: Why not permanent license plates for his van? The penitent Rino explained that he wanted to drive solo in the express lane during commute hours, and he figured that if he only had temporary paper plates, the CHP would be less likely to pull him over.

After the arraignment the FBI continued to get cooperation from the subjects—one reason why McKinney, for one, had little sympathy for the criticism of Bray by his former colleagues. "The Marinos and some of the others blamed Bray for all their problems," said the agent. "They should blame greed, not Bray. They shouldn't feel betrayed. They all ended up doing what he did: giving guys up. They made the same decision he did."

More seizures took place. The FBI and IRS confiscated another $340,000 in cash, including $110,000 from the Marinos. The *Bada Bing* became government property and was eventually sold, and since the bust occurred before the Marinos could take delivery of the *Casa de la Mare*, Greg and John never got the chance to put it in the water. The Marinos' biggest property loss was their house. Maura Fahy filed forfeiture papers on the day of the takedown but the actual transfer of assets did not occur until nearly a year later. The "stipulation for compromise settlement and forfeiture," as this document is formally called, stated that the Marinos were giving up all claims to the house, that it would be sold to pay the $410,000 owed by the family for back taxes, and that the remainder of the proceeds after taxes belonged to Uncle Sam. The entire Marino family including Andrea, who flew to San Diego to be present for the occasion, signed the nine-page document. The last person to sign was the man who had signed so many other names falsely. For his own signature, Greg writes his first name smaller than his last, and the most prominent letter by far is the *M* in Marino, suggesting his strong identification with family.

The filing of this form signified that the Marinos' dream of a house in the hills was officially dead. Even so, considering how much money the family had made from the scam, officials expressed surprise and a little dismay that the government's haul was not larger. "After the takedown we looked at all their assets," said Fahy. "Except for the house and boat and some cash, they basically had no money left for restitution purposes. They had spent most of what they earned." Despite Gloria's best efforts to curb her sons' spending, money still flew out of the house as if on wings.

Little Ricky's Magnum PI car got seized. So did Bray's Harley Sportster with the racing pipes. Wayne stood outside his house and smoked a cigarette and watched as the agents rolled the bike out of his garage up onto the bed of a truck. He said nothing until he saw one of the agents eyeing his Mustang Cobra as if he was thinking about confiscating it too. "No way," said Bray, stepping forward. "I was driving that way before this ever started." The agents kept their paws off the Cobra but took his collection of Rolexes and diamond jewelry.

The government seized the contents of Nate Harrison's $35,000 E*Trade account and one of his two houses. His other house he had to sell to pay attorney's fees and back taxes. In the months after the takedown Nate cooperated with the FBI to set up a dealer named Anthony Marino (no relation to Greg and his family), arranging for him to pick up $25,000 in counterfeit goods at LNN Enterprises. When Anthony appeared, Nate explained he had a friend who was in the business like them and that he wanted Anthony to meet him. Anthony said okay and Nate called Tim Fitzsimmons, who was waiting nearby. When Fitzsimmons, posing as a crooked dealer and wearing a wire, showed up, Nate made up some excuse as to why he had to leave, and split. After Fitzsimmons got Anthony to admit he was moving fake goods, a flock of FBI agents swooped in, Fitzsimmons revealed his true identity, and one more player was out of the game and on his way to prison.

Partly because of his help in bringing down Anthony Marino, Nate succeeded in reducing his prison sentence to one year. Ironically, he spent more time behind bars than his mentor in the autograph trade. The United States Attorney's Office recommended a sentence of one year for Bray but the judge did not follow this advice. Citing Bray's decision to come forward and cooperate with the FBI, and saying how the government wished that other subjects in criminal cases would do the same, the judge sentenced him to six months in a halfway house not far from San Diego. When the Marinos and some of the others heard about this, it dug the knife in a little deeper. Kathy received probation; Gloria and Angelo got eight months apiece in prison; and John and Greg each received a sentence of three years, five months in federal prison.

On April 11, 2000, seven months after the takedown, the FBI, IRS and United States Attorney's Office held a joint press conference to announce the takedown of the ring. The government got the show it always wanted, and it made the most of it. Little Ricky's gleaming red Ferrari was wheeled in for the day and served as a centerpiece for the gaudy stacks of counterfeit merchandise on display. Hanging along one window was a row of twenty-five pro jerseys, including some team-signed jerseys of Greg's favorite, the Yankees. On tables covered by blue cloth were rows and rows of bats, baseballs, basketballs and footballs. As if there was not enough room on the tables to hold all the merchandise the government wanted to show off, the Ferrari doubled as a display space with cartons of baseballs and packages of cuts arranged on its hood. Leaning against one side of the car were beautifully framed photos of Ruth, DiMaggio, Williams, Mantle and Marilyn Monroe wrapped in white fur. Beaming FBI and IRS agents posed by the Ferrari and had souvenir pictures taken.

During his remarks to the press the FBI's Special Agent in Charge held up the Mother Teresa baseball for the cameras to see, thereby creating an instant media sensation. Mention of the ball with the forged signature of a probable future saint on it appeared in virtually every story about the case. It was the lead, the hook, the sound bite—what got people talking. CNN "Headline News" led with a reference to it. It popped up at the top of the AP wire story. Barbara Walters used it in her lead-in for the "20/20" piece, and it came up again on a companion story run by "Primetime Thursday." As perhaps even stronger evidence that the ball had touched a chord in the national consciousness, Jay Leno did a riff on it on "The Tonight Show": "Hear about this? The FBI busted up what they say is the biggest fake sport memorabilia ring in the United States. And one of the items they confiscated was a baseball signed by Mother Teresa. [Audience laughter] I'm not making this up. They said it was authentic. What idiot buys a baseball autographed by Mother Teresa? Oh sure, that'll look good on my mantle next to my hockey puck signed by Jesus." Similarly, "Dilbert" ran a series of strips in which the characters were shown buying and selling sports equipment signed by Jesus and other religious figures.

For some in the media, the Mother Teresa forgery seemed to say something larger about the men and women involved in the ring—their "brazen" and "outrageous" nature, as *Reader's Digest* put it. Other media accounts characterized the group as a kind of gang-that-couldn't-shoot-straight, failing to mention that they had been in business five years and it had taken nearly three of those years for the FBI to bring them down.

Another prominent name to receive wide play in the media coverage (though nothing compared to Mother Teresa) was Tony Gwynn. The widely admired Padres star and hometown hero had come to the press conference at the invitation of the FBI and, although hobbling from the bad knees that would force him to retire after the 2001 season, he told the media about walking into his team's gift shop one day and seeing a window display of baseballs supposedly signed by him. Upon closer inspection he discovered them all to be forgeries. He informed the team management about this and eventually, the FBI.

Some in the media inaccurately reported that Gwynn was the one who tipped the FBI off to the existence of forgeries. But Fitzsimmons and McKinney had been on the case for two years before Gwynn ever walked into that shop, and the Chicago FBI had started investigating sports memorabilia fraud well before San Diego. Gwynn did lend a hand by helping to identify forgeries of his signature, meeting Fitzsimmons on several occasions at Qualcomm Stadium, and his appearance at the press conference gave some celebrity shine to the event. The other baseball superstar who participated in the case, the publicity-shy Mark McGwire, declined to appear at the press conference.

A more interesting and important misconception about the case emerged from the press conference. Reporters received a thick packet of FBI-prepared material as well as a seventy-two-page document known as "the Information." Similar to an indictment, the Information listed the specific crimes committed by the ring and a chronology of events leading up to the bust.

John Ferreira's name never appears in the Information, although his identity did surface in later press accounts. The document refers to him only as "a government undercover agent," and his meets at the Nihon Trading Company and elsewhere appear frequently in the chronology. Relying mainly on government sources, the media gave credit to the FBI undercover operation for bringing down the ring. ABC News was typical in this regard: "Federal agents, based in San Diego, established themselves as dealers in sports forgeries, ultimately infiltrating what federal authorities call the most extensive network of sports counterfeiters ever uncovered." *Sports Illustrated* echoed the theme: "The feds set up a front called the Nihon Trading Company, and although it was no more authentic than the Mother Teresa-autographed baseball the operation uncovered, it fooled members of a nationwide ring whose allegedly incriminating statements now fill more than 1,000 FBI audio tapes."

The FBI publicized the fact that it made more than 1,000 undercover tapes, which it presented as a sign of investigative thoroughness and competence. What the FBI neglected to mention was that many of the tapes made by its undercover agent failed to do the job they were supposed to do—i.e., get admissions. The best undercover tapes in the case were made by Bray.

The name of the FBI's star cooperating witness appears extensively in the Information but only as a criminal doing criminal activities. In fact the Justice Department and FBI distributed a flow chart to the media placing him at the center of the gang's operations, with Bray as the sun and Greg Marino and everybody else revolving around him like the planets. Bray's role as the person who broke the case open received nary a mention. This was the story the government told, and this was the story that got reported.

After he went to prison, Bray was watching TV when a story came on the news about how the FBI had just busted a multimillion dollar counterfeit card factory in Los Angeles. The report went on to say that one of the operation's ringleaders was…Wayne Bray. "So there I am in prison, sitting in a room with a hundred other guys watching TV and I hear how I'm this big dealer of fake cards," he said with barely controlled anger. "Man, I'm the guy who helped bring it down. I delivered Barry Goldberg on a silver platter to the FBI."

Bray had it right and the TV report had it wrong: The FBI's bust of the counterfeit card factory would not have occurred without him. On takedown day, Goldberg, despite having boxes of counterfeit cards in his possession, would admit nothing until he first spoke to an attorney. After tough negotiations with the government, he eventually agreed to cooperate and put on a wire to get admissions from his partner in the scheme, Hank Benner.

"Benner and Goldberg worked together," said McKinney. "Barry was buying the cards from him." Once Goldberg jammed up Benner on tape, the FBI raided Benner's house in El Segundo, and Benner gave up the name of the printer: Vincent Ferrucio of Ferrucio and Associates, a Gardena printing company. With his employees working after hours, Ferrucio and Associates had produced tens of thousands of the near-perfect counterfeit McGwire, Sosa, Gwynn, Elway and Marino cards.

Taking over from Goldberg, Benner put on a wire as part of the FBI's plan to nail Ferrucio. Trouble was, the plant had ceased production of the fakes and was no longer in the counterfeit business. "But we wanted to catch him in the act, get the presses started up again," said McKinney, who oversaw this phase of the investigation. "We wanted to have the ink wet on the presses when we walked in."

To accomplish this, Benner placed a big order for the fake Sosa and McGwire cards, and Ferrucio agreed to do another run. The cards were running off the presses, still in sheets, and the ink on them was fresh when Benner walked into the plant and paid Ferrucio with a wad of hundred dollar bills. When Benner walked out a dozen federal agents walked in, and what they found inside made them feel awful.

Ferrucio, in McKinney's words, was "a good person who made a mistake, a legitimate businessman who slid into crime"—one more victim of the slippery slope. In his early sixties, he was a former Boy Scout troop leader and a grandfather whose son was in the Navy. A picture of his son, in his dress whites, hung on the wall of Ferrucio's office along with photos of the Little League teams his company had sponsored over the years. Also framed on the wall was a copy of the Gettysburg Address.

A soft touch as a boss, Ferrucio had run the printing plant for decades, employing the same people for many years. His employees depended on him for a job, and he was loyal to them, not wanting to lay anyone off.

When his business hit hard times he saw the counterfeiting scheme as a way to keep the money coming in.

The FBI said several of the employees at the plant could have been charged with crimes because they had worked on the presses at night and almost certainly knew what was going on. But Ferrucio refused to implicate anyone else and accepted all the blame. He spent four months in prison, Goldberg nine months, and Benner a year and three months.

26

This should have been the end of the story. Bray and the Marino brothers in prison or on their way, their comrades busted and in disgrace, the counterfeit card factory shut down. But that wasn't the end of it. The story takes another turn, largely because of Tim Fitzsimmons and two leading Bullpen figures whose run on the other side of the law ended with the takedown.

One of them was Dave Tabb. Twice before Tabb had been busted or cited for selling counterfeit memorabilia, but on each of those occasions he had returned to the racket after the law enforcement pressure had lifted. This time was different. There would be no easing of the pressure—legally, emotionally or financially. Selling fakes was his primary way of making money, how he helped pay for his nice house and nice clothes and the nice SUV where he kept his bankroll in a clip stashed behind the sun visor. Now, all his money was going straight to his attorney. On top of this were his personal problems—first and foremost, getting straight with his wife. She was another of the wives who knew nothing about the racket, intent as she was on living her life and building her career. Now, in addition to the possible prison time he was facing, they worried about her not being able to get a job in the fallout after the bust. With his income drying up and hers so tentative, their beautifully constructed Orange County lifestyle appeared in danger of cracking apart.

A month after the takedown Tabb was still reeling, still trying to figure a way out of the jam he was in. Then he met Fitzsimmons, and things started to change for him. Tabb appreciated what the agent had to say, and the no b.s. way in which he said it. "I started to feel like everything was going to be okay. I got a sense of what to do and how to get back to living my life." The flim-flam man of Hollywood Dreams was going straight—and this time he wasn't conning anybody about it, including himself. "I felt relieved," he said. "I was glad it was all over. I started sleeping better."

Tabb offered to cooperate with the FBI but at this late stage in the game, Fitzsimmons wasn't sure about the value in it. "He was very insistent on getting involved," said the agent. "I told him no, this is not just catching guys doing forgeries. You have to do business with them, talk to them on the phone, produce merchandise for them to sign. But Tabb was persistent, and finally I agreed."

Beginning in January 2000, Tabb began to monitor fraudulent memorabilia sales activity online and report back to Fitzsimmons. In their post-takedown interviews the FBI had asked ring members about the future direction of the counterfeit racket. To a man they answered, "eBay." The future had clearly arrived as Tabb, sitting at home in front of his computer, scrolled down the lists of autographed material being offered for sale on the site, material he knew to be indisputably fake. He sent e-mails to these dealers, asking questions about the merchandise and making purchases and gaining their confidence. He borrowed a trick from John Ferreira, saying the stuff he was buying was going overseas and so there was no reason to worry about it.

Tabb saved every piece of electronic correspondence in a binder under the dealer's name. Once he got the dealer's phone number he called to chat him up, not happening to mention that their conversation was being recorded. The master of subtext who never made a taped admission to Ferreira found that he was good at getting bogus dealers to make admissions to him. With some dealers, he didn't have to spend a dime with them to get them to say they were selling frauds. He gave the tapes he made to the FBI and kept copies for his own files, storing them with the e-mails in the binders he was compiling on each case he was working.

On every tape Tabb carefully noted the time and date of the conversation. The number of subjects he was investigating kept growing, as did the thickness of his binders. He took all of this very seriously, as did his wife and family who knew what it could potentially mean to him. His father took over his car payments, and his parents and other family members helped him and his wife financially so that he could work basically full-time for the FBI without pay. By the April 2000 press conference, in which he was named as a major player in the biggest forgery ring in the U.S., he had already made more than one hundred undercover tapes for the FBI.

Three months later, in June 2000, Tabb pled guilty in federal court. But his sentencing date was postponed because of his undercover work—work he was doing without any guarantees from the FBI. "I cooperated without being guaranteed anything," he said. "Because if you ever have to testify in a criminal case [which he later did], the judge will ask you if you've received any guarantees for your cooperation. The answer has to be no. Because if you did get any guarantees, it would taint your testimony."

If he had followed the path of his confederates, he would have likely gone to prison in the fall. Instead he was tracking forgers and shady dealers on eBay and other Internet sites. One of his early subjects, a Middleboro, Massachusetts shop owner and forger named Dave Hammond, used four different screen names to cloak his identity. But Tabb picked up on him through other means. "Forgers change their screen names but their habits don't change—the patterns of items they sign, the objects they like to sign. They know a certain area of the business so they stick with it and their forgery style remains the same. Because of this, you can pick up what they're doing."

One Texas dealer, Robert Yancey Lawhorn, operated under the screen name of GuntherTheGreat. He sold autographs of Muhammad Ali, George Foreman, Joe Frazier, Larry Holmes, Evander Holyfield, Lennox Lewis, Ken Norton and Mike Tyson—all of them, combo-style, on boxing gloves and trunks. Then there were the two Ohio State students, Kumba Alafi and Jeffrey Coffman, who sold combo- and single-signed counterfeits, perhaps to offset the high cost of college tuition. At the behest of Fitzsimmons, whose idea it was, Tabb sent them a photograph of Joe DiMaggio and "this other guy," as Tabb put it in a note to them. In the note Tabb said he didn't know who this other guy was, only that he worked in the federal government "a long time ago."

Showing off the benefits of a higher education, the students recognized this other guy right away. Dressed in a suit and tie and smiling for the camera with his arm around Joe's shoulder, he was J. Edgar Hoover.

"Do you know who that other guy is?" One of the students, probably Kumba, asked Tabb over the phone.

"No," he said, playing dumb.

"He ran the FBI for years and years, and now he's dead."

"Does that mean you won't forge the picture?" Tabb asked.

"Nah," came the reply. "We'll do it. We just wanted you to know."

Whereas Tabb described John Ferreira's undercover style as "business-like," his was more "scumbag-like." Falling back on his old acting chops, he pretended to be various characters, adopting different accents according to the role he was playing. He frequently changed aliases to keep his identity hidden, though the people he was dealing with knew he lived in the same general area as the site of the big Operation Bullpen bust. But some of them thought they were safe because they lived in other parts of the country.

"They said they didn't worry because they were in Texas or Massachusetts or wherever," said Tabb. "Then they'd send their stuff to San Diego, which put them in the San Diego FBI's jurisdiction."

One of the bigger cases Tabb worked was that of James Ferrazzano. Based in Suffern, Long Island, about a half hour outside New York City, Ferrazzano's business was called Truly Unique Collectibles. Its web site and catalog featured more than 10,000 autographed items—a sure sign that not everything being sold was truly unique or legitimate. The catalog offered the "genuine hand-signed autographs" mainly of movie and TV stars, including dozens of sexy young Hollywood starlets, many of them in scantily clad attire, often with the sig placed in a suggestive position across their body. Apparently the autograph was not the only thing that Ferrazzano's customers found titillating.

One of the stars whose signed photo was being sold by Truly Unique was David Duchovny. Hollywood forgeries are as rife as those in sports, but unlike in sports, where many prominent and not-so-prominent athletes derive considerable income from paid signings, TV and movie stars tend to be more blasé about the issue. Duchovny, then at the height of his "X-Files" fame, proved an exception to this rule, filing suit against Ferrazzano to stop him from selling what the actor claimed were blatant frauds. But when the matter went to trial and Duchovny took the stand to testify, Ferrazzano's attorney produced different examples of Duchovny's signature for him to look at—some genuine, some not. Did you sign this? the attorney asked. Yes? Well, what about this one? You didn't sign this? Are you sure, Mr. Duchovny, because this fake one here looks an awful lot like this genuine one over here, don't you agree? Under cross-examination the actor could not say with absolute certainty which of his signatures were genuine and which were not, and the judge ruled against him, even ordering him to pay minor damages to Ferrazzano for bringing the failed complaint.

Ferrazzano's evasion showed again why the FBI needed those all-important admissions, and why Tabb had become such a valuable man in what came to be known as phase two of Operation Bullpen. On his first call to Truly Unique, Tabb spoke to an employee, Danny, identifying himself with one alias. On his next call, also to Danny, Tabb used a different alias, though Danny didn't realize he was speaking to the same man. On both calls Tabb asked how Truly Unique acquired its merchandise, noting that some of its signatures were of celebrities who were dead.

"We pay people to go out and get things signed," said Danny, dredging up the age-old fable of the autograph runner.

"How do you get the signatures of dead people then?" asked Tabb.

Danny replied that it took two to three weeks to special order dead people.

Located in Dana Point, California, the Movie Market is a leading stock house for celebrity photographs. Ferrazzano had been a customer for years, so it was no surprise when Movie Market received a fax from him ordering the photographs of Kurt Cobain, Audrey Hepburn and other dead celebs. What was different from past Ferrazzano orders, however, was the person assisting with it on the other end. Since Dana Point is only an hour north of San Diego, Fitzsimmons drove up to the Movie Market for the day. With the company's cooperation he put black light markings in the corners of the Cobain and Hepburn photos before they were shipped off to Long Island.

A little later Tabb went on the Truly Unique web site and noticed how it was selling two signed Kurt Cobain photos. He bought them both, and they were sent to a mailing address in San Diego County. Bingo! When placed under a black light they were revealed to have the secret markings. At this point the other Bullpen figure working undercover for the FBI stepped in to do his thing. This was Rick Mitchell.

In the brief, tumultuous period after the takedown, Mitchell had grown a great deal, but this growth had not come without pain—pain to himself, pain to his wife, pain to the people he loved most in life. Humiliated by what he had done and the hurt he had caused others, he genuinely sought to make amends, though obviously a large part of his motivation in cooperating was the same as Tabb's: He hoped to get a lighter rap or perhaps no rap at all when his sentencing came before a judge.

And so, after the bust, he was inspired to do what Tabb was doing: go on the Net and hunt for guys who were still in the racket. They were not hard to find, nor were their bogus products. Though Mitchell could not yet prove it. To do that he needed to keep hunting, and so he approached Fitzsimmons with an offer similar to the one Tabb had made. But the agent turned him down for the same reasons he first said no to Tabb. Disappointed but unwilling to give up, Mitchell continued to dig up information on suspicious eBay operators. Then he went back to Fitzsimmons and shared his discoveries. This time the agent said yes, and hooked him up with Tabb.

With Fitzsimmons guiding their activities, the two became undercover sidekicks of a sort—Tabb in the lead, Mitchell backing him up, each with his own complementary interests and strengths. Dave was the Hollywood guy, Rick the sports guy. If Tabb came across someone who was dealing in sports he kicked him over to Mitchell, who returned the favor when he came across a celebrity junkman. Many times they worked as a tag team, such as for Ferrazzano.

After Tabb bought the bad Kurt Cobains, Mitchell called Truly Unique and placed an order for a signed Audrey Hepburn photo. He of course said nothing about Tabb's previous order; his pose was simply that of a customer interested in buying a keepsake from the star of "Breakfast at Tiffany's." When the photo arrived in San Diego it carried the telltale black light markings, prompting Mitchell to order four signed David Duchovny pictures. Truly Unique ordered the blanks from the Movie Market, where Fitzsimmons marked them. The stock house sent them to Truly Unique and when they came bouncing back to Fitzsimmons and Mitchell, they were shown to be the same photos that had been blank before, only now they had Duchnovy's signature on them. In a fitting gesture, Fitzsimmons sent the photos to Duchovny for his personal review. The star was not wishy-washy this time: These were fakes, pure and simple.

In his late twenties or early thirties, good looking, with wispy blond hair and blue eyes, Shawn Jackson built a name for himself in the autograph world as a man with inside access to celebrities. From his home near St. Louis, he jetted off to New York and Hollywood to be at events and parties where celebrities gathered. (One of his must-attend events every year was the Academy Awards.) To gain entry to these events, he frequently made donations or paid the sponsors, and when this didn't work he sometimes badged his way in with a fake FBI ID with his photo on it. Once on the inside he made sure to have his picture taken with whatever celebrities happened to be present, and get their autographs. He sold legitimate as well as illegitimate autographs, and the real provided cover for the fake.

Tabb first made contact with a friend of Jackson's, who put him in touch with the man himself. When Tabb asked how he obtained his merchandise, Jackson said he paid celebrities to sign at private sessions.

"Well," said Tabb, "you're going to have to hold a séance because many of the people I want are dead."

That Tabb was looking for dead people did not bother Jackson, who seemed to understand what the request was really for. He said he thought they could work together but with one stipulation: They first needed to meet in person. Once they did that and everything checked out, Jackson would be able to supply the names on Tabb's wish list—no séance needed. They agreed to meet on Jackson's next trip to LA, which was coming up presently.

First the meet was to take place at the Hilton Hotel on Century Boulevard. Then Shawn changed his mind and rescheduled it for the

Holiday Inn at LAX. When Tabb called to confirm this new spot, Jackson changed the location one more time—back to Century Boulevard, only now in the parking lot of a McDonald's. The time: after midnight. Clearly Jackson was feeling a little antsy about the man he was about to meet, for when they finally did get together he fully patted Tabb down, even going so far as to peer down the front of his trousers. "He looked in and peered around to see if I had a wire down there," said Tabb with a smile. "I mean, he saw my whole package, if you know what I'm saying."

For his undercover meets Tabb, a heavyset man who had put on pounds after the takedown, then lost weight once he started working for the FBI and got his life back on track, generally liked to place the recorder in the small of his back and run the microphone wires up around to his chest. But because this was their first meet and Jackson was so obviously tweaking, he showed up without a wire. This fact, combined with the show he put on—pulling up in his late model SUV, wearing bling, looking rich, coming on like a real scumbag—persuaded Jackson that this was a man he could trust.

At their next meeting in LA, the country's biggest in-person autograph collector loosened up some and confided to Tabb that he had been breaking the law all his life but had never spent a day in jail. He also mentioned that his wife felt strongly that Tabb should not be trusted. Shawn should have listened to his wife because Tabb was now wearing a wire and recording everything they said.

When Jackson returned to Missouri, he sent a package of autographs to Tabb in California. Although ordinarily he did not use the Postal Service because of worries about mail fraud, Jackson said he'd make an exception in this case. "You're not a fed," he told Tabb confidently, and he was right: Tabb wasn't a fed, just working with them.

Another major target of Tabb's was a big-time forger named John Fried, who lived in the colorfully named Long Island hamlet of Ronkonkoma. In nine months from late 1998 to 1999, according to records obtained by the FBI, Fried sold $364,000 in merchandise on eBay. He later bragged in a recorded conversation that he was making nearly $1 million a year. As soon as Tabb got onto him he asked for samples of his work. Asking for samples was a cheap way to obtain evidence of forgery. Laying it on thick in this first conversation, Tabb established a quick rapport with Fried, who told him that he could tell right off that Tabb wasn't FBI, saying he was too smooth with too many street smarts to be a federal agent.

"If we were FBI agents," joked Tabb, "we'd be the two best in the country." Fried laughed, and said he'd put some samples in the mail to him right away.

As he frequently did after making the first contact with a subject, Tabb told Fried that he had a friend who was also interested in buying memorabilia and asked if it'd be all right if this friend called him. When Fried said yes, he unknowingly gave his blessing to two undercover operatives getting into his business at the same time.

Since Mitchell's expertise was sports, he asked for sports autographs from Fried, who told Tabb in a separate conversation that he hoped Mitchell didn't send him lots of sports orders because he was "not good with most of those sigs." Despite his reservations, Fried gamely did his best, sending a package of cuts to Mitchell of Ruth, Gehrig, Mel Ott and Nellie Fox. There was no question these were forgeries because three of the sheets of paper contained no less than eight Gehrig sigs. Fried also enclosed a note that said, "I am practicing buddy!" apologizing to his new client because these were rough drafts. If Mitchell had any genuine exemplars of these autographs, Fried said, he'd appreciate seeing them because they would improve the quality of his work.

Mitchell placed another order for some Mantle cuts, and after the conscientious Ronkonkoma forger filled it, Rick sent him a couple hundred bucks in payment. A couple hundred bucks? You kidding me? A guy making a million a year doesn't need to jack around with penny ante nonsense like that, and Fried fired off an angry e-mail to Mitchell. He thought Mitchell was going to do real business with him, so what was up with this lousy two hundred bucks?

A liar is often a great promiser, and Mitchell kept spinning lies and promises in order to keep Fried happy. He told him he hadn't yet seen his Mantles, so he didn't know how valuable they were. Once he checked them out to determine their merit, he'd buy more. Still miffed, Fried said he wasn't doing any more sigs for Mitchell unless he received top dollar for his work. Meanwhile, an employee at General Pictures, Fried's company, sent Mitchell a product list of cuts, ranging from a low of twenty dollars for Walt Alston to a high of $2,200 for Ed Plank. Every sig came with a General Pictures certificate of authenticity, which Fried bragged about as being a joke.

In going back and forth between Mitchell and Tabb, Fried blundered by sending a joke e-mail to them and fourteen of his associates, all counterfeit dealers. The address portion of the e-mail carried their names and e-mail addresses, and Mitchell-Tabb captured all this contact information, cross-referencing the names with eBay sellers. One of the names on the list belonged to a Rhode Island dealer by the name of Steve Lyons. Lyons, said Fried, wasn't buying from him so much anymore because he "now has his own little forgery ring." Adding sagely, "You can't stop people from forging."

Lyons and his ring subsequently became Mitchell's prime investigative target. "He had a huge number of items for sale that Dave and I could tell immediately were forgeries," said Mitchell. "So Dave was talking to Fried and he mentioned Lyons's name to him, saying, 'Wow, he's really talented. Can we use him?' Fried said no problem. Fried was so overworked he didn't really need our business anyway. Dave made the first call to Lyons, and the story was that he was very interested in seeing Steve's talent but that he was going to Canada and could I call him? Lyons said yeah, and that began my involvement with him."

On their first call Mitchell expressed a desire to see what Lyons's "quality was like," and he sent him three movie posters—"Star Wars Trilogy," "The Matrix" and "Independence Day"—with a recommendation letter from Tabb and some cash "for your time," as Rick wrote in a note. In less than a week the posters, now cast-signed, came zipping back to San Diego, and Mitchell knew he was onto something good. Both he and Tabb eventually got damaging admissions from Lyons.

In explaining why counterfeit dealers were willing to open up to them, Mitchell said, "We know what to say and what to do. We've been there so we know how to talk to these guys. You use the word 'talent,' for instance. 'We want to see your talent.' In other words, let's see how good your forgeries are. Another thing you say is, 'We want to use you.' How else is a guy going to be used except can he produce the goods?"

In one case, Mitchell and Tabb switched identities. Mitchell was working a subject over the phone using an alias. Then an undercover meet was arranged with this subject. But it was Tabb, not Mitchell, who did the meet, using Mitchell's alias and posing as him. The subject never knew the difference.

Perhaps the most colorful character they worked was an ailing, tough-talking New Yorker named Billy Costa. Costa lived on 64th Street in Brooklyn with his aged mother. Fitzsimmons ran Costa's record and noted numerous arrests, including two convictions for forgery and possession of forged instruments. He was clearly still in the game because on one of his early calls with Tabb, he explained he had more than 1,000 signed Mantle balls for sale. Each was going for forty bucks, far below what a genuine one would cost. He was also offering Mantle jerseys for one hundred-fifty apiece—again, well below market. Saying he was interested in a deal, Tabb sent Costa some blank index cards so Billy could show him some samples of his talent. But the savvy old-timer didn't fall for it. He said he wouldn't sign any blank memorabilia from Tabb until he met him in person and knew for sure he wasn't the law. In another call he went even further, flatly accusing Tabb of working for the FBI. "You're going to have to work harder if you want to bust me," he said in his thick Brooklyn accent. He added, "The only way you're going to stop me [from forging] is by cutting off my hands."

Later Costa said that even putting steel gloves on his hands wouldn't stop him, and he continued to accuse Tabb, and then Mitchell, of being undercover FBI. During one conversation Costa remarked on "the big raid" in San Diego and wondered why Mitchell had escaped being busted while so many other dealers in the area had been brought down. Rick said he had avoided arrest by being a small dealer.

Funny, profane and deeply sarcastic, Costa speculated once on how he'd react if the FBI showed up at his apartment: "If I'm in the right mood, I'll take a couple of secanols and throw a couple of shots through the door. Then I'll take a couple more secanols, right until I'm at the point where I'm James Cagney. Right, you talking to me. I'll come out there shooting. You'll see me on television."

Besides being a fan of old gangster movies, Costa was an ingenious and resourceful forger, creating replica stamps for the old Federal League, Bronx Bombers, Babe Ruth and others. His New York Highlanders stamp was modeled on an actual 1904 Highlanders ticket stub. Then he'd strip the trademarks off old baseballs, re-sand the horsehide and apply these fake stamps to them. He even had fake old-time boxes made for the balls.

Mitchell once sent Costa some vintage stuff in exchange for some of his signed pieces. But Billy, suspecting a trick, refused to send him what he wanted and kept Mitchell's things, saying he was going to hang onto them as a bargaining chip in their negotiations. When Rick complained that the old baseballs were genuine and very valuable, Costa brushed him off, saying it was easy to make vintage balls. "All you have to do is strip down the ball and re-stamp it," he said.

As old school as Billy was, he had found a home in the new technology, selling to a steady stream of eBay customers using the screen name of "sportsmanattic." He sent Mitchell a package with fake-vintage baseballs with fake sigs, inside of which was a note: "If you want more, any name $125 each." He duplicated a special edition Joe DiMaggio trademark for a baseball and signed Marilyn Monroe's autograph on it. After buying this ball Mitchell playfully sent Costa a picture of Marilyn inscribed, "To Billy, With Love, Marilyn." The next time they spoke Costa asked Mitchell who did the Marilyn sig. When Mitchell said he had, Billy advised him to only use a red pen for Marilyn because that was how she always signed her pictures.

When Mitchell, the creator of the dipping method for the Bray-Marino crew, complimented him on his ball restoration work, Billy repeated how easy it was to do. He explained how to scrub down a new ball to make it look old (Oxyclean and steel wool), and how to use cotton and bleach to get rid of the date on some Mantle photographs printed after his death so they would appear to have been made while he was still alive. Despite his dealings with them Costa never stopped suspecting Mitchell and Tabb of having a secret agenda, frequently poking fun at them. When Tabb told him he wanted to buy only high quality stuff, Costa replied, "You mean it makes a difference whether it's good quality or bad quality?" He said he thought Tabb and the FBI should investigate all crooks, both good and bad. When Tabb pressed him on some cuts Costa had promised to send, Billy joked that they had all gone up in a big barn fire.

To prove he was a true crook, Mitchell sent Costa a copy of his phone bill to show that he was making all these calls from home, not the FBI. Even so, Costa asked if Mitchell and the FBI could delay arresting him for another year. He claimed to have sources within the Bureau who had told him that more Operation Bullpen busts were on the way. But he wasn't worried. If the feds came knocking at his door they'd get his balls, bats, pens and stamps—but not him. He'd pull a vanishing act before anyone put him in prison.

"You don't make money in this world without getting in trouble," he said.

As events showed, Billy was right. The two Californians pestering him on the phone were working for the FBI, which was indeed planning to make more busts. But before the FBI moved on Costa and the others in phase two, Tabb alighted upon the name of Chuck Wepner. A one-time professional boxer, Wepner occupied a small but colorful niche in ring history. Known as the Bayonne Bleeder, he had squared off against Muhammad Ali in a 1975 heavyweight title fight and knocked him down in the ninth round. Although he lost the fight, this unlikely scenario—big, white, working class pug going fifteen heroic rounds with the great black champion—was said to be the inspiration for "Rocky," the Oscar-winning movie that made Sylvester Stallone a star. But what was most interesting to Tabb was that "the real-life Rocky," as Wepner billed himself, was now selling fake Ali and Stallone memorabilia. It was a matter worth looking into some more.

27

The trail to the Bayonne Bleeder began in late 2000 when Tabb, working the Internet beat as usual, noticed that a Brooklyn resident named Mike DeSola was selling Ali memorabilia that appeared to be not entirely on the square. DeSola worked as a marketing and sales rep for a company called Madison Sports, whose offices were on Queens Boulevard in Forest Hills on Long Island. Tabb checked out its website. Madison Sports, it said, was "involved in many areas of sports marketing, consulting, sports-related promotions and sports product merchandising." Another area of involvement was autographed memorabilia. "Madison provides the broadest inventory from Joe DiMaggio to Joe Namath to Larry Bird," the site continued, "and our product is guaranteed authentic. If there are unique products we can develop for you, just let us know." Curiously though, the site contained no e-mail address, no phone, no fax, no street address or post office box for people to inquire about those unique products.

Nevertheless, Tabb, with Fitzsimmons's help, found DeSola's number. He called him and the two got down to business right away. DeSola said he could get his hands on four hundred Mantle baseballs and similar amounts of DiMaggio material with a turnaround time of one day. What's more, he had five hundred pairs of Ali boxing gloves in stock and said he could set up a signing with Ali at any time. When they talked again a few days later, DeSola bragged about a private signing he was about to do with Ali and Joe Frazier in Atlanta.

Eager to bag a new client with lots of cash (or so he thought), DeSola offered Tabb four hundred signed Ali photos for $4,000. And, he said, he'd knock the price down if Tabb did not need certs with the pictures.

To Tabb and Fitzsimmons, DeSola was plainly selling fakes. Nobody can deliver hundreds of Mantle balls in a day or has stacks of signed Ali pictures sitting around his office—not genuine ones, anyhow. Additionally, Shelly Jaffe had told the FBI that he had sold Greg Marino's Ali forgeries to DeSola. John Fried also mentioned to Tabb in a taped conversation that he had supplied fakes to Madison Sports in the past. Yet another source was Ali's agent, Harlan Werner, who called Fitzsimmons in February 2001 concerned about the widespread forging of his famous client's autograph. Ali supports himself in part by selling his autographed memorabilia, and the forgeries were punching a hole in his income. With so many low-cost fakes in the marketplace, they were crowding out the more expensive legitimate stuff. Werner told Fitzsimmons that he had long believed that Madison Sports sold counterfeits, and that the company claimed to get its Ali memorabilia from Chuck Wepner. He said Ali had not done any signings with Madison Sports for years, nor would he in the future.

Anxious to cooperate with the investigation, Werner said that if the FBI needed Ali to verify signatures for authenticity, he'd be happy to do it. (The champ did later fly to San Diego to inspect some of the evidence acquired in the case.) Another helpful thing Werner did was send the FBI a rare photograph of Ali and the Japanese wrestler Antonio Inoki. In the late seventies, while still heavyweight champ, Ali had fought Anoki in a closed circuit TV exhibition match that ended in a fifteen-round draw. The picture showed Ali, fading as a boxer but still strong and powerful, with his gloves raised and seeming to yell at Inoki, who was falling backwards on the canvas. Never in his life had Ali signed one of these photographs, Werner said. Thus it would be a tall task for DeSola or anyone else to produce one with a genuine signature.

With Ali and Werner now squarely in their corner, Fitzsimmons and his undercover man moved aggressively ahead. Tabb called DeSola back to tell him that he had gotten hold of a batch of Ali photos and that he wanted them signed. "I want them as cheap and as good looking as possible," he said, adding that he planned to sell them in Japan.

Tabb sent two samples of the photo to Brooklyn. When they arrived DeSola said he didn't recognize the guy in the ring with Ali. Tabb patiently explained he was a Japanese wrestler. Thus satisfied, DeSola said that Wepner would get them signed by Ali and that the certs would come from Brian Ginsberg, the president of Laura's Cartoons and Collectibles in Huntington, Long Island. Fitzsimmons pulled Ginsberg's chart from eBay and found that he had moved more than $500,000 of goods on the site from March 1999 through October 2000. Clearly active in the racket, Ginsberg became a prime target of the investigation.

Once he came in on the negotiations, Ginsberg pushed the deal strongly forward, calling Tabb to assure him that Ali would be in New York on April 6 for a private session, that he'd sign in silver, and the cost per picture would be one hundred thirty-five dollars.

"I'm more concerned about the price of the sigs than their quality," Tabb said, a clear reference to forgery that did not upset his listener at all. Tabb talked the price down to one hundred dollars per picture and shipped off the entire order—more than two hundred numbered Ali-Anoki pictures—to Huntington. Included in the package was $2,000 in cash—the first installment, said Tabb, of a total payment of $20,000 once the job was done and all the photos were signed.

On April 7, the day after the session was supposed to take place, Ginsberg called Tabb to let him know that everything had gone as expected and that Ali had signed all the photos. The one change was that he had signed not in silver but in gold. DeSola, who was one of Ginsberg's prime customers, followed up with a call to Tabb saying that the New York papers had even carried an item about how Muhammad was in town that day.

These were all lies. The signing session never happened, not in New York or anywhere else. Ali was in Miami that day, consulting on the Will Smith movie about his life that was being shot there. But Tabb said nothing about this, asking Ginsberg to send him some signed photographs from the session so he could see what they looked like. If they checked out, Tabb said, Ginsberg would be paid in full. Ginsberg happily agreed and shipped a half-dozen photos west, but unhappily for him, no money came east.

Here, things got testy. Having delivered some signed Ali shots as requested, Ginsberg expected Tabb to pay up, at which point Ginsberg would send him the rest of the order. But Tabb and Fitzsimmons had no intention of paying twenty grand or anything close to it to the New Yorkers, so Tabb invented a new, impossible-to-fulfill demand: He wanted to see a picture of Ali actually signing the photographs.

Ginsberg blew up when he heard this, giving Tabb a ration over the phone, saying they had a deal and he had delivered on his end and he wanted his money...now!

Coming on like a crook at first without actually saying so, Tabb had now switched to playing it straight. He said that some of his Japanese buyers were questioning the signing because they had heard that Ali was in Florida that day, not New York.

Ginsberg replied that he was sure that Wepner took the photos to Ali, and for the money Tabb was paying, Chuck might have flown to Florida to get them signed.

Tabb was unimpressed. "I gotta see it," he said evenly. "I need verification." No verification, no money.

After an exasperated Ginsberg got off the line, his tag team partner, equally ticked, took over. "I laid out money for the Ali signing and I want to get paid," DeSola demanded. Three thousand miles away on the other side of the continent, the Californian calmly replied that if he couldn't get a photograph of Ali signing, he wanted to see something in writing from Wepner confirming the session took place. DeSola said he wasn't listening to any more of his friggin' demands, and hung up.

But twenty grand is twenty grand, and in a few minutes a calmer DeSola was back on the line saying that what Tabb was asking for was impossible. Wepner never provided written certs for signings.

"Unless I get some proof to the contrary, it's clear to me the photos are fakes," said Tabb.

More heated cross-country calls ensued. A disgusted DeSola said that he had already paid Wepner for his part in the deal and that if Tabb didn't buy the photos he'd simply "dump them." Later that afternoon, however, a package arrived in San Diego from Laura's Cartoons and Collectibles. Inside were more Ali-Inoki photos, all supposedly signed by Ali. Ginsberg also e-mailed a sample cert to Tabb who, continuing to push, asked Ginsberg to state the time and date of the nonexistent signing on the document. Ginsberg agreed. Then, finally giving Tabb everything he wanted, he said he'd get Chuck Wepner to call him.

In his fourteen-year pro career, Chuck Wepner sparred with Joe Frazier, knocked down George Foreman (though Foreman eventually bloodied him and won on a TKO), fought Andre the Giant, defeated one-time heavyweight champion Ernie Terrell, and held his own in a savage brawl with one of the hardest punchers of all time, Sonny Liston. After the fight with Liston, the last of Sonny's career, doctors needed fifty-seven stitches to put the Bayonne Bleeder's face back together. But the fight with Ali in 1975 was by far the biggest of his life. "Here's a guy who knows he got lucky," said one writer. "He got one big break in his life, and is still riding it all of these years later."

Before the fight, a close-up of Wepner's face appeared on the cover of *Sports Illustrated,* and it was truly impressive: a real fighter's mug with thick brow bones overshadowing deep-set eyes and a nose that had been broken more than once. With slightly thinning hair on top and a thick mustache, Wepner stood six-foot-six inches tall and weighed two hundred-fifty pounds, a formidable if lumbering presence in the ring with big arms and a powerful chest and shoulders. Ring observers said that his height and size were largely why he gave Ali so much trouble. That, and the fact that the champ, like the fictional Apollo Creed, may have underestimated him, figuring to put on a show and dance away with a nice payday. But, refusing to quit despite taking a terrible whipping, the thirty-seven-year-old, one-time New Jersey street kid put Ali down in the ninth (though Ali claimed Wepner stepped on his foot and made him slip) and earned widespread admiration for the way he stayed on his feet and battled all the way to the end in a losing cause. "There's not another human being in the world that can go fifteen rounds like that," an exhausted Ali reportedly said afterward.

Watching this fight on TV was an unemployed thirty-year-old actor who had appeared in a bit role in "The Lords of Flatbush" and not much else. Inspired by what he had just seen, he knocked out a movie script in a few days about a underdog working class fighter named Rocky Balboa who gets a shot at the heavyweight title. Then, according to show biz legend, the actor hit the jackpot, selling his screenplay to Hollywood for a sizable sum and signing on to play the lead role himself. The next year "Rocky" became a surprise box office success, winning the Oscar for best picture and launching the career of the suddenly very employable Sylvester Stallone. Although Stallone has said that the movie was based on the lives of several boxers, not just Wepner's, Wepner served as its technical advisor. But the wealth and fame that followed Stallone after "Rocky" mostly passed its technical advisor by, and a few years later Wepner was out of the fight game and looking for a way to make a buck.

His main occupation was as a liquor salesman, but in the mid-eighties Wepner got into a different sort of high. "I was socially addicted to cocaine," he told *Playboy* in an article published in 1999, the year before the FBI began investigating him for memorabilia fraud. "I was doing it a lot. I had some heavy friends, and was running with some crazy people." Some of those heavy friends, according to Wepner, asked him one day to deliver a package containing drugs. He did it—and got busted in a law enforcement sting operation. Pleading guilty to one count of possession of three ounces of cocaine, and one count of conspiracy to distribute, he received a ten-year prison sentence that could have been reduced significantly if he had chosen to inform on his past associates. "But," he said, "my makeup could never allow me to become a rat. I did the crime. I had to do the time." Befriended in prison, said the article, by "a group of Italian mobsters," Wepner served eighteen months behind bars and then another twenty months of home detention in Bayonne, in east New Jersey, where he grew up and where he has lived his entire life.

After putting prison behind him, Wepner struck up a friendship with a fellow New Jersey resident named John Olson. Olson cannot recall precisely, but he thinks they may have met while Wepner was still on probation from his cocaine rap. In his late twenties, Olson was a couple of decades younger than Wepner, but the two had a great deal in common. Raised in nearby Jersey City, Olson was no choirboy himself. He was an amateur boxer as a teenager and, as he described himself, "notoriously a tough guy" in an area where tough guys abound. But he found a calling for himself as a sports agent, forming a company, with Wepner, called Power Sports. He represented the man who had stood toe-to-toe with Ali and inspired Stallone, and traveled around the country with him appearing at card shows and other events. Additionally they sold memorabilia mainly in the New York-New Jersey area.

"I know Wepner really good," said Olson, who was also running a printing and lithography business during this time, which fit well with their memorabilia activities. "I ran with him for ten years." In time their association brought him other clients, and he represented dozens of retired and active champions in boxing and pro wrestling. His duties for them included booking appearances, arranging for travel and negotiating contracts. His clients made up to $5,000 per appearance, which often coincided with an appearance by boxing's star of stars. "We piggybacked onto Ali a lot," he said. "If Ali is appearing somewhere, maybe the promoter wants more boxers. So they'd call Chuck or John Olson."

Their clients invariably signed autographs at these appearances, usually a specific number of items or for a set amount of time. One part of Olson's agreements with his clients was that they often signed photos for him as well, and he sold or traded these with other promoters and collectors. Gradually he became a collector himself, building up his own personal cache of signed material. "See, over the years I was with all the guys anyway. I had their legitimate sigs. Maybe we'd run out of photos so I'd have them sign index cards. I carried index cards with me all the time because we were always running out of photos."

For a former neighborhood tough guy, it was an exciting life—flying around the country with Chuck and other famous people, meeting and partying with celebrities, visiting the great Ali in his hotel room on three separate occasions. "Ali signed things for me because Ali knew I was associated with Chuck," recalled Olson with pride. Money was no problem, and he dated Hollywood starlets and a Playboy bunny. He had it all going on.

Then, in late 1995 or early 1996, Wepner asked his partner to print some copies of a boxing poster called "Champions Forever." Based on a video of the same name, it showed five boxing champions posed together—Ali, Frazier, Foreman, Larry Holmes and Ken Norton—all dressed in tuxedos, each with a boxing glove hanging over one shoulder. The original idea was to get the boxers to sign the posters printed by Olson, and then sell them. But both Olson and Wepner agreed the logistics of this were impossible. You'd have to get all five men together again, or take copies around to each of them individually. That'd take forever. Next they discussed having each man sign the same poster once, then run off some copies and sell them with preprinted autographs. But Olson knew this was a bad idea because collectors would cetainly see that the sigs were mass-produced and not buy them.

Finally it was decided that the thing to do was forge the signatures and sell the posters as if they'd actually been autographed by the fighters.

As for who would vouch for the authenticity of the sigs, that was obvious. Wepner's reputation—the fact he knew all these guys and had sparred and fought against three of them—would provide the cover.

As for who would do the forging, well, that was also obvious. With his sizable collection of legitimate autographs, Olson already had the exemplars. Plus they could use his light table from his lithograpy business. When placing a signed document on the table, the light shined upward through it and let Olson closely study the intricate curving lines and marks of an autograph. Even more important perhaps, the younger man had a knack. "I used to forge my mother's name on my school notes," he said. "I've been doing this since like I'm eight years old. Give me an hour and I can look at a person's signature and I can master it. It's like a gift. But I used it for the wrong reason. It's like a gift from God but it's also like the devil made me do it."

Thus inspired, Olson signed all five sigs in gold ink on a big stack of posters. They sold them to Darren Prince, the self-styled "Prince of Cards," and another dealer on the East Coast, and "all of a sudden," recalled Olson with wonder, "the money started pouring in." A boxing industry person told him that the five champs had actually signed some of these posters, so there were genuine ones in the marketplace. This fact "kinda helped us with our story," he said. "For us to pump out five hundred of them, it was still believable."

But not so believable to some. In August 1996, Rocky Landsverk of *Sports Collectors Digest* wrote an article saying that collectors needed to be wary of buying forged Champions Forever posters signed in gold ink. Representatives of the boxers told Landsverk that they had signed a few but not many of these posters, and Larry Holmes's manager said his client's autograph on the ones he'd seen was an out-and-out fake. Named as one of the dealers selling the posters, the Prince of Cards—singled out by the FBI in 2000 as a former client of Mike Lopez and a dealer who did business with Shelly Jaffe, according to Jaffe—said his source was Chuck Wepner. "What more reliable source can you get?" said Prince. He said that Wepner had shown him pictures of him and Olson with Ali at Joe Frazier's fiftieth birthday party in New York and that had helped convince him the posters were legit. Adding, "Even experts can be fooled. I've done five signings with Ali and these autographs are a spot-on match." Prince said he was offering refunds to his customers and that he was returning any posters he still had to Wepner.

Wepner complained that he'd been scammed as well. "We're going to have to get the money back from the guy that sold them to us, and he's going to have to get the money back from the guy who said he got them signed," he told the magazine. "John [Olson] is a good kid. He buys things in good faith and sometimes he gets stuck."

Not long after this, the kid who sometimes got stuck attended the seventy-fifth anniversary celebration for *Ring* Magazine in New York. Numerous boxing luminaries attended, and Olson sat at a table with a group of them. "I sat with these fighters and even though there was this bad publicity about me, people could see that clearly John still knows these people and gets along with them." One of the people who saw this was Brian Ginsberg, who had a table at the benefit selling signed memorabilia. Evidently undaunted by the cloud of suspicion hanging over Olson, Ginsberg gave him his business card and told him to call him.

Olson did, and that was how he and Wepner got hooked up with Ginsberg, a talented salesman and a real go-getter in the trade. After Prince returned the tainted Champions Forever posters to Olson and Wepner, they turned them over to the president of Laura's Cartoons and Collectibles, who sold up to three hundred of them. This was only the first of many deals to come. Olson estimated that over the years he forged close to 10,000 items for Ginsberg, mainly of Muhammad Ali.

"It was crazy. We went on for years after that. People saying, 'I want to buy five hundred Ali photographs. I want to buy a thousand Ali photographs.'"

To meet these demands, John did the forging, Brian did the selling, and Chuck did the vouching. "Chuck would say we had five hundred photos signed by Ali and we'd show them a photo of Chuck and Ali together. If someone said something about it, Chuck would say, 'Oh no, I was with Ali personally.' He also sometimes gave letters of authenticity. But he didn't like doing that because he knew that'd catch up with him," said Olson.

And if someone questioned their wares, they'd spin a story. "Whether it was me coming up with a story or him, we always had a story."

Wepner told their customers that he sent things to be signed to Ali's home in Berrien Springs, Michigan. That Ali was a close personal friend and that was why he signed for him. That Ali did the signings "off the books," for cash, and behind the back of the unsuspecting Harlan Werner. That Ali sometimes signed free for him. Once, when questioned by a skeptical customer about the Champions Forever posters Wepner was pushing, Chuck said he'd "swear on a stack of Bibles" that the sigs were authentic.

Olson and Wepner always had photos of them taken with the famous fighters they represented. These proved that yes, they had access to the people whose autographs they were selling. But the chief reason they were successful was Wepner. Now in his late sixties, he is a well-known, well-liked and well-connected figure in New Jersey. "The King of Bayonne," one newspaper has described him. Everyone in town calls him "Champ," and that is what the vanity plates on his Lincoln Town Car say. Old-timers still remember when he represented Jersey in the Golden Gloves in his early twenties and slugged his way to a national title. Back then they called him the Bayonne Brawler, before an unfortunate tendency to bleed caused a change in his nickname.

For Wepner and Ginsberg, Olson forged mainly Ali, "but we branched out into other guys," mostly other big-name fighters like the ones on the Champions Forever poster. Their chief stock in trade were photographs, especially 16x20s of Ali paired with celebrities—Ali and the Beatles, Ali and Elvis Presley and of course, Ali in his fight with Wepner. Olsen and Wepner charged Ginsberg ten to fifty dollars per forgery, and Ginsberg sold them to the public for whatever the market would bear—as much as $1,000 apiece or more, depending on the item. They also sold signed boxing posters, boxing gloves, boxing trunks, headgear, ring gongs (the bells used to signal the end of a round), even hand-wraps. Sometimes Olson would pack up a box of photos and stuff for Wepner, who'd sell it out of the trunk of his car while he was making his rounds as a liquor salesman.

Usually, in Olson's telling, Ginsberg placed his order through him. He relayed it on to Wepner, who put up the front money for the blank merchandise. Olson bought the blanks, signed them and delivered them to Ginsberg, who liked to pay by checks. Typically John and Chuck—Olson almost always calls him "Chuck," seldom by his last name—went to the bank together to cash the check and divvy up the spoils. After Wepner deducted the money he had put up for the blanks, the split was eighty-twenty: eighty percent to the older man, twenty percent to the younger.

Olson's work—"My stuff was pretty good, really close," he said, assessing himself as a forger—included Stallone photos and some "Rocky" posters as well. "I used to do a lot of Stallone stuff for Chuck," said Olson. "And I met Stallone with Chuck."

They handled Stallone sigs much the way they did Ali. Wepner and Olson would appear at a card show, bringing some forged photos of Ali with them. "Say we had some shots of Ali that were already signed," he said. "So you're standing there on line waiting to get Chuck's autograph, and Chuck signs his name to the picture and you see him do it. So you're going to say that the Ali sig that's on the photo is fake? I don't think so. We did the same thing with Stallone pictures."

One time Wepner and Olson were at a shop and they ran out of signed Ali photos. Taking a break for a moment, they went outside to Wepner's car where there were more Ali photos stored in the trunk. Trouble was, they were unsigned, so Chuck offered to sign them himself. But Olson said that was crazy because somebody in the shop might notice that the Ali sigs on these photos were different than the ones they'd been selling. So he ended up doing the job. They returned to the shop with a fresh batch of signed Alis, and Wepner sat down again and started signing his name to them.

As a "doer" in the racket, Olson kept current on other doers. "I knew about Bray and Marino. Their names are always thrown around in the industry. I knew their work. When you end up being a doer and a forger, you know. You can look at something and you know it's bad. Everybody knew who everybody was. We didn't buy from them and they didn't buy from us. Why should they? They had their own thing. They got in with these big dealers all across the country."

Much of the business he and Wepner did, said Olson, was in cash. "Everything was good. By the term 'good,' I mean we were making illegal money." Though all three of them, Ginsberg included, were aware that things could turn bad for them. And if this ever happened, they had worked out a code for how to handle it. "If one of us called the other and the first thing he said was, 'I hope the stuff you sold me was good,' then that was code that the FBI was onto us," said Olson.

In his negotiations over the Ali-Inoki photos, Ginsberg arranged for Olson to speak to Tabb, and Olson said he would. Identifying himself only as John, he told Tabb that he had worked for Wepner for more than ten years and yes, Chuck had been at the much-discussed Ali signing in New York. Olson said he'd ask Wepner to supply a certification letter for the signing, and that was the end of their conversation. That was the only time Olson spoke to Tabb in the latter's undercover calls for the FBI, and he revealed nothing about being a forger or his relationship with Wepner and Ginsberg.

Olson signed Ali's name to every one of the two hundred Ali-Inoki photos sent by Tabb to Ginsberg. As he was doing so, he noticed numbers on the back of each picture. To him this seemed suspicious, but when he pointed it out to Ginsberg and Wepner, they dismissed it as unimportant.

Unaware of Olson's role in the enterprise, Tabb focused much of his investigative energies on Wepner, with the idea of getting him on tape and jamming him up. But Ginsberg and DeSola kept getting in the way. At one point DeSola asked Tabb what was up with all the questions about the Ali signing. He wondered if Tabb would be satisfied if Wepner told him when, where and how Ali signed the pictures.

Shifting back from being a straight dealer to a crooked one, Tabb said no, he didn't want that. "I know the pictures are forgeries," he said. "I just want Wepner to lie about it."

DeSola and Ginsberg were plainly suspicious of Tabb because they called to ask if his address was in the San Diego area, trying to determine if he was part of Operation Bullpen. Tabb threw them quickly back on the defensive by demanding that Ginsberg give him Harlan Werner's phone number. If he didn't give it to him, Tabb threatened to call Werner to see if Ali had really signed the photos.

Fed up with Tabb's endless list of reasons as to why he couldn't pay them the twenty grand he owed them, an irritated Ginsberg said that he worked with Wepner, and that Wepner worked for Ali. As proof, he sent a letter to Tabb signed by Wepner in which Chuck stated that the photos were "signed by Ali for me while I was with Ali." Still pushing, Tabb demanded more. A few weeks later Ginsberg sent another letter signed by him and Wepner vouching for the authenticity of the sigs and, in a novel touch, the letter was notarized.

Sensing an opening, Tabb asked how Ginsberg had gotten a notarized letter. Ginsberg said the notary worked in his building. Tabb questioned whether Wepner really signed the letter. Under more questioning, Ginsberg admitted that yes, the notary only saw him signing the document. (Wepner's sig, in this case, was almost certainly forged.)

In September, Tabb finally got through to Wepner by simply going to his website, where Wepner was selling signed Ali material. Tabb called the number listed on the site and left a message, saying he was interested in buying some memorabilia. Less than an hour later Wepner called back, and they talked prices. Wepner said he had a bunch of signed Ali photos available for as little as thirty-five dollars apiece, repeating his story of how he got things signed by Ali by sending them to his home in Michigan.

Fitzsimmons double-checked this claim with Ali's personal secretary. She said she had never received nor sent any mail to Wepner in the seven years she'd worked for Ali. And she knew Wepner, so she would have remembered if there had been any correspondence with him.

Wepner also said he was selling signed copies of the Champions Forever poster that he had bought from a dealer some years ago. The posters had been stored in a warehouse and although they normally sold for more than $2,000 apiece, he'd be willing to sell Tabb one for three hundred bucks.

"Can I pay in cash?" Tabb asked. "I prefer to pay in cash so I don't have to pay taxes on my profits."

Not a problem, said Wepner. He added that if you write checks you have to pay taxes, but if you use cash you don't have to pay taxes.

The next day Tabb received an e-mail from Wepner with the prices for several items of signed memorabilia, including the combo-signed Champions Forever poster. A follow-up e-mail explained that Tabb should send the cash to Wepner's home in Bayonne. Tabb did so, and in a week or so a package from Bayonne arrived at his mailing address in San Diego. It contained the poster, signed in gold.

That same month, Tabb's investigative sidekick, Rick Mitchell, who had also been working DeSola and Ginsberg under a phony name, rang up Wepner for a little chat, quizzing him about the notarized letter produced by Ginsberg. Chuck responded that he never signed it and that he never attended the Ali-Inoki signing. Further, he said he had quit dealing with both men. Even so, he did happen to have some Champions Forever posters, signed in gold, that he was willing to part with for the right price.

"Those are forgeries," said Mitchell, commenting how it was well known that the posters signed in gold were fake.

Reconsidering, Wepner said he thought they were "maybe" signed in silver.

Mitchell said he didn't care either way. Silver or gold, it made no difference to him. Wepner agreed, confiding that the posters were stored under his bed for safekeeping. Later he sent Mitchell an e-mail noting that the posters were indeed signed in gold.

Mitchell and Wepner spoke again a while later, and Chuck offered to sell him a few of the Ali-Inoki photos and some other things. Mitchell liked the sound of that and dropped a money order in the mail to him. In turn Wepner shipped off the forged photos and a certificate of authenticity signed by him to an address within the jurisdiction of the San Diego FBI. The real-life Rocky didn't know it yet, but life had just bloodied him again.

EPILOGUE

In March 2002 FBI Special Agents Tim Fitzsimmons and Adam Lee, IRS Special Agents Dave White and Elizabeth Winn, Assistant United States Attorney Phil Halpern, and Dave Tabb flew to New York to continue their investigations in phase two of Operation Bullpen. The group stayed at the Waldorf Astoria Hotel on Park Avenue, a site chosen to convey the image of Tabb as a man with money to spend. "We wanted to do it right and put Tabb across as a big-time memorabilia dealer," said Lee. "The Waldorf was essentially a prop to give him credibility."

Once assigned to the lowly role of listening to the Bray-Marino wire, Lee's responsibilities in the case had grown. He was now its "ops guy," helping to plot the strategy for Tabb's undercover meets. One of those meets took place in the elegant Waldorf Astoria lobby, and the subject was Mike DeSola. He arrived carrying some samples of the merchandise he was selling, unaware that four undercover government agents were watching him and Tabb. Lee sat casually in a cushy armchair reading a paper, Fitzsimmons stood nearby, and Winn and White posed as a vacationing couple taking pictures of the historic clock in the lobby. Unlike most tourists, though, they carried weapons. "We dressed in civilian clothes and took pictures of the clock," said White. "The clock was good because it's popular with tourists so we could be there and not excite suspicion."

Tabb went on six or so other meets in New York, including one with Chuck Wepner, who sold him some Ali fakes. Tabb's usual technique was to have the recorder placed in the small of his back, the wires running up and over his shoulders to the two mics attached to his chest. Other times he wore a pager that wasn't a pager: "It looks like a standard pager clipped to your belt but it's actually a recorder." Unlike the more laid-back, casually dressed flip-flop mafia of California, the New Yorkers Tabb dealt with were "more image conscious. They wore suits and business attire and were more into the history and storytelling. They'd tell you about the time they rode in a limo with Joe DiMaggio. They were more arrogant, too. And harder to break than the Californians."

The first week, Tabb and the agents focused on his undercover meets and recorded calls, with Tabb proposing $100,000 deals that were never going to happen. The second week saw the agents and Halpern, who was back in his old Hudson County stomping grounds where he had started as a prosecutor, scrambling around New Jersey and New York preparing affidavits for the searches. "Normally in an investigation the affidavit process can take months," said Lee. "But New York was as close as it gets to the stuff you see in the movies. We flew in, wired Tabb, set up meetings, taped conversations, built the case, developed probable cause, drafted search warrants, took them to a judge, got them signed and executed the searches—all in a matter of days."

The San Diego agents and FBI and IRS field agents in New Jersey and New York culminated this hectic round of activity with raids on the homes and businesses of DeSola, Brian Ginsberg, John Fried, James Ferrazzano and Billy Costa. At the same time the FBI and IRS conducted coordinated raids on Steve Lyons in Rhode Island, Shawn Jackson in Missouri, Robert Yancey Lawhorn in Texas, Kumba Ardali and Jeff Coffman in Ohio, and other phase two subjects in Massachusetts, Mississippi and California.

One of those also busted in the raids was Wepner. Lee acted as team leader for the Wepner search, describing him as "charming and nice, almost like a politician" when federal agents appeared at his Bayonne condo on March 11. One of the New Jersey search agents was a weightlifter and fan of Wepner's, and their friendly, good-natured banter helped keep things light despite the discovery of a trove of fake memorabilia under Wepner's bed: twenty-one Ali-Liston photos, thirty-seven Ali-Frazier posters, nearly fifty Ali-Elvis photos, one hundred-twenty Ali-Beatles photos and forty-five Champions Forever posters—all bearing the forgeries of John Olson.

Wepner told the FBI during the search that he got involved in the scam through Olson, saying he loaned him money to buy memorabilia. After the goods were sold, Olson would repay Wepner, though never in cash, he claimed. Wepner described Brian Ginsberg as "a crook," saying he never made arrangements for the Ali-Inoki photos to be signed. He again labeled Ginsberg's notarized letter as a fake. He did admit, however, to selling the notorious Champions Forever posters. But he thought they were legitimate because Larry Holmes had told him they were. Larry, said Chuck, had signed in gold. Wepner said he also talked to Ken Norton who said he autographed some of the posters too.

When asked by the agents why he kept selling the posters after acknowledging to *Sports Collectors Digest* that they were fake, Wepner had "no answer," according to government records.

Going along with requests from the FBI, Wepner made recorded calls to Ginsberg, DeSola and Olson. Olson wasn't home that morning, and when he picked up his messages later in the day he heard Chuck's voice on the line.

"John," he said, using the coded warning. "I hope the stuff you sold me was good."

The FBI did not know where Olson lived, giving him time to destroy evidence. "I was nervous," he said. "I threw out all this incriminating stuff, hundreds of blank and forged photos." The next day he met with Wepner in Wepner's car outside the Dunkin' Donuts in Jersey City, not knowing that his ex-partner, having apparently reconsidered his opposition to becoming a government informant, was wearing a recording device and secretly taping their conversation. After they finished talking, Olson got out of the car and immediately two FBI agents confronted him, though he confessed nothing at the time. That only occurred months later when he started talking extensively with Fitzsimmons and came to realize that if he didn't tell his side of the story, the rap for the whole thing might land on him. "Mr. Fitzsimmons treated me like a man," said Olson. "He treated me like a human being. He never treated me like a criminal, though I was one. I respected him."

Coming forward in June, he met Fitzsimmons and another agent he trusted at the Newark office of the FBI. They asked him, "Who was the forger?"

"Me," he said.

From that point on he cooperated fully with the FBI, admitting that he forged countless pieces for Wepner and Ginsberg, including the Ali-Inoki photos that Fitzsimmons, Tabb and Mitchell used to catch him. In a turnabout, Olson put on a wire for an undercover meet with Wepner to develop information on him. His cell phone was the listening device and a money clip he wore was the recorder, he said.

Like many others in this case, Olson has sought to reform his life since the bust. "It was hard for me in the beginning," he said. "For the first year I was like a mess. I was drinking a lot. But you know what, I got to straighten out my shit. I went back to being a working stiff. I haven't touched a drop in two years. Financially, it's been really tough. I knew I was doing wrong but when the money's coming in, who cares? But now I can look myself in the mirror."

Olson received probation for his crimes. Because of his cooperation with the government and because he has decided to tell his story in this book, he says he has fears for his safety. He has moved several times since 2002 to keep his whereabouts a mystery. He spoke to this writer without revealing where he was living or what number he was calling from.

Asked to comment on Olson's charges or any of the issues and events discussed in this book, Chuck Wepner declined, referring all questions to his attorneys. "They'll give you whatever information you need," he said. "I'm not supposed to be saying anything. They'll tell you who's really involved with this." But his attorneys failed to respond to calls and requests for information.

Wepner appeared in U.S. District Court in San Diego in 2005 and pled guilty to conspiring to commit mail fraud. (Mail and wire fraud are typically how counterfeit memorabilia cases are charged under the federal system.) He stipulated to the judge that, starting in 1996 and ending with the FBI raid, he had sold and authenticated $117,000 worth of forged memorabilia. In Wepner's sentencing hearing held a year later, Assistant United States Attorney Melanie Pierson argued that the victims of the scam actually lost closer to $600,000 because after Wepner and Olson sold the forgeries to Ginsberg, Ginsberg marked the price up and resold them to his customers. Further, Pierson said, the dollar loss was likely higher still because the threesome had worked largely in cash and as a result it was impossible for investigators to trace all their fraudulent activity. Anthony Fusco, Wepner's attorney who has represented Mike Tyson and others in the fight game, rejected this and other assertions by the government. He argued, among other things, that his client deserved leniency because he has "demonstrated a laudable commitment to repair and rebuild his life" and "has solidly established himself as a highly respected and successful member of the community." Wepner, in effect, had turned his life around too.

The judge agreed with the defense. Wepner, who could have received up to five years in prison, got ninety days of home detention, a $2,000 fine and three years' probation. His sentence included one day in jail, which he had already served. "We didn't think the case warranted jail time," a jubilant Fusco told Wepner's hometown Bayonne paper. "He was very minimally involved. We're very happy it's behind us."

Unresolved at this date is Wepner's ongoing legal fight with Sly Stallone. In November 2003, a year after the FBI busted him for selling counterfeit Stallone memorabilia, Wepner filed suit in New Jersey Superior Court claiming that Stallone had unfairly profited from his life story for "Rocky" and its four sequels, and that he deserved financial compensation. Late the next year Stallone's attorneys failed to get the suit thrown out of court, although two of Wepner's claims against the star were dismissed. Stallone is now reportedly starring in another "Rocky" sequel, dubbed "Rocky Balboa," with a tentative release date of 2007. A documentary on Wepner's life is also said to be in the works.

In the summer of 2005, two months after Wepner pled guilty, the United States Attorney's Office filed a thirteen-count indictment against Ginsberg for selling and distributing counterfeit memorabilia. He has pled guilty and at the time of this writing, has not yet been sentenced, although he is expected to go to prison.

Mike DeSola also confessed, and received probation.

Of the other phase two subjects mentioned in the last two chapters, David Hammond spent close to three years in prison; James Ferrazzano, fifteen months; John Fried, a year and a half; Robert Yancey Lawhorn, a little over a year; Shawn Jackson, nine months. One of the Ohio State students, Kumba Alafi, went to prison for three months; his partner Jeff Coffman got probation.

When federal agents searched Billy Costa's place, they found an abundance of the fruits, evidence and instrumentalities of forgery at his home. What they also found was a sick old man. Although in his youth Billy may have resembled the tough-talking Jimmy Cagney, those days had long since passed. Authorities never charged him in the case due to his failing health, and he is now dead.

A harsher legal fate awaited Steve Lyons, who, alone among all the Bullpen subjects in either phase one or phase two, took his case all the way to a jury trial. Operating on eBay under several different screen names, the Rhode Island dealer sold Rick Mitchell a "Star Wars" poster with the forged signature of Anthony Daniels on it. At Lyons's trial in San Diego in late 2003, Daniels, who played C3PO in the movies, testified for the prosecution, identifying his signature on the poster as fake. Also testifying at the trial were the two men who jammed Lyons up, Tabb and Mitchell. "I testified for two days," Mitchell recalled. "Four hours on Monday and four more on Wednesday. Dave testified before me. When I was on the stand his attorney tried to make it seem like we were targeting Lyons, which was a joke. We were working thirty-five other cases at the time. We didn't press any of them. There were so many forgers out there wanting to do business with us, we didn't need to."

To Mitchell, the red-haired Lyons appeared to be so nervous that his face and neck had broken out in a rash. The jury went out for two hours and returned a guilty verdict on all ten counts of mail fraud. He was sentenced to three years in prison. When the verdict was announced an officer placed him in handcuffs and led him out of the courtroom. He subsequently appealed his sentence and has been released from prison, pending resolution of the appeal.

Curiously, one of the names brought up during the Lyons trial was Donald Frangipani. The FBI singled out the Brooklyn authenticator by name in 2000. In its evidence files are cuts of Abraham Lincoln, James Monroe, Herbert Hoover and Richard Nixon—all Greg Marino forgeries certified as authentic by Frangipani. Nevertheless, he stayed in business after the original takedown and two years later, Brian Ginsberg offered to have Frangipani certify the forged Ali-Inoki photographs. In his defense, Frangipani maintains that some of his certs were stolen by counterfeiters and faked, and this was why his COAs fell into the hands of crooks. He has never been charged in the case.

Another authenticator, Jim Bellino, also steadfastly maintains his innocence. Though his authentication firm, Forensic Document Services, closed its doors after the bust, Bellino told a reporter that he was "neither tried nor convicted of any crime because I never would knowingly buy or sell an illegitimate or forged autograph." Feeling sure he would be vindicated if his case went to trial, he declined to take the matter to court, citing the high cost of litigation and the length of time involved. Instead he accepted a deal with the government that gave him probation and expunged his record. He cannot, however, return to the memorabilia business without obtaining an order from the court.

Jim DiMaggio served seven months in prison. After getting out of prison he ran a restaurant, his occupation before Bullpen. He now lives in Florida.

It was DiMaggio who certified the infamous Mother Teresa baseball. The man who placed the order for this ball on behalf of a client, Rino Ruberti, spent fifteen months in prison as part of an agreement that kept his wife Karen out of jail. "Rino Ruberti is a hero in my book," said Dave White, who worked his case. "He was very remorseful, very repentant after the takedown. He cried a lot. But he stood up like a man and took the rap for his wife." Karen received only probation, as did her parents, Scott and Mary Louise Harris.

Rino's one-time partner, Mike Moses, spent nearly two years in prison. Like Rino, he made a deal with the government to add time to his sentence to keep his wife out of jail. That way Robyn, who received probation, could continue taking care of their young children. Since leaving prison Moses has dropped out of the collecting scene to make a fresh start in life.

The FBI raided Stan Fitzgerald's home and business in Caldwell, New Jersey on October 13, 1999, but after the bust his case began a slow march through the legal system. Five years later, in April 2004, Stan, his wife Donna and his mother Josephine were indicted and arraigned on seventeen counts of mail fraud, conspiracy and money laundering. As part of their plea agreement they forfeited possession of their two homes in Caldwell and the house on the Jersey Shore that Stan had bought with a $500,000 down payment the week after the takedown. They also paid $80,000 in restitution to some of their victims.

Josephine and Donna received probation. The judge originally sentenced Stan to up to seven years in federal prison, but this was reduced considerably due to his cooperation in criminal cases on the East Coast. Relying on his experience as a former deputy sheriff, he went undercover to gather evidence that led to several convictions and removed illegal guns from the streets. Considering the danger of Stan's undercover work, the judge reduced his sentence to a year and three months. He began serving his term in early 2006.

Like Stan Fitzgerald, the cases of Doc and Phil Scheinman have taken years to bring to a close. In January 2004 the United States District Court of the Southern District of California convened a grand jury that issued an eight-count indictment against them. Father and son have since both pled guilty. Doc received house arrest for six months. Phil's rabbi appeared in court to speak on his behalf for the religious service he has done to atone for his errant deeds. Phil got ten months in prison.

Another large retailer brought down in the case, Barry Albert, operated a chain of card and memorabilia shops in southern California. One day Dave White was listening to Dr. Laura Schlesinger on the radio when he heard Albert's voice come on the air, asking for advice on how to explain to his daughters that he was going to prison. He did not mention what his crimes were, and Dr. Laura discretely did not ask. "You just tell them that Daddy did something wrong," she said, "and now you're going away for a while because of it." Daddy went away to prison for nine months and then came back home.

Jon Hall, the owner of Del Mar Sports Cards, felt so bad about the crimes he'd committed that he sold his house and moved in with a family member to raise money to pay back the people he had defrauded. The sentencing judge took this into consideration and gave him only probation. Others receiving probation were Lowell Katz, Bruce Gaston, Frosty Golembeske and Mike Tapales, aka Mikey the Runner.

Two members of the inner circle, Big Ricky Weimer and Dick Laughlin, went to prison for five months, as did Jack Morgenstern and Chip Lombardo. Chip's buddy Mike Bowler received a one-year sentence and served about nine months of it.

Shelly Jaffe logged six months in lock-up, returning home to Tustin to resume his long-time career as a steel and metals broker. Both he and Nate

Harrison have done consulting work in autographs, authenticating signed memorabilia for estate sales and auctions. Some collectors have criticized this as inappropriate, saying the two shouldn't be able to make money in an industry they exploited. But Jaffe and Harrison may be uniquely qualified to assess and evaluate forgeries, having seen so many in their lives.

Ever the sharp-tongued iconoclast, Jaffe is not impressed with industry reforms of recent years. In one high-ticket auction in which he, Harrison and another authenticator consulted, they rejected nearly three-quarters of the signed material they saw as fakes. But the auction house ultimately sold these pieces anyway. "Nobody wants to hear that the signatures are bad because there's so much money in them," said Jaffe.

According to Jaffe, authenticators may review only a small percentage of what is being sold at an auction. But the image fostered by the auction's sponsors is that all the lots have passed inspection and been certified as genuine. Jaffe is equally unimpressed with the post-takedown changes instituted by the online auction sites. To show this writer how bogus sigs are still being sold these days, he scrolled down a list of ten Mantle autographs that were up for auction on eBay on the day we spoke. All but one, he said, was a certain fake. "Dealers are still dealing crap," he said. "You warn and warn and warn people and tell them a thousand times and they still don't care. So screw it. Let the buyer beware."

Surprisingly perhaps, Jeff McKinney agrees to some extent with Jaffe, saying that fraudulent memorabilia investigations are potentially endless. "We rolled these guys, who could tell us about six more guys, who could tell us about six more guys, and this could go on forever," he said. But, he added, "We succeeded in taking out the major players at the time. This helped raise public awareness and the autograph industry has since taken steps to protect itself better. The FBI did its job." McKinney went from Operation Bullpen to oversee with another agent a major fraud investigation of Michael Fanghella's PinnFund USA, a southern California mortgage company that bilked investors for hundreds of millions of dollars. Fanghella and some of his associates were convicted and sent to prison. The man who helped put them there is now a supervisory special agent for the San Diego FBI, targeting cyber crime,

Assistant United States Attorney Phil Halpern feels that the greater goal of the investigation—"to educate and deter"—was achieved. "People should know by this time that if they bought a Mark McGwire autograph during the home run chase, it's a counterfeit," he said. "It just is." A one-time marathoner, the energetic prosecutor has moved onto racing bicycles, including a five hundred-miler across the Mojave Desert. Within the United States Attorney's Office he recently prosecuted a case concerning illegal dietary supplements, while other prosecutors in his office have taken on the phase two cases brought by the FBI.

Maura Fahy is now a supervisory special agent in the Laguna Niguel field office of the Los Angeles IRS. Her chief right hand man for Operation Bullpen, Dave White, became the lead IRS agent for phase two and continues to investigate fraud and tax evasion cases for the San Diego IRS.

Adam Lee parlayed his experience in Bullpen by becoming the case agent for Operation Good Samaritan, which busted up a $50 million fraud and money-laundering ring that defrauded investors around the nation. During this investigation he called upon the talents of Dave Tabb, who made a number of taped calls and undercover meets in the case. Lee has taken his love for cloak and dagger undercover ops to FBI Headquarters in Washington D.C., where he is a supervisory special agent.

Anthony West, the Upper Deck investigator whose original subject lists aided the investigations of both the Chicago and San Diego FBI, has since left the company and is now a welfare fraud investigator in Riverside County.

John Ferreira feels vindicated that his undercover approach to the Bullpen ring was the right one despite not being able to crack the tight Bray-Marino inner circle. "The nice guy approach worked with most of the guys," he said, pointing to the many subjects, including Tabb, he helped bring to justice. After the 1999 takedown he returned to Eugene and resumed working cases full-time in his specialty of eco-terrorism. In early 2006 the Justice Department announced the indictments of a ring of environmental terrorists allegedly responsible for the attacks on the Detroit Ranger Station, Oakridge Ranger Station and other crimes in the Northwest. Ferreira has since retired from the FBI, and he remains, as ever, an avid autograph collector.

In law enforcement parlance, a career case is one that defines an investigator's career. For Tim Fitzsimmons, Operation Bullpen is his career case. He has received national commendation from FBI Headquarters for his achievements. All told, his investigations have bagged sixty-three charges and convictions, the dismantling of eighteen forgery rings around the U.S., the seizure of nearly $5 million in criminal assets and more than $300,000 paid in restitution to victims. Tabb, Mitchell and John Olson give him full credit for helping to turn their lives around after they were busted. As an aside, in the summer of 2005, the San Diego FBI gave away tens of thousands of forged baseballs that were confiscated during the case to local Boys Clubs and other youth organizations. Volunteers and FBI agents marked up the balls before they were handed over to the kids.

Today Fitzsimmons remains on the fraudulent memorabilia beat for the San Diego FBI, though he admits his investigations are "winding down" and changing to some degree. Because many crooks are now hip to the fact that if they send forged memorabilia to San Diego County they will fall under his purview, he helps police and FBI in other parts of the country bring cases in their respective areas. These investigations are centered in the places where the fraud is being committed, and the subjects are charged there. Since 1997, when he opened Operation Bullpen, Fitzsimmons believes that the autograph industry, particularly in sports, has made valuable reforms. Even so, the Internet auction sites—eBay, Yahoo, Amazon, to name only the biggest ones—are "still a huge problem," he said. "Generally speaking, what's sold there is worse than what is in the stores."

In 2000, weeks after the original Bullpen press conference, a San Diego law firm filed a class action lawsuit against eBay, claiming it should be held liable for the counterfeit merchandise sold on its site. The suit, Gentry vs. eBay, listed individuals in seven states that had bought bogus stuff from Stan's and Smokey's, with the certs being supplied by the J. DiMaggio Company, Donald Frangipani and Wayne Bray's SCAA. Ebay vigorously opposed it, saying it was not a traditional auctioneer overseeing what was bought and sold; rather, it was a venue or platform with "no control over the quality, safety or legality of the items," as the company's user agreement states. The company, which earns $1 billion annually in sports merchandise alone, said it was not obligated to check on the authenticity of the thousands of autographed items it auctions every day, nor the tens of millions of other items it lists on its site. Thus, it was not responsible for the frauds perpetrated by the Bullpen ring. A year later a Superior Court judge agreed with eBay's argument and dismissed the suit. Nevertheless, the issue remains a thorny one for Pierre Omidyar's creation. Tiffany & Co. has filed suit against the company, alleging that counterfeit jewelry is being sold on the site and that eBay is not doing enough to stop it. Other companies selling other types of products have also complained about the counterfeits being sold there.

Fitzsimmons has worked extensively over the years with eBay investigator Kevin Kamimoto. Kamimoto testified at the Steve Lyons trial and has helped the FBI garner "the last thirty convictions we've had in the case," said the agent. Ebay conducts a little-known program called VeRO in which legitimate individuals and companies can remove counterfeit or black market material from the site. He described eBay's anti-crime efforts as "extremely helpful," saying that fraudulent memorabilia activity is worse on the other auction sites. "Cyberspace in general lends itself to certain types of fraud," said Fitzsimmons. "People can be relatively anonymous on it. Start-up costs are minimal. We've had subjects who are essentially operating out of their bedroom."

At the 2000 Bullpen press conference, officials estimated that as high as ninety percent of all autographs sold were fake. After many in the industry complained that this figure was wildly exaggerated, the estimate was reduced to fifty percent. The truth is, nobody knows and nobody will ever know how many fakes are circulating in the marketplace today. Nor can anyone know how much of the work of Messrs. Marino, Moses, Lopez, Lombardo, Schwarz, Walsh, Fried, Jackson, Costa, Olson, et al. is still out there, hanging on office and bedroom walls and being offered for sale at auctions and stores.

HBO's "Real Sports" recently did an investigative piece that exposed—once more—the dubious authentication practices of Donald Frangipani and others. In this piece Shelly Jaffe, working with the program and the FBI, pointed out that an Upper Deck signature card contained a Walter Johnson forgery produced by Greg Marino. On the same card was a Babe Ruth sig done by an unidentified forger. The card sold for $85,000 on eBay, and questions have been raised about the authenticity of similar Upper Deck signature cards. The HBO investigation highlighted anew some stubborn truths about the autograph industry: that authentication can be a refuge for scoundrels, that counterfeits remain a lucrative enterprise despite the efforts of law enforcement, and that the work of Greg Marino is still making money for people and ripping off consumers, even though the man himself has retired his Sharpie.

John Olson said he still sees his stuff being sold today. Many of the people who buy it either do not realize or do not care to realize that what they own is a beautiful fraud. Others have money invested in counterfeits and are not about to say anything because they want to sell them. Many dealers who owned material certified by J. DiMaggio Company and SCAA at the time of the original takedown simply replaced these bad pieces of paper with their own store-made pieces of paper and sold the bogus items anyway. "Most authenticators are dealers too," says Olson. "And they all bought from counterfeit dealers and forgers like myself." Some authenticators who sell signed material are much tougher in assessing other people's memorabilia and less willing to certify it because it competes with their own products, says Olson.

Fitzsimmons considers a COA issued by the store or dealer who is selling the merchandise as "nothing more than a receipt, a piece of paper." He feels strongly that consumers need to establish "a chain of custody" for the things they buy, before they buy them. In the collecting industry this is called "provenance," which is essentially a history of ownership. In recent years several sports and memorabilia companies have begun witnessed signings and other programs to establish provenance and reassure buyers of the legitimacy of their products. With some companies, the autographed items they sell are affixed with holographic serial numbers indicating the date and place of the signing, and are registered online. But a holograph by itself is no guarantee of authenticity. Don Steiger, aka "Hollywood Don," was a Massachusetts forger brought down in phase two who sold lots of fake stuff using numbered holograms. Fitzsimmons says the key to any claim of authenticity, be it with holograms or anything else, is being able to log into an online system and see for yourself that yes, Kobe Bryant or Alex Rodriguez or Peyton Manning did indeed sign on that given day and here is the evidence to prove it.

For autographs that predate the current era of witnessed signings, holographs and online registry, he recommends hiring an expert third-party authenticator, although he recognizes that the experts are often fooled, too. "Greg Marino could get some of his stuff authenticated by every authenticator in the business, including the legitimate ones, because it was so good," said the agent.

Due to his high level of cooperation and the undercover work he did for the FBI, Rick Mitchell received probation and never went to prison. He remains married to his schoolteacher wife, and they have two children. He sells golf clubs and other goods on consignment on eBay, and during the holidays, manages Christmas tree lots in the San Diego area. He still loves sports and collecting, but he has sworn off gambling and now views blackjack as an evil game. "I'm not ashamed of my story," he said after agreeing to talk to this writer. "What happened to us, could have happened to anybody."

Mitchell feels strongly that his life is far better than before, although to some degree he has become disillusioned by his work for the government. "Dave and I brought down not just one ring but lots of rings. But I'm tired of busting people. Am I deterring anyone by doing it?"

Dave Tabb, who largely helped bring down John Fried, James Ferrazzano, Shawn Jackson, Brian Ginsberg, John Olson, Chuck Wepner and others, estimates he built cases on nearly one hundred-sixty subjects for phase two of Operation Bullpen. "I've gotten lots of admissions from them, frequently on the very first call I made with them," he said. "But how many have actually been charged? Fifteen, twenty maybe. The reason is, you have to have a prosecutor who's willing to take the case, and for a variety of reasons they may not be willing to do that. I've done business with lots of phonies who may never be charged."

He also admits to being discouraged by this: "At some point, you must move on. You've done your job. The public is aware of the problem. What more do you need to do?"

Tabb has certainly moved on in his undercover work for the FBI. At last count he had done, all on a volunteer basis, more than 5,000 hours of criminal undercover investigations, including at least two for the San Diego FBI—Operation Bullpen and Operation Good Samaritan—and a software piracy case for the Santa Ana FBI. These cases have required him to make some 1,700 calls, 1,200 tapes and numerous in-person meets—probably the most undercover tapes and in-person meetings ever done by a non-FBI agent for criminal investigations. His life was threatened in one of the cases he worked. He is now on undercover assignment for the FBI for a white collar fraud case with investor losses of more than $100 million. The FBI has invited him to come to Washington, D.C. to speak to special agents on how to use e-mail to approach and cultivate subjects during an investigation. He has also performed six hundred-fifty hours of community service apart from his undercover work, and paid $100,000 in refunds to the customers he burned while running scams for Hollywood Dreams. His sentencing date was postponed eight times until finally he received straight probation—no jail time. His ultimate goal is to clear his record completely.

"I've flipped the coin from who I was then to who am I today," he said. "And what I'm doing now erases the bad. I feel good about myself."

In their investigations, both Tabb and Mitchell saw the work of many top forgers around the U.S. Both maintain that Greg Marino was the best of them all. Tabb still owns three Marino pieces, done at the height of his powers: Elvis Presley, Marilyn Monroe, Alfred Hitchcock. Calling on his talents as an artist, Marino drew a sketch of Hitch's fabled profile as part of the signature. Tabb regards these forgeries much like works of art, and he has them framed and hanging in his house.

Other examples of Marino's forgeries are on display at the FBI Laboratory in Quantico, Virginia. They are shown to members of the public who take the lab's tour.

One of the greatest forgers in American history now works as a cashier at a grocery warehouse store in New England. He went to prison in Nevada, same as his brother John, and they both served two years. When they got out each clocked six more months at a halfway house in Boston. Both returned to the East to get far away from California and to start the next chapters in their lives with a clean slate. Angelo and Gloria took turns serving their respective sentences. When Gloria went to jail, Angelo was out; when Gloria got out, Angelo went in. The reason for this was so that one of them could care for John's children while their father was away. After prison Angelo and Gloria moved to be close to their daughter Andrea and her husband. Greg and Kathy and John and his children now all live in the same area as well.

Though not in the dream house they once envisioned for themselves, the Marinos are, once again, together.

Angelo loves to paint as always and maintains a website to sell his lithographs—signed only by him. Except for his interviews for this book, Greg has stayed away from the media and the collecting world. But he remains an ardent Yankees fan and lives and dies with the team's fortunes on the field.

After Nate Harrison spent nearly a year in prison, he returned to North County and managed a 7-Eleven store for a while. At last check he had left that job and was handling sales for an automotive shop in Escondido. "I'm pretty much broke now," he says. Still he's not the type to hold a grudge, and he has let go of his anger toward the man who persuaded him to join the racket in the first place. "I'm not a vindictive person," he says with a shrug. "Wayne's my friend."

Bray served six months in a halfway house near the Mexican border, doing menial work for the government. Upon being released he returned to San Marcos and ran a sports card shop, the same thing he was doing when the scam started. He has since left this and become the owner of a jewelry store, a long-held dream of his. As he has since he was a teenager, Wayne chooses to tell the significant stories of his life through his body art. He had a tattoo done in recognition of Operation Bullpen's impact on his life. Occupying a ten-inch long section of his back near his right shoulder, it depicts the skull of a bull whose horns are trapped in a spider's web. Piercing the bull's skull is a pen.

Despite the FBI's assurances that what he did was right, and despite the fact that so many others in the case also ended up cooperating with the government, Bray cannot escape the feeling that he let his friends down, people who trusted him and counted on him, particularly Nate and Greg. Though he and Nate have made amends, the cut was too deep for Greg, who will have nothing to do with his one-time forgery brother. "If you see Greg," Wayne told this writer at the end of one of our last conversations, "tell him I'm sorry."

SOURCES AND ACKNOWLEDGMENTS

I became interested in the Bullpen story after the birth of my first son. Left over from research on one of my previous books, I had a wonderful photograph of Hank Aaron hitting a home run. Thinking it would make a nice keepsake, I sent the photo to Aaron at his Atlanta Braves' office asking him to inscribe it to my son, whose first name is also Hank. I have reason to believe that Aaron did in fact sign the photo and that the autograph is genuine.

Sometime after that my wife's sister, thinking along the same lines as me, bought an Aaron-signed baseball online and gave it to my son as a present. The ball, signed on the sweet spot, came with a certificate of authenticity stating that the autograph was genuine. But when I compared the signature on the ball with the one on the photograph, they appeared different. That's odd, I thought.

At the time I had no idea that much of the memorabilia purportedly signed by sports stars and Hollywood celebrities is not signed by them at all. But I didn't think anymore about the ball until I started doing research for *The Golden Game* and began hearing about Operation Bullpen from some of the collectors I was interviewing. This was two years after the big FBI press conference announcing the takedown of the ring. Even so, people were still talking about the case. My curiosity sparked, I decided to look into the story further.

This began my involvement with the book you have in your hands. In early 2003 I called the San Diego FBI asking to speak to someone about the case. Since I was a member of the media, FBI Headquarters in Washington had to first give its approval before a field agent could talk to me. I faxed a statement about myself to Rex Tomb in the FBI Office of Public Affairs, and eventually an associate of his gave me the name of Tim Fitzsimmons, Operation Bullpen's case agent. I called Fitzsimmons and flew to San Diego for a series of interviews with him and other officials in the investigation. Later I went back for another extensive round of interviews.

My gratitude goes to Special Agents Tim Fitzsimmons, Jeff McKinney, Adam Lee, Caroline Hoag and Jan Caldwell for their cooperation and assistance. I spoke to Assistant United States Attorney Phil Halpern in his downtown Federal Building office, and his candor and insight are greatly appreciated. From my home in northern California, I drove to Eugene and spent the better part of a day and a half with John Ferreira. He was friendly, generous with his knowledge and equally candid. He bought me lunch and gave me some of the evidence he had collected during the case, including back issues of collecting magazines that I used for background information.

My interviews in southern California included IRS Special Agents Maura Fahy and Dave White, who were both extremely helpful. Tami Stine of the IRS set these interviews up for me. On another of my trips to Southern California I had a long lunch with investigator Anthony White, who filled me in on Operation Foul Ball and graciously handed over his newspaper files on the case.

Despite all this cooperation, however, I knew I only had one side of the story. In order to tell this story the way I wanted to, I needed to talk to the guys in the ring. I felt then, as I do now, that this was an important story, a story that deserved to be told—a great American story about crime and redemption, and about friendship and family and trust and the breaking of that trust. The crime angle drew me into the case, but once I dug deeper into it, I felt I had to know more about the people who pulled off the scam.

It's one thing if you're a government official and want the media to hear about a success of yours. But it's quite another thing to talk to a writer after you've committed a crime and gone to prison for it. When I began my research, most everyone in the original Bullpen ring had been sentenced and done their time. They didn't need to sit down with a person who wished to revisit those old, bad memories.

Fortunately, though, many of them did. I had a freewheeling conversation with Shelly Jaffe in his house while he worked on his computer. I interviewed Dave Tabb at a restaurant near where he lived, and we have talked several times after that as well. It took a while to connect with Rick Mitchell but we eventually had several solid conversations together. At first Wayne Bray didn't see the point of talking to me. When he finally consented and I showed up at his shop, he said, "That was my first mistake. I should have never let you see me." But he invited me into the back and we sat down and talked the rest of the afternoon. He seemed glad to get some things off his chest, as if he'd been carrying them around a long time. We spoke a half-dozen or so more times after that. Once Wayne spoke to me, Nate Harrison, who still remains loyal to his friend in some deep way, agreed to be interviewed and share his version of events.

I spoke several times with Kathy and Greg Marino. True to his easy-going nature, Greg spoke freely and without calculation, to my knowledge the first and only time that he has spoken to a reporter about his experiences as a forger and at the center of the ring. John Olson talked to me about his participation in the crimes, and how he has changed his life since being busted. I am grateful to all of them—John, Greg, Kathy, Nate, Wayne, Rick, Dave and Shelly. They didn't have to talk to me but they did. I wish them only the best.

Others involved in the ring have dropped out of sight, and I wasn't able to reach them. Others were still going through the justice process and their cases were not yet resolved when I was doing my writing and research. Now that this book is out, if any of them wish to contact me, I'd be happy to talk to them and update their stories. Please contact me at the publisher's website, www.operationbullpen.com. The site contains more photographs of forgeries and other information about the book and the investigation.

I must thank Lillian Kaiser, Pamela Hood, Gesher Calmenson, David Nelson, David Baker, Gary Grillo, Rebecca LeGates, Alison Barnsley, Christine Mayall, Lorraine Rath, Larry Gordon, Annette Kaiser, Peytie Schuler, and other family and friends for their advice, encouragement and support during this project. And, of course, as always, Jennifer.

—Kevin Nelson

ABOUT THE AUTHOR

Kevin Nelson spent three years researching and writing *Operation Bullpen: The Inside Story of the Biggest Forgery Ring in American History*. He obtained exclusive interviews with the forgers and counterfeit dealers involved in the ring, as well as the FBI, IRS and Justice Department officials who brought them down.

Nelson is the author of eighteen books and numerous magazine, newspaper and online articles. His previous book, *The Golden Game: The Story of California Baseball,* was named one of the top ten books of the year by National Public Radio and the *San Francisco Chronicle,* and was featured on "The Today Show." He lives in the San Francisco Bay Area with his wife and children.